THE STILLNESS OF SOLITUDE

Traditions in American Cinema
Series Editors Linda Badley and R. Barton Palmer

Titles in the series include:

The 'War on Terror' and American Film: 9/11 Frames Per Second
Terence McSweeney

American Postfeminist Cinema: Women, Romance and Contemporary Culture
Michele Schreiber

In Secrecy's Shadow: The OSS and CIA in Hollywood Cinema 1941–1979
Simon Willmetts

Indie Reframed: Women's Filmmaking and Contemporary American Independent Cinema
Linda Badley, Claire Perkins and Michele Schreiber (eds)

Vampires, Race and Transnational Hollywoods
Dale Hudson

Who's in the Money? The Great Depression Musicals and Hollywood's New Deal
Harvey G. Cohen

Engaging Dialogue: Cinematic Verbalism in American Independent Cinema
Jennifer O'Meara

Cold War Film Genres
Homer B. Pettey (ed.)

The Style of Sleaze: The American Exploitation Film, 1959–1977
Calum Waddell

The Franchise Era: Managing Media in the Digital Economy
James Fleury, Stephen Mamber and Bryan Hartzheim (eds)

The Stillness of Solitude: Romanticism and Contemporary American Independent Film
Michelle Devereaux

edinburghuniversitypress.com/series/tiac

THE STILLNESS OF SOLITUDE
Romanticism and Contemporary American Independent Film

Michelle Devereaux

EDINBURGH
University Press

For David and Jaxon

Edinburgh University Press is one of the leading university presses in the UK. We publish academic books and journals in our selected subject areas across the humanities and social sciences, combining cutting-edge scholarship with high editorial and production values to produce academic works of lasting importance. For more information visit our website: edinburghuniversitypress.com

© Michelle Devereaux, 2019,2021
Portions of this book previously appeared in issue three of *MAI: Feminism & Visual Culture*.

Edinburgh University Press Ltd
The Tun – Holyrood Road, 12(2f) Jackson's Entry, Edinburgh EH8 8PJ

First published in hardback by Edinburgh University Press 2019

Typeset in 10/12.5 Adobe Sabon by
IDSUK (DataConnection) Ltd

A CIP record for this book is available from the British Library

ISBN 978 1 4744 4604 4 (hardback)
ISBN 9781474446051 (paperback)
ISBN 978 1 4744 4606 8 (webready PDF)
ISBN 978 1 4744 4607 5 (epub)

The right of Michelle Devereaux to be identified as the author of this work has been asserted in accordance with the Copyright, Designs and Patents Act 1988, and the Copyright and Related Rights Regulations 2003 (SI No. 2498).

CONTENTS

List of Figures   viii

Introduction: Filmmaking as a Romantic Quest   1
    What is 'Romantic'?   2
    Imagination and the Romantic Sensibility   8
    Romanticism, Sincerity and Authenticity: A Problem of Identity   10
    'Metamodernism' and Romantic Irony   13
    From the New Wave to New Hollywood to Now   16
    Chapter Overviews   23

PART I. ROMANTIC CLARITY AND CONFUSION

1. Beauty Among the Ruins: The Painful Picturesque and Sentimental Sublime in Wes Anderson's Aesthetics   29
    The Sublime and the Beautiful in Eighteenth-century Aesthetics   30
    The Royal Tenenbaums and the Painful Picturesque   33
    Trapped in a Never-ending Play: Anderson's Use of Diegetic Space   38
    A Search for Meaning Within Postmodern Pastiche   41
    The Middle-aged Man and the Sea: *The Life Aquatic* and the Sentimental Sublime   43
    The Camp Cathedral: Eclecticism in Anderson's Mise-en-scène and Dialogue   49
    Conclusion   52

2. 'An endless succession of mirrors': Irony, Ambiguity and the Crisis
of Authenticity in Charlie Kaufman's *Synecdoche, New York* ... 54
    Romantic Irony: From Kant and Schlegel to Byron and Beyond ... 56
    Embracing Irony and Undermining Realism in *Synecdoche, New York* ... 59
    'A series of mad visions perhaps': The Screen as the Site of Confused Subjectivity ... 64
    The Mise en Abyme and the Mathematical Sublime ... 71
    Conclusion ... 76

PART II. EMOTION, IMAGINATION AND THE FEMININE SUBLIME

3. Oh! You Pretty Things: The Egotistical and Feminine Sublimes in Sofia Coppola's *The Virgin Suicides* ... 81
    Gendered Expressions of Sublimity: The Egotistical and Feminine Sublimes ... 82
    Staging Sublimity in 1970s Suburbia ... 84
    Mood Creation and the Emotional Core of the Film ... 86
    The Aesthetics and Politics of 'Pretty' ... 92
    'Preparing to give assault': Creating the 'Pseudo-political' Gothic ... 96
    Conclusion ... 98

4. Girlfriend in the Machine: Intersubjectivity and the Sublime Limits of Representation in Spike Jonze's *Her* ... 100
    The Role of Will in the Romantic Imagination ... 102
    Sublime Obscurity and the Mind's Eye ... 106
    Photographing Sound in a Disembodied Mise-en-scène ... 108
    'The light of sense goes out': Intersubjectivity and the Acknowledgement of Others ... 112
    Conclusion ... 117

PART III. CHILDHOOD, (R)EVOLUTION AND IMAGINARY HISTORY

5. 'Because I'm a wild animal': Nature Versus Nurture in Wes Anderson's *Fantastic Mr. Fox* ... 121
    Romantic Conceptions of Childhood and Nature ... 123
    Digging for the Middle Ground: *Fantastic Mr. Fox* and American Pastoralism ... 127
    'A native blend of myth and reality': The Landscape of Imagination ... 133
    Little Savages in the Garden: Ash, Kristofferson and the Romantic Child ... 136
    Mourning the Loss of Animal Nature ... 140
    Conclusion ... 143

6. 'It's not too much, is it?': Keats, Fancy and the Ethics of Pleasurable
   Excess in Sofia Coppola's *Marie Antoinette* 144
   Fancy and Material Excess as Alternative Romantic Discourse 147
   Marie Antoinette and the 'Material Sublime' 153
   The 'Romantic Ethic', Daydreaming and Modern Consumption . . 158
   Revolution, Modernity and Shifting Personal Identities 161
   'Like a little piece of cake': The Body, Consumption and
      Moral Utility 163
   'Dying into life': Embracing the Romantic Depth Model? 167
   Conclusion 171

Conclusion: On Endings and New Beginnings 172
   The Romantic Relationship to Reality: A Questioning of Absolutes . . 174
   The Battle Between Self-consciousness and Solipsism 176
   'Bravery in the midst of indeterminacy': Emotion as a Form
      of Revolution 178

Notes 181
Filmography 190
Bibliography 193
Index 209

FIGURES

1.1 The film's mise-en-scène links Margot Tenenbaum to images of wildness, exoticism and performative beauty — 36
1.2 Richie instructs Etheline to hang his portrait of Margot in a seemingly haphazard place on the wall of the ballroom — 37
1.3 A sublime point-of-view shot of Richie's bleeding wrists offers a counterpoint to Anderson's penchant for pleasantly constructed overhead shots of static objects — 38
1.4 The bisected set of *The Life Aquatic*'s *Belafonte* — 40
1.5 A medium shot of Esteban emphasises the artificiality of the underwater realm as well as the theatricality of its presentation — 44
2.1 The eternally burning house fire creates confusion in the spectator and serves to keep the film squarely in the realm of the fantastic — 62
2.2 Caden's grand theatre project involves geographical impossibility: creating infinite life-size replicas of New York City within a warehouse in New York City — 71
2.3 Caden and Hazel observe their doppelgängers as they act in a play that has essentially become the only form of existence for their real and fictional selves — 74
3.1 Early images of Lux and Cecilia create a sense of conflicting emotional presentation — 87
3.2 The use of split screen emphasises both physical distance and intersubjective connection through 'touch' — 90
3.3 Coppola creates a confrontational image of femininity with excessively ornamental mise-en-scène — 94

4.1	Theodore walks home from work alone, adrift in a sea of isolated bodies beneath a phalanx of oppressive skyscrapers	105
4.2	Jonze's camera often focuses on Theodore's face in close-up, rendering it both sympathetic and beautiful in the Burkean sense	109
4.3	Theodore and Amy's rooftop meeting suggests an alternative, feminine sublime is also available to humans	116
5.1	In a pivotal moment, literal machines in the garden destroy Mr Fox's dream of pastoral plenitude	129
5.2	In its final supermarket scene, *Fantastic Mr. Fox* calls attention to its artifice and the circular nature of existence	131
5.3	The film's cave paintings evoke the 'primitive' origins of humanity	135
6.1	Marie's point of view of the sneering, sceptical royal court is quickly contrasted with images of her studying herself as object of their gaze	151
6.2	The film's first image sets up its discourse on excess regarding both femininity and consumption	152
6.3	The 'I Want Candy' montage sequence links pleasurable consumption to fleeting desire, historical anachronism and the female body	155
6.4	Coppola emphasises the power of touch, which alludes to both sensual interconnection and the eternal grasping emanating from desire	163

INTRODUCTION: FILMMAKING AS A ROMANTIC QUEST

The choice of subject matter of this book might seem curious to some. What could the great pantheon of poets, philosophers and artists of the various eighteenth- and nineteenth-century Romantic movements have to do with modern American independent filmmaking? After all, the first commercial film screening was nearly a hundred years off when Wordsworth's *The Prelude* was first published in 1799 and Romanticism was arguably at its height. It is difficult to know what the Romantics might have made of the cinema itself, its reliance on technology and money uncomfortably married to the concept of single-minded auteurist vision. (Would Keats have picked up a 16mm Bolex as a teen and made films instead of poems if given the chance?) But in many ways, the world in which the Romantics lived and worked is not terribly removed from our own. In the Romantic era, political revolution, the birth of modern capitalism and the Industrial Revolution created conditions of change both 'profound and sweeping' (Mellor 1980: 3) and 'violent and inclusive' (Abrams 1970: 92), enabling the questioning of societal 'progress', the creation of new modes of being and feeling, and the consideration of how to navigate them.

This time around, geopolitical and environmental turmoil, economic globalisation resulting from late capitalism, and the 'electronic revolution' of the information age situate our own era in a similar societal landscape of uncertainty (Botting 1999: 99, 101). Such profound social changes 'promise massive global transformations which repeat revolutionary and romantic gestures while at the same time threatening the human subject and the modernity sustaining it' (1999: 99). As Fred Botting writes, the neoromantic turn, one I argue is present in contemporary American independent cinema, is as much a product of a desire for societal and political change as it is one for self-realisation and interpersonal connection:

> The exhumation of Romanticism, the calling up of a ghost already haunting the present, constitutes another nostalgic appeal to a lost past, a gesture of mourning that recognizes a lack and vainly calls up an autonomous political agent who can resist the present state of things. (Botting 1999: 103)

True to the contradictions inherent in Romanticism, this study of seven films from four contemporary American directors – Wes Anderson, Charlie Kaufman, Sofia Coppola and Spike Jonze – is predicated on each being very much of its moment yet also greatly removed from it, existing in its own imaginary time and place. While they all 'resist the present state of things', they do so in oblique ways. The films are simultaneously *here*, in the tumultuous early twenty-first century, and *nowhere*, in a reimagined past conjured purely from the spirits of their creators and their collaborators.

While the myth of the information age is one of transparency and instantaneous global connection, the reality is often one of 'near-endless repetition' (Hartman 2002: 193) and a cacophony of often-meaningless symbols. The filmmakers I consider try to combat the despair of such a postmodern 'disenchantment that is final, or self-perpetuating' (2002: 138) through varying approaches to intersubjectivity, self-consciousness, sympathetic emotional engagement and imaginative creation, but all approach them in what can be defined as Romantic terms. Just what does this turn to so-called 'neoromanticism' say both about the films themselves and about the contemporary age in which they were created? Before exploring that question, it is necessary to define the parameters of Romanticism, a nebulous, misinterpreted concept if there ever was one.

What is 'Romantic'?

The term *Romantic* is often utilised and just as often misunderstood. What exactly does it mean to say something is Romantic, specifically in terms of a canon of Romantic artistic works? Most often the Romantic age has been defined as a historically bound movement stretching from 1789, the year of the French Revolution, to 1832, the year of the Reform Act in Britain (Bainbridge 2008: 6). Some scholars, however, contend the period lasted until the mid-nineteenth century (George 1955: xi). Romanticism was not simply one movement, but a collection of them, from the Jena School German Romanticism of the 1790s to the French Romantic novelists of the 1820s. The heterogeneous nature of Romanticism leads Seamus Perry to claim it as a 'posthumous invention' (1997: 4). In fact, the use of *Romantic* to describe a particular style or outlook did not become popular until the later nineteenth century in Britain and was not cemented until the critical reappraisals of the twentieth century (Bainbridge 2008: 4).

In the 1940s, René Wellek influentially characterised British Romantic literature as employing 'imagination for the view of poetry, nature for the view of the world, and symbol and myth for poetic style' (qtd in Bainbridge 2008: 4). Wellek's proposed corpus was notoriously narrow, which helped solidify the Romantic canon as a handful of British poets – William Wordsworth, Samuel Taylor Coleridge, Lord Byron, Percy Bysshe Shelley, John Keats and William Blake – and neglected scores of other poets and writers of the era (2008: 4).

Wellek's definition, while a good starting point, is vague, and the body of work he cites fails to include non-British Romantic works entirely. Arthur Lovejoy famously proposes that instead of 'Romanticism', we should speak in terms of a 'plurality of Romanticisms' (qtd in Bainbridge 2008: 5). Similarly, Jerome McGann acknowledges that 'a systemic or comprehensive accounting of Romanticism – of its works or ideology – is an impossibility: indeed, it is a contradiction in terms' (1983: 47). For McGann, that contradiction lies in Romanticism's aspiration toward completeness and its simultaneous acknowledgement of the impossibility of perfection (1983: 47). German Romantic poet and philosopher Novalis's definition of Romanticism is more descriptive: 'By endowing the commonplace with a higher meaning, the ordinary with mysterious respect, the known with the dignity of the unknown, the finite with the appearance of the infinite, I am making it Romantic' (1997: 60). Fundamentally, the qualities of Romantic works represent a 'cataclysmic coming-into-being of the world' (Abrams 1953: 93). The Romantic, it follows, is located within the 'mysterious' experience of a phenomenological becoming – a constant hoping, striving and doing related to a steadfast Romantic longing – rather than in the impossible completion of such a quest.

There are many familiar and more obscure Romantic strains running through the films I consider. These include a preoccupation with personal history and memory; a deep undercurrent of emotion and a reliance on mood and tone to convey it; a foregrounding of the creative process and the all-important imagination; and an ambivalent relationship to both the natural world and civilised society. In terms of aesthetics, they depend on qualities of the beautiful, the picturesque and (most importantly) the sublime to elicit complex emotional responses in their characters and their audiences. Above all, they represent a preoccupation with subjectivity and self-consciousness, the latter not necessarily in the sense of metatextual and reflexive analysis (although there is plenty of that evident in these films) but in the more Romantic sense: the coming to personal self-consciousness that creates a rift between the individual subject and the greater sense of a social self (Bloom 1970: 6).

Harold Bloom considers subjectivity, or self-consciousness, 'the salient problem of Romanticism' (1970: 1). Similarly, when Geoffrey Hartman writes that 'Wordsworth cannot find his theme because he already has it: himself' (1970: 53), he highlights the problematic solipsism shadowing the subjectivity of Romantic thought. Echoing both Bloom's and Hartman's sentiments, Philip Shaw contends, 'the Wordsworthian mind is self-contained, serving no other purpose than itself' (2005: 102). While the Romantic movement (in the personal sense) is a journey from nature to the 'imagination's freedom' – the unleashing of visionary subjectivity beyond and above that of nature – it is also a move that can lead to the 'destruction of the social self':

> The quest is to widen consciousness as well as intensify it, but the quest is shadowed by a spirit that tends to narrow consciousness to an acute pre-occupation with self. This shadow of the imagination is solipsism, what Shelley calls the Spirit of Solitude. (Bloom 1970: 6)

The resulting realisation of such self-consciousness entails giving up a feeling of totality, a connection with the external world, a world that includes other consciousness – that is, other people. How does one negotiate between such an all-important visionary self and a social self? This divide between self and other results in fractured selves left to the solitude of their own subjective consciousness. The title of this book paraphrases a line from Shelley's 1816 poem that Bloom references, *Alastor; Or, The Spirit of Solitude*, in which a lone poet retreats to nature to discover what lies beyond it ('One human step alone, has never broken / The stillness of its solitude'). With it, I hope to highlight the principle of this self-consciousness and the fissures it potentially creates between self and world. I argue that this Romantic principle, and the perpetual desire to establish intersubjective connection that this self-consciousness can impede, forms the implicit Romantic theme in the films that I discuss.

For the purposes of my study, I consider the term *Romantic* as both an artistic mode of expression(s) as well as a historically situated age where such expressions were principally fomented. (Because it is defined principally by its epoch, I have chosen to capitalise the term except when used in its most everyday sense.) While the filmmakers I consider are all American, their cultural and artistic influences are much more global in outlook, one of the reasons I have chosen to correlate them with the Romantic movements of a variety of nations. This also allows for a greater understanding of the pluralities of Romanticism Lovejoy references. I draw not only from the work of the famous English poets Wellek discusses, but also German Romantics such as Schlegel and Novalis, writers of gothic fiction such as Anne Radcliffe and Mary Shelley, American Romantics such as Ralph Waldo Emerson and Henry David Thoreau, and British women authors such as Felicia Hemens and Charlotte Smith.

Some (the German Jena Romantics) predate the British canon, while others (the American Transcendentalists) follow it; still others, such as Smith and Mary Shelley, were more or less contemporaries and often critically engaged with the work of their more historically celebrated counterparts. I use Romantic philosophy, texts and critical theory as a foundation for engagement with the films I discuss. I combine this with a larger theoretical framework utilising medium-specific analysis of the films. I have chosen to focus on films at least co-written by their directors because the idea of 'authenticity of origins', directly linked to filmic auteur theory, is in essence a fundamentally Romantic principle. While this is not an auteurist study per se, it relies upon the Romantic focus on the origins and intentions of a more or less singular consciousness – a somewhat absurd notion given the collaborative nature of filmmaking, but one inextricable with the theories of authorship and romanticised notions of artistic practice that these filmmakers often embrace.

This book does not involve dissecting conceptions of romance as they relate to generic conventions like the 'love story', although Romantic love does play a role. Rather, I engage with twentieth- and twenty-first-century critical interpretations of European and American Romantic artworks, principally poetry and literature. I have chosen, for practical purposes, not to engage with the differences between factions of Romantic criticism, neither in discourse nor in method of approach (for example, New Historicism versus formalism). More important is my selection of films – this is not a study of Romanticism or artists from the Romantic period, but rather one about how those artists' conceptions of Romanticism are expressed in contemporary American 'art-house' film. (By 'contemporary' I refer to work made in our current century: the oldest film I discuss is Sofia Coppola's 1999 debut *The Virgin Suicides*, while the most recent is Spike Jonze's *Her*, released in 2013.)

By utilising the work of theorists and critics such as Harold Bloom, M. H. Abrams, Anne Mellor, Geoffrey Hartman, Jerome McGann and other major and minor scholars of the past and present century, I hope to emphasise the historical trajectory of Romantic thought – one that has endured to the twenty-first century as presented in the work of the filmmakers I have chosen to write about. Just as I am looking back to the past in order to analyse the present state of film, Romantic artists themselves were in part inspired by looking back to the mythmaking past of medieval and chivalric romances (Snell 2013: 1) and were preoccupied by personal and cultural history in general (Milnes and Sinanan 2010: 4). Present realities are, of course, just as important. The Romanticism of these filmmakers is shaped as much by the historical and cultural realities in which they operate as Wordsworth or Keats or Mary Shelley were shaped by their own time, so much of my project focuses on how these filmmakers have adapted, altered, affirmed or challenged such thought, however unwittingly.

None of this is to necessarily suggest these filmmakers have consciously chosen to engage with Romantic aesthetics and philosophy; rather, just as Romanticism was in part a 'conversation with [. . .] the unconscious' (Snell 2013: 7), I argue that Romantic concepts form the very fabric of these works in mostly unconscious ways.[1,2] The films of Coppola, Jonze, Anderson and Kaufman are steeped in a Romantic tradition that follows from many of their filmic and larger artistic influences, including European New Wave cinema, New Hollywood Romanticism and filmic surrealism, as well as twentieth-century literature and photography. These traditions permeate the general landscape of European and American culture and have had an enduring role in shaping art beyond the Romantic era. These earlier artists' Romantic tendencies engage in a dialogue with modernism, as an aesthetic movement, and modernity, as the historical reality of their time.[3] To a large extent, the films I discuss express similar preoccupations. However, they are generally less political and experimental and more personal, even solipsistic, a trend that continues the 'personal politics' of what Jeffrey Sconce refers to as American 1990s 'smart cinema' (Sconce 2002: 352).

Unlike their cinematic forebears of the 1960s and 1970s, who often focused on the 'social politics of power, institutions, representations and subjectivity', the filmmakers I discuss shift attention to the interpersonal relations of 'power, communication, emotional dysfunction and identity in white middle-class culture' (2002: 352). They are all fundamentally concerned with the matter of the alienated self and its relation to the external world, and that sense of alienation is expressed in the various emotional states their films convey: melancholy, restlessness, confusion, despair. But they also often express a sense of hope: bursts of joyous naïveté or intersubjective expressions of deep feeling, just as '[t]he Romantics glimpsed the darkness to come, yet a principle of hope prevailed' (Hartman 2002: 167–8). Their characters may act blasé or disaffected, but they all fundamentally care, even as they remain isolated within the solitude of their self-consciousness and occasional solipsism (Mayshark 2009: 188).

The Romantic conception of the power of individual imagination to expand social imagination explains these filmmakers' imaginative, often fantastical 'redescriptions' (Rorty 2016: 72) of reality, and it also speaks to their qualified hopeful spirit. Far from cynical or nihilistic stabs in the dark at an uncaring universe, these films and their characters 'rarely succumb to hopelessness' (Mayshark 2009: 12). They engage on a deeply moral and ethical level, mostly through problems of the alienated individual's relation to their personal social network (usually the family) and society as a whole (2009: 5).

Fundamentally, the films exhibit a preoccupation with self-identity: the notion of self and its definition in relation to other selves, and even to what constitutes a self. Since the Romantic era, the idea of an authentic self has become degraded, a casualty of postmodernism and poststructuralism (Jameson 1992: 62). This 'post-structuralist attack' (Henderson 1996: 2) – that such self-identity is simply an illusion and there is no 'core' self – in many ways spurs a certain conservative, consoling mode in the films I consider. Characters often personify a more reactionary strain of Romanticism in their evocation of what Wordsworth in *The Prelude* refers to as the 'anxiety of hope', a longing to return to the harmony present in pre-self-consciousness – or the belief that 'the idea of unity has to be recovered or reborn' (McGann 1983: 40). Characters incessantly search for the means by which to reassert and reiterate their own identities as a way to protect themselves from a sense of inauthenticity, even as the very notion of the authentic now seems moot. They re-enact their own growth personally or through others (especially children), or they engage in a continual process of reinvention in order to stumble upon their 'real' selves. This generally amounts to a series of false starts and failed attempts.

The films themselves often appear as imaginative recreations of impossible pasts as a protection against uncertain futures. From Caden Cotard's relentless desire to embalm his entire life through his art; to Richie, Margot and Chas Tenenbaum's attempts to recapture the faded glory of their childhoods, which were miserable in the first place; to *The Virgin Suicides*' nameless boys' quest to forensically recreate the magical allure of their objects of affection, who they never even really knew, characters continually plumb their histories with the intention of self-discovery. Often they are just as deeply mired in self-delusion and seem incapable of meaningfully engaging in their day-to-day lives.

Despite their obsession with the past, the films' Romantic inclinations are grounded in their own idealised historical time and place. Many of their stories seem to take place in a nebulous, transhistorical otherworld that does not quite correspond to our own. Leo Marx terms such a place 'moral geography', an ideal, mythic landscape used to work through subjective fascinations (1964: 245). Grappling with the anxiety of indeterminacy and 'weakening of historicity' that signifies the postmodern condition (Jameson 1992: 58), the filmmakers, through their art, exhibit a yearning for a past acknowledged as imaginary. While utilising irony, they take aim at that irony's 'tyranny' by injecting their narratives with sincere sympathy (Mayshark 2009: 5, 7). Their films are overly concerned with reconstruction (2009: 6), even as they recognise that these attempted reconstructions are bound to fail because they are reconstructions of imaginative illusions.

According to Jesse Mayshark, 'If there is a defining dialectic [in the films] it is between the self and the world' (2009: 11). In many ways that is the way their characters prefer things, but the status quo of solitude has intense and unasked-for repercussions. Ultimately, the characters in these films reflect the filmmakers', and our own, grappling with this sense of alienation and estrangement: alone even in a crowd, they are solitary figures, strangers not only to family, friends, partners and co-workers, but also to themselves. While they represent a partially conservative turn (King 2014: 7) toward a past modernism – with its utopian vision, a 'standstill' of life perfected through utility (Benjamin 1969: 170) – they embrace many of the seemingly inescapable tenets of postmodernism, such as fragmented subjectivity, irony and self-consciousness (Waugh 1992: 5). Their turn toward the past is a turn toward renewed meaning. Ironically, it represents a desire for progress, even as the notion itself is called into question. It is this very oscillation between the poles of modernism and postmodernism that defines their particular historically based brand of Romanticism (Vermeulen and van den Akker 2010). In the following pages I will elucidate the twentieth- and twenty-first-century critical responses to several major components of Romantic philosophy and art works in order to form an initial theoretical framework for my corpus. I start with one of the most important ideas: the concept of the Romantic Imagination.

Imagination and the Romantic Sensibility

In his 1841 essay 'Circles', Ralph Waldo Emerson writes that a Romantic view of individual life, and human history, is of a cyclical, unending progression akin to an ever-turning wheel powered by individual imagination:

> The life of man is a self-evolving circle, which, from a ring imperceptibly small, rushes on all sides outwards to new and larger circles, and that without end. The extent to which this generation of circles, wheel without wheel, will go, depends on the force or truth of the individual soul. (Emerson 1841: 10.5)

This passage speaks to the Romantic belief in the endless inquiry of the human imagination and its limitless potential, that '[e]very ultimate fact is only the first of a new series' (1841: 10.6). Such a belief encompasses the idea that '[w]e shall never find descriptions so perfect that imaginative redescription will become pointless' (Rorty 2016: 71). It describes a perpetual motion machine of inspiration and hopeful renewal, but, unlike Enlightenment conceptions of progress, it denies ultimate knowledge, instead affirming an unending epistemological quest (2016: 71).

Critically, it also expresses the idea that imagination is the key to human advancement; it is the 'principle vehicle of human progress' (2016: 71). This emphasis on individual imaginative power was evidenced by a 'growing self-consciousness in art' in the late eighteenth century (Bate 1970: 169). Fundamentally, it is indicative of the emphasis on the 'cult of individual genius' (Hamilton 1999: 18), an acknowledgement that poets are, as Shelley wrote, 'the unacknowledged legislators of the world' ([1840] 1921: 48) and share a special visionary access to hidden fundamental truths that ordinary people do not (McGann 1983: 114). Genius is the ingredient that 'arrests the moving fantasms, the material and images of beggardly day dreaming, the corrupting movements of romance delirium' and renders the Romantic imagination's 'evident light and truth' in its place (Botting 1999: 108) – it expands fanciful illusion to a sublime state of reason. Such poetic genius was only accessible through a combination of lived experience, deep feeling and patient reflection (Bate 1970: 164).

If theories of the Enlightenment considered imagination merely as a 'function of memory, the recollection of decaying sensory data that was to be brought forth to mind after its objects were gone', the Romantic artist sought to reintroduce the power of the 'active mind' in an attempt to break the bonds of materialism (Wolf 2012: 20). For the Romantic, the imagination was the source of sympathy for others (Bate 1970: 162) and a 'touchstone of stability and order' for the self (McGann 1983: 68). It was even cast in quasi-divine terms, in the conviction that it would 'transcend historical divisions' and see 'into the life of things in a secular age' (1983: 98, 101). Both Coleridge and Wordsworth 'wished to make imagination not merely creative but a power for apprehending truth' (Pottle 1970: 283), and Blake went so far as to align the poet's imaginative power with the 'creative power of God' (Frye 1970: 130). In accordance with such a project, the Romantics embraced myth and mythmaking as protection against the rationality they thought inhibited true vision (Bate 1970: 151).

Artistic mythmaking becomes 'a means to resist the intelligence intelligently' (Hartman 1970: 50), a higher calling than the mere functionalism of intellect. Through imaginative power, the artist resists spiritually deadening rationality to arrive at something greater and more exultant. Under this rubric, fiction, not the objective scientific enquiry of Enlightenment, holds the key to enlightened truth. While Romantic thought is rooted in hope, that hope 'has been shifted from the history of mankind' to 'the mind of the single individual' (Abrams 1970: 111). It is, in some ways, an emancipatory attitude that focuses on the power of the individual through creative freedom.

While imagination, along with emotion, 'began to destroy the perfect balance and the harmony which neo-classic art had sought' (Monk 1970: 28), it also unbalanced (or perhaps simply brought into stark relief) the separation between self and world. Geoffrey Hartman contends that the Romantic poet harnessed the 'sympathetic imagination' within in order to counteract solipsism and 'entice the brooding soul out of itself, toward nature first, then toward humanity' (1970: 55). This is related to Harold Bloom's conception of the 'quest romance', comprising a series of stages in which immature and wild creative impulses are channelled into the pointedly self-actualising imagination of the Romantic poet (Bloom 1970: 3). The first phase requires a 'radical withdrawal of self' that can result in 'visionary solipsism' (Rzepka 1986: 9), but such solipsism is eventually overcome in favour of the 'Real Man' or 'Imagination' stage Bloom characterises as 'the outward turning of the triumphant Imagination' toward a larger humanity (Bloom 1970: 17).

In contrast, Charles Rzepka refers to the Romantic imagination as 'the self as mind' (1986: 5); enraptured by his own power, '[t]he Romantic poet turned away, not from society to nature, but from nature to what was more integral than nature, within himself' (1986: 16). The traditional Romantic view of sublimity, sometimes called the 'Wordsworthian' or 'egotistical' sublime, exemplifies this notion. Developed from ideas of sublimity espoused by both Edmund Burke (in relation to sublime objects and the soliciting of emotion) and Immanuel Kant (in relation to imagination's role in sublimity), the Romantic sublime is based on the subjective perception of the individual, in a fundamental shift 'from world to mind' (Shaw 2005: 73). In this way, 'it is not the object itself' that now possesses the characteristics of sublimity, 'but the manner in which that mind apprehends that object' (2005: 79). For Wordsworth the imagination itself becomes sublime – its power is 'awful' and has the capacity to obliterate both external reality and the mind's experience of that reality, but it is also the source of poetic vision (2005: 101). As such, the imagination must be contained in order to protect a sense of self (2005: 102).

Because subjectivity is so central to Romantic thought, the self is tasked with living 'authentically' above all else: the Romantic was 'a person of true sensibility, possessed of a passionate and impetuous nature which would simply not permit dissembling or hypocrisy' (Campbell 2005: 177). In the Romantic age, ideas of sincerity and authenticity were being re-evaluated and reconstructed in enduring ways, ways integral to the realisation of the Romantic identity.

Romanticism, Sincerity and Authenticity: A Problem of Identity

The idea of the 'authentic' versus 'in-authentic' self (Miles and Sinanan 2010: 6) is another key 'problem' of Romanticism. Much engagement with canonical Romantic writing presumes a model of psychological depth – the idea that a fundamental core of being exists (Henderson 1996: 4). That idea of the core self had a profound influence on new notions of authenticity in the Romantic era. Authenticity became a matter of moral strength not based on any external authority but on that of personal subjectivity: 'authority moves indoors' and 'being oneself' takes on primary significance (Milnes and Sinanan 2010: 5). This is the birth of the modern conception of authenticity – and by relation, sincerity – one that finds its source in the 'authorizing origins' of the subject (2010: 5). Authenticity is no longer related to a realistic depiction of the world but instead to the 'truth' of the mind's eye, 'something that really proceeds from its origin' (2010: 6). Sincerity relates to the outward expression of such an authenticity; it becomes essentially the social practice of authenticity (2010: 4).

The critical function of sincerity now becomes the 'burden' of bridging the widening gap between an authentic self and the world (2010: 6). Autobiography becomes a key mode of expression in this 'Age of Feeling' (Richardson 1988: 13), allowing a correspondence between the artist and audience that becomes a signature of sincerity (Milnes and Sinanan 2010: 13). In *Walden*, Thoreau expresses a desire for a 'simple and sincere account of his own life' (Thoreau [1854] 1999: 5–6). When in his *Preface to Lyrical Ballads* Wordsworth claims, 'all good poetry is the spontaneous overflow of powerful feelings' ([1800] 1957: 6) which should be delivered in the unfettered, naturalistic language of ordinary life, he relates the idea of authenticity as integrally an intuitive and direct quality (Milnes and Sinanan 2010: 19).

In much the same way as the filmmakers I discuss have been branded as socially disengaged and self-absorbed, the Romantics have often been accused of celebrating modes of escapism. But M. H. Abrams insists they 'were obsessed with the realities of their era' (1970: 110). With the burgeoning economic realities of capitalism taking hold, and Europe embroiled in a series of Napoleonic wars, in the beginning of the nineteenth century the social and political realms were undoubtedly unstable. Caught up in the sublime political upheaval of revolution in America and, especially, France, Romantic writers embraced its potential and 'unbounded and hence impossible hopes' (1970: 110). When they were ultimately disappointed by revolution's unfulfilled promises, they turned their hope and desire for change toward themselves, making it personal.

There were, of course, political differences between nations and even within them – Hazlitt, Hunt, Shelley and Byron reportedly admired Napoleon (Nemoianu 1998: 188), and Emerson, unlike most, embraced the technological advances that came with the machine age (Marx 1964: 231). But all were a product of an age of new frontiers. Wordsworth, especially, shifted focus from this uncertain and foreboding societal future to what Abrams calls the 'egalitarian revolution of the spirit [. . .] of the equivalence of souls, the heroic dimensions of common life, and the grandeur of the ordinary and the trivial in Nature' (1970: 117). In a sense, Romanticism embraced the inverse of the adage 'the personal is political', popularised by mid-twentieth-century identity politics activists (Hanisch 1970). For Wordsworth and others, the political became personal. This 'spiritual quietism' eschewed 'overt political action' in favour of passivity and acts of imagination (Abrams 1970: 110, 111). The revolution became one from within.

Rzepka considers that publication of the 1800 edition of *Lyrical Ballads* marks a fundamental shift from 'the world as an object of knowledge [. . .] to the thinking subject's point of view on the world' (1986: 10). Personal feeling and sympathy replace objectivity in a quest for truth and both are linked to expressions of authenticity. Thomas Pfau suggests that these expressions were 'attempts to trace political, economic, and spiritual history back to its manifestation as emotional experience' (2005: 2), that is, to source the feelings that lead to the facts. If 'sincere feeling is *in* the language before it is produced by reflecting *on* it' (Miles and Sinanan 2010: 11; original emphasis), the author's emotional sincerity is expressed by 'contagion', a sympathetic communion that starts with the direct expression of feeling in the writing itself, leading to a similar emotional experience in the perceiver (Pfau 2005: 3).

Whereas the previous 'age of sensibility' (Abrams 1970: 98) was attuned to the standards of societal convention and feigned emotion, the Romantic age associates 'emotional susceptibility' with goodness and 'make[s] custom and etiquette the source of all that is undesirable [. . .] leading to the contrasting of "self" and "society"' (Campbell 2005: 177). Sympathy becomes an expression of individual sensibility, removed from the inauthentic organising principles of socially proscribed norms and rules (2005: 7). In contrast to the social constrictions of civilisation, nature was often viewed, in the fashion of proto-Romantic Jean-Jacques Rousseau, as an 'authentic voice' (Grayson 1986: 81) removed from society's hypocrisy. Childhood was linked to authentic nature, as it exists in a state of 'sensation unmediated by intellect' (1986: 85). The very idea of whether a 'social self' can be authentic is thrown into question (Miles and Sinanan 2010: 10).

Just as Jerome McGann sees different 'phases' of English Romanticism, moving from a 'visionary' mode to one focused on revision and self-critique (1983: 108, 109), Angela Esterhammer posits that some Romantic works actually 'interpret sincerity as a code or convention' (2010: 104) by emphasising its performative dimensions. Tim Milnes and Kerry Sinanan contrast Wordsworth's 'spontaneous outpouring as the fiat of "authentic" selfhood' with Byron's later 'tireless *performance* of selfhood' (2010: 3, 4; original emphasis). Far from being a simple expression of inner authenticity, in this later mode, sincerity becomes 'fictional, imaginary or even downright false' (Esterhammer 2010: 110). If sincerity is something that needs to be 'embodied' – that is, expressed physically by verbal and other physical signs – its experience is unavoidably both spontaneous and theatrical: 'This paradoxical notion of sincerity as a *socially accessible and physically engaged performance of interior emotion* is paradigmatic for late-Romantic poetry' (2010: 113; original emphasis).

The progression from the 'essential' sincerity of Wordsworth to the 'constructed' sincerity of later Romantic works reveals that newly redefined notions of sincerity and authenticity in the Romantic period were already being problematised by the early nineteenth century (2010: 105). For instance, Letitia Landon's 1829 poem 'History of the Lyre' reveals 'whether sincere or insincere, the mental states of others are unknowable except by the indirect evidence of appearance, language, and other external or publicly shared conventions' (2010: 116). (I discuss this 'problem of other minds' in

Chapter 4.) This newfound reflexivity within the text engages in an uneasy dialectic of performance and sincerity, which is the case in many of the films I study. Their characters often suffer from extreme crises of identity, exemplifying a Romantic grappling with the idea of authentic selfhood.

If expressions of sincerity, which were being called into question, were 'fused' with ideas of authenticity in the Romantic era (Milnes and Sinanan 2010: 2), it now seemed possible the 'depth model' of authenticity was itself questionable, and one's 'own "likeness" or image is all [. . .] there ever is to lose' (Esterhammer 2010: 114). Perhaps, it was entertained, there is no 'core' self at all. As Tim Milnes and Kerry Sinanan show, the 'desire to discover a holistic self at the heart of writing' was a key Romantic project, but 'authentic selfhood remain[ed] elusive, disappearing even as it is grasped' (Milnes and Sinanan 2010: 2). Geoffrey Hartman considers that the 'ethos of self-fashioning', defined by Coleridge via Shakespeare, might lead to 'a restless identity search' (Hartman 2002: 33). For some later Romantics, especially Keats, what Hartman calls 'anti-self-consciousness' (1970: 46) offers an alternative to such a crisis. For Keats, the authentic poet 'has no Identity [. . .] he has no self' (Keats 1970: 157). Instead, a celebration of physical phenomena results in what he calls the 'material sublime' (Keats 1976: 237), an overabundance of sensation leading to vertiginous bliss that goes 'beyond' individual subjectivity (Gigante 2002: 441).

Internal conflict is endemic in much of Romantic thought and its attendant works, especially in terms of its key tenets of imagination, authenticity and subjectivity. In many ways, 'Romanticism [. . .] initiates the conflict between modernity's homesick longing for authenticity and its dogged pursuit of critique' (Milnes and Sinanan 2010: 17). The films discussed in this book exemplify many of these struggles with identity and the alienation between self and world. The paradoxical state between unmediated authenticity and self-criticism can best be delineated via a discussion of Romantic irony. In contemporary terms, it is evident in what has been termed the 'metamodernist' sensibility of the twenty-first century.

'Metamodernism' and Romantic Irony

Timotheus Vermeulen and Robin van den Akker outline the key traits of what they consider 'the romantic turn in contemporary aesthetics', which they dub 'metamodernism' (2010). Just as in many ways modernism was a reaction to Romanticism (Whitworth 2007: 63),[4] postmodernism offers a rebuke of the holistic utopian philosophies of modernism, resulting in a sense of 'indeterminacy' which can 'allow for an exemplary respect for the particular' (Hamilton 1999: 19). But postmodernism soon comes to describe a feeling that Jean-François Lyotard calls the condition of 'and what now?' (1993b: 246). Vermeulen and van den Akker claim that postmodernism's 'years of plenty, pastiche, and parataxis' (2010) – its reliance on ironic detachment, knowing reflexivity and fragmented subjectivity – have reached an epistemological dead end, with seemingly nothing able or willing to take their place.

Pointing to the effects of a degraded ecosystem, geo-political turmoil and the financial chaos of neoliberal globalisation, Vermeulen and van den Akker argue that postmodernism's 'death' has seen the emergence of what they call 'metamodernism'. Metamodernism teeters between the poles of modernism and postmodernism without ever achieving any form of 'balance' between the two: it 'oscillates between a modern enthusiasm and a postmodern irony, between hope and melancholy, between naïveté and knowingness, empathy and apathy, unity and plurality, totality and fragmentation, purity and ambiguity' (Vermeulen and van den Akker 2010).

These oscillations create a profound sense of anxiety caused by 'unyielding tension' – the metamodernist work operates within a framework of desire for meaning and acknowledgement that meaning, reason and rationality are elusive at best, and absent at worst (Vermeulen and van den Akker 2010). The authors are quick to make a link between metamodernism and Romanticism; this tension or conflict is, in fact, fundamentally Romantic. They highlight the 'general idea of the Romantic as oscillating between attempt and failure' (Vermeulen and van den Akker 2010) and argue that Friedrich Schlegel's definition of Romantic irony includes such an oscillation between 'enthusiasm and irony' (Vermeulen and van den Akker 2010) – it is irony that contains its obverse, sincerity, within its very mode of expression.

According to Ernst Behler, such irony is an integral part of the self-consciousness that Romanticism implies, which creates endless shifts between experience and reflection. For Behler, Romantic irony comprises 'an infinite mental spiral in which the individual mental ego hovers between naïve experiences and critical reflections on its experiences while viewing its own passions with disillusioned detachment' (1988: 43). Such an 'intellectual attitude' allows the 'vulnerable personality' a distance from immersive negative feelings of 'melancholy, loneliness and profound suffering' while still acknowledging their reality (1988: 43). For Schlegel, Romantic irony is not a detriment, but a 'propelling force' similar to Emerson's imaginative circles, one that allows for a continual becoming and renewal (Behler 1988: 62). Still, the Romantic ironist partly resides outside of personal experience, not wholly engaging in the immediacy of action and emotion, which signals a fragmented, partially alienated subject.

For Fredric Jameson, this 'fragmentation of the subject' is characteristic of postmodernism (1984: 63). Indeed, in this sense postmodernism can be considered a 'remoulding of Romanticism [. . .] a mutation of the original stock' (Larrissy 1999: 1). If, as Lyotard does, we take postmodernism to be not an epoch as such (à la 'postmodern era') but a descriptive mode (Roberts 1999: 142), we can more easily consider the coexistence of different modes – the Romantic, the modern and the postmodern – within the same text (1999: 142). As Vermeulen and van den Akker suggest, this coexistence resonates in metamodernist works. Just as 'Romantic poetry incorporates Romantic Ideology as a drama of the contradictions which are inherent in that ideology' (McGann 1983: 2) – the 'spontaneity and recollection in Wordsworth', the 'spiritual tone' without specific religious context (Thorlby 1988: 147) – metamodernism incorporates its own contradictions, demonstrating a Romantic 'working out' of those contradictions without any kind of structural resolution or synthesis.

Although they do mention two filmmakers I discuss, Jonze and Anderson, Vermeulen and van den Akker primarily elucidate the metamodernist influence in visual art and architecture. (Their 2017 edited collection, *Metamodernism: Historicity, Affect, and Depth After Postmodernism*, expounds on its relation to film criticism via an essay by James MacDowell.) Their conclusions, however, can be readily applied to all these films, both in terms of mise-en-scène and narrative. For instance, the authors point to the structures designed by Ader and Rubsamen as employing 'materials and methods' not ideally suited to their task, hypothesising that their intention is 'not to fulfill it', but rather to represent an 'attempt to fulfill it in spite of its "unfulfillableness"' (Vermeulen and van den Akker 2010). The architects realise structurally the failed attempt at the unity of the 'good forms' of modernism – forms that holistically serve their purpose, offering a nostalgic sense of 'solace and pleasure' – while still visualising the attempt itself (Lyotard 1992: 45). A similar conclusion can be made with the use of antiquated forms such as stop-motion animation and other practical effects in the creations of Anderson and Jonze. It also characterises the actions of a vast majority of the films' characters, who continually embark on quixotic plans and quests to fulfil desires with an air of premature defeat.

This sense of the unfulfillable links metamodernism to the paradox found in Romantic irony, which engenders simultaneous 'creation and de-creation':

> The authentic romantic ironist is as filled with enthusiasm as with scepticism. Having ironically acknowledged the fictiveness of his own patterning of human experience, he romantically engages in the creative process of life by eagerly constructing new forms, new myths. (Mellor 1980: 5)

For Anne Mellor, Romantic irony creates new forms and myths in order to puncture them. It acknowledges the game it is playing but plays it anyway, moving forward in a continuing cycle of 'self-creation and self-destruction' (Behler 1988: 61) and recognition of the unending struggle that fuels imaginative power. (I discuss Romantic irony at length in Chapter 2.)

Metamodernism is, in essence, an attempt to traverse the gap between modernism's discredited, utopian expectations of totality – a belief in 'good forms' (Lyotard 1992: 45), grand 'metanarratives' of social progress (Lyotard

1997: xxiv), 'scientistic' ideological abstraction that feigns ideological neutrality (Docherty 1993: 25), and the 'fantasies of realism' (Lyotard 1992: 41) – and postmodernism's fragmenting and fracturing of them through the creation of 'new myths' (Vermeulen and van den Akker 2010). This attempted traversal forever fails, but it is in the attempt that metamodernism wages its own war against what Jameson calls postmodernism's 'waning of affect' – the obliteration of subjectivity leading to the end of 'unique and personal' style and the death of feeling 'since there is no longer a self present to do the feeling' (Jameson 1992: 64).

In its place, it creates a new 'narrative of longing' for something it can never achieve; as such 'the metamodern discourse consciously commits itself to an impossible possibility' (Vermeulen and van den Akker 2010). Metamodernism, in fact, marks a new return to a Romantic sensibility, one that grapples with the incommensurability of feeling and action, self and other. It is not merely postmodern pastiche or an arch wink toward the past from the knowing present:

> If these artists look back at the Romantic it is neither because they simply want to laugh at it (parody) nor because they wish to cry for it (nostalgia). They look back instead in order to perceive anew a future that was lost from sight. Metamodern neoromanticism should not merely be understood as re-appropriation; it should be interpreted as re-signification. (Vermeulen and van den Akker 2010)

The filmmakers in question all seem intent on such a process of re-signification. They create narratives that depict spirits in solitude moving through brave new liminal worlds of personal mythmaking in attempts at meaning-making: desperate for intersubjective connection, unable to totally fulfil their desires, yet continuing to struggle with the re-signification of their relationships and their own identities. I now turn to an overview of the filmmakers I discuss and connect them to this theoretical framework.

From the New Wave to New Hollywood to Now

While these filmmakers have no official organising principles, they are connected to each other professionally and personally in many ways.[5] Jonze and Coppola met early in their respective careers and were briefly married; Jonze directed two films from scripts written by Kaufman. They frequently use the same cast members and crew, such as actors Bill Murray and Jason Schwartzman (Anderson and Coppola), production designer K. K. Barrett (Jonze and Coppola), and cinematographer Lance Acord (Jonze and Coppola). They also share a similar working milieu. Some, such as Coppola, largely finance their films independently, but all are affiliated in one way or another with major Hollywood studios and their subsidiaries, sometimes referred to as 'Indiewood' (King 2014: 7).

There is a neat correlation between these filmmakers and the famous 'New Hollywood' filmmakers of the late 1960s and 1970s, who include, among others, Martin Scorsese, Roman Polanski, Francis Ford Coppola, Terrence Malick, Robert Altman, Hal Ashby and Brian De Palma (Biskind 1999: 15). In many ways the filmmakers I discuss owe a large debt to their predecessors' institutionalisation of a 'relative (but not radical) alterity' (King 2014: 31). Robert Phillip Kolker considers the New Hollywood era a fleeting period in American filmmaking when filmmakers were able to 'pursue the romantic possibility that there can still be individual interventions in the homogeneity of film' (1988: xiii). Falling somewhere between the avant-garde and the more formally and socially conservative product of the Hollywood studio era, New Hollywood filmmakers were 'unembarrassed [. . .] to assume the mantle of the artist, nor did they shrink from developing personal styles that distinguished their work from other directors' (Biskind 1999: 15). They 'maintained that directors are to movies what poets are to poems' (1999: 16), echoing the sentiments of French film critic Alexandre Astruc, who in 1948 coined the phrase 'la caméra-stylo' (camera pen) in reference to a new age, or 'tendency' of cinema.

For Astruc, after decades of simply being a 'fairground attraction', cinema was now 'a form in which and by which an artist can express his thoughts, however abstract they may be, or translate his obsessions exactly as he does in the contemporary essay or novel' (Astruc 1948). A director was no longer simply an 'illustrator' or 'presenter'; he (almost exclusively a 'he' in Astruc's time, and sadly still today) was a 'film-maker/author [who] writes with his camera as a writer writes with his pen' (Astruc 1948). This conception of filmmaking as 'personal obsession' is, of course, highly influenced by the Romantic principle of the particular 'insight and vision' that was the 'poet's privilege' (McGann 1983: 114). Astruc and the auteur theory born of his idea helped popularise the notion of film as art, and the filmmaker as an artist on par with the poet, writer of great literature and master painter.

'Authenticity' was a watchword for New Hollywood: its actors often trained in the Method acting style (Biskind 1999: 16) and its narratives embraced character-driven stories and anti-heroes and 'challenged the tyranny of technical correctness' through an embrace of European art cinema techniques that flew in the face of the classical Hollywood filmmaking style (1999: 17, 21, 15). But while these filmmakers, who were given a heretofore unknown level of creative freedom in Hollywood, were interested in upending a studio system that was already coming crashing down around them (1999: 17), decades later, their filmic descendants maintain a much more symbiotic relationship to the commercial system. If, in 1960s and 1970s Hollywood, 'Everything old was bad, everything new was good' and 'nothing was sacred' (1999: 14), by the end of the twentieth century, much self-conscious filmmaking style began to look back to the past for its inspiration. It embraced a less revolutionary stance, embodying an ethos and style Brendan Kredell calls the 'cinema of gentrification' (2012: 84).

Writing in the late 1980s, Kolker declares, 'the brief time of the Hollywood *auteur* is gone' (1988: xii). But his pronouncement seems premature. Now largely operating within a system of subsidiaries of major studios, 'mini-majors' such as Focus Features, Sony Pictures Classics and Fox Searchlight, the filmmakers covered in this book are often given a broad amount of creative control like their maverick cinematic forebears (Biskind 1999: 3). This is thanks in part to the prestige they engender (if not necessarily because of the box office receipts they garner) (King 2014: 282) and their relatively modest budgets compared with Hollywood 'blockbusters'. All are generally critically praised, with varying degrees of commercial success. With their markers of quality, they can be considered what Yannis Tzioumakis calls 'speciality' cinema (2006: 282).

Some in this group acknowledge their debt to New Hollywood, but they are just as likely, if not more so, to reference their affection for the twentieth-century European art cinema that itself inspired New Hollywood, especially in the case of Anderson. He references the French New Wave in films such as *Fantastic Mr. Fox* (François Truffaut) and *Moonrise Kingdom* (Truffaut and Jean-Luc Godard), and his general aesthetic owes a large debt to the wistful melancholia of Truffaut's decidedly less arch films. Coppola has said that as a teenager Godard's *À bout de souffle* (Les Films Impéria, 1960) was her favourite film (*Festival de Cannes Daily* 2014). It is possible to draw a line from the *Nouvelle Vague*, champions of *politique des auteurs* and renouncers of the socially conscious, mainstream 'prestige' pictures of *cinéma du papa* (Caughie 1981: 35), to the filmmakers being considered here (the so-called 'Left Bank' filmmakers, more formally daring and politically conscious, notwithstanding) (Roud 1977: 143).

The New Wave filmmakers' free-spirited personal portrayals of 'solitude, aimlessness, introspection, aggression and failure' sometimes saw them accused of a 'reactionary' politics (Caughie 1981: 38, 35). Their rebuke of the stuffy, melodramatic 'Tradition of Quality' was somehow both 'modernist' and 'elegiac', backward- and forward-looking (Vincendeau 2010: 136). In much the same way, the new 'neoromantic' American filmmakers infuse their films with an idiosyncratic, highly personalised subjectivity that has led to their own accusations of being 'reactionary' (MacDowell 2014: 159), 'tedious' and 'boring' (French 2006), or 'self-satisfied' and 'solipsistic' (Moats 2009). But unlike the filmmakers of the French New Wave, they do not have a stodgy tradition to overturn so much as a Romantic tradition to rebuild.

Kaufman, the oldest filmmaker by more than a decade, is the only one of the four to have formally studied film – Anderson has a philosophy degree

(Collin 2014), Coppola learned the craft while shadowing her father on his film sets growing up and Jonze got his start making amateur skateboarding and BMX videos. In contrast to the 'movie brats' of the 1970s – Scorsese, Coppola, Spielberg, Lucas, et al. – who all attended film school (Biskind 1999: 15), these filmmakers continue a trend emerging in the 1990s of what Jeffrey Sconce considers a scepticism of the 'consecrating functions' of a formal artistic education (2002: 357).

This idea encapsulates a Romantic inclination of the more simplistic variety – a resistance to the civilising forces of society on individual expression, a belief in a Rousseauian 'untutored and original genius' (Bate 1970: 150), or perhaps a 'revolutionary' upheaval of the old guard, as Truffaut himself railed against *cinéma du papa* in the 1950s. However, it is difficult to consider any of these filmmakers or their films in the context of revolution. Coppola's very own *papa*, Francis Ford Coppola, made an indelible mark on the cinema, but she and her contemporaries do not appear interested in the social upheaval that often coloured the work of the elder Coppola's generation (Sconce 2002: 352). Despite their idiosyncrasies and formal inventiveness, their films are usually commercially viable, if not necessarily universally appealing.

The sobriquets applied to these films have been numerous. Variously referring to them as 'quirky' cinema (MacDowell 2010), 'smart' cinema (Sconce 2002), the 'new sincerity' (Buckland 2012) and 'post-pop' (Mayshark 2009), these critical appraisals mostly define the various aesthetic and thematic traits the films exhibit rather than attaching them to any underlying, unifying principle or philosophy. Instead, the films are described as having a discursive, 'highly unstable [. . .] tendency' defined mostly by tone (Perkins 2012: 14). Jeffrey Sconce writes of 'smart' film's use of irony as one that identifies a 'semiotic chasm' dividing a 'structure of feeling that sees everything in quotation marks' from one that 'still looks for art to equal sincerity, positivity, commitment, action and responsibility' (2002: 358).

Writing in 2002, Sconce focuses on American films of the 1990s, which he claims exhibit a commitment to 'irony, black humor, fatalism, relativism and, yes, even nihilism' (2002: 350). Fundamentally, smart films exhibit a distrust of 'ultimate positions of truth or reason' (Perkins 2012: 14). Building on Sconce's thesis, Claire Perkins identifies in smart film a depiction of 'post-youth' culture: a culture defined by those members of so-called 'Generation X' who are 'over-educated, underemployed and over-invested in popular culture' (2012: 7). Except for Kaufman, born in 1958, the filmmakers I consider are all members of this generation temporally, if not necessary descriptively. All are, in multiple ways, concerned with familial and interpersonal breakdown of a complacently bourgeois society (Sconce 2002: 358).

Sconce contends these films express an overwhelming scepticism, one informed by 'a fundamental break in the narrative of "revolutionary potential" advanced by the events and ideas of the 1950s, 1960s and 1970s' (2002: 6) due to a degraded social and cultural milieu – and what Jesse Mayshark calls 'a sense of domestic life as a nexus of abandonment, alienation, and frustration' (2009: 9) – that removes a search for meaning and replaces it with a myopic 'interest in the politics of taste, consumerism and identity' (Sconce 2002: 358). Aesthetically, they project a 'blankness' – a 'sense of dampened affect' – that jibes with their disaffected worldview (2002: 358). As Perkins writes, 'the signature blankness of the smart film is a compelling illustration of a generation with "nothing" to say' (2012: 8). Both Sconce's and Perkins's conception of smart film seems incomplete, however, if not incorrect. In fairness to Sconce, some of the films he discusses, especially those of Quentin Tarantino, Neil LaBute and perhaps Todd Solondz, apply more to this rubric; but the 'smart' impression is lacking in his assessments of Anderson's films and the 'matter-of-fact surrealism' (2002: 350) of Jonze and Kaufman.

It seems obvious that not nearly so much critical attention would be paid to a certain 'tendency' in American cinema if it really had 'nothing' to say, nor even if it postured as such. Most if not all of these films, in fact, are about the struggle to express what that very 'saying' is, to articulate a deep well of feeling frustrated by a culture of alienation that delimits a search for meaning. Sconce tellingly refers to Wes Anderson's films *Bottle Rocket* (Columbia Pictures, 1996), *Rushmore* (American Empirical, 1998) and *The Royal Tenenbaums* (American Empirical, 2001) as 'bittersweet' (2002: 350). But his conception of 'smart' seems to rely far more on the bitter to the detriment of the sweet. Likewise, Perkins alludes to smart film as part of a 'therapy culture', which ascribes 'the tendency in contemporary culture to make sense of the world through the prism of emotion' (2012: 10). This notion seems antithetical to smart films' pure adherence to the principles of ironic distance and disaffected apathy, and certainly to 'dampened affect'. Could it be that many (if not all) of these films are instead attempting to bridge that 'semiotic chasm' between apathy and emotion, feeling and futility?

I join MacDowell and Buckland to emphatically argue 'yes'. They are, in fact, about the struggle to create grand statements on the loss of grand narratives, even as the very idea seems antiquated. Warren Buckland identifies this breed of films as the 'new sincerity', in contrast to the original meaning of the term as defined by Jim Collins (Collins 1993: 243). Buckland suggests that, rather than a simplistic rejection of irony and return to sincerity, as Collins suggests, the new sincerity offers a response to, not a disavowal of, postmodern irony: 'in a dialectical move, new sincerity incorporates postmodern irony and cynicism; it operates in conjunction with irony' (2012: 2). MacDowell offers a similar perspective on this tendency's ambivalent tonal register. As in Sconce's definition of smart film, MacDowell's concept of quirky cinema is based mainly on the 'notoriously tricky concept' (MacDowell 2010: 2) of tone but is much more circumspect. Key to the sensibility of quirky is 'a commitment to a certain comedic mode' (2010: 3). Akin to the aesthetic 'blankness' of smart cinema (Sconce 2002: 359), it relies on 'deadpan', which MacDowell defines as 'dry, perfunctory, excessively functional, taking a situation and line that we might expect to be made dramatic [. . .] and downplaying them to the point of absurdity' (2010: 3).

Blankness and deadpan both relate to smart film's 'dampening' of affect. However, for MacDowell, quirky cinema's reliance on comedic address 'requires we view the fiction as simultaneously absurd *and* moving, the characters as pathetic *and* likeable, the world as manifestly artificial *and* believable' (2010: 4). The films are sincere, but just as in the late-Romantic critique of sincerity as performative, their sincerity is 'best understood as a rhetorical construct rather than the "natural" expression of inner truth implied in its traditional usage' (King 2014: 60). Authenticity is, as in the New Hollywood, of renewed importance. As Coppola says, 'I don't want my movies to feel like movies [. . .] I want them to feel like life' (Rickey 2013). Of course, such a desire is realised by a very subjective idea of exactly how life 'feels'. (It is important to note the potential discrepancy between onscreen portrayals of emotion and those emotions being embodied by the spectator, an issue I address in Chapters 2 and 3.) For Coppola and her compatriots, feeling, not mimetic reproduction, is indicative of authenticity. According to MacDowell, the quirky film's sense of ironic detachment combined with 'sincere emotional engagement' operates on the level where both structures of feeling are 'made different' as they inform each other (2010: 12). The simultaneous engagement with both creates an underlying sense of anxiety and uncertainty.

Like smart cinema, quirky film turns on depictions of arrested development – adults in these films often 'behave like children' or are plagued by childhood trauma; protagonists are often 'chaste romantic dreamers' (2010: 9, 10). Combined with a mise-en-scène MacDowell sees as exemplary of the desire to conform the world into a 'less chaotic, more simplified' version of reality, it signals a nostalgic, 'quasi-magical voyage into the past [. . .] made to appear both melancholic and comforting' (2010: 7, 9). It is clear that MacDowell sees the films of quirky not just as pastiche and quotation 'born of ironic distance' (Sconce 2002: 358), but as something much more than the sum of their quirks.

MacDowell's discussion of quirky cinema is, in many respects, an excellent starting point for a discussion of Romanticism in film, particularly the films I discuss. But it is also, again, somewhat limiting in this context. These films depict varying levels of comic overtones and undertones, with Anderson being the most consistently deadpan as MacDowell defines it. MacDowell references films from Anderson, Jonze and Kaufman, including the latter's directorial debut, *Synecdoche, New York* (Sidney Kimmel Entertainment, 2008). But in that film, along with Coppola's *The Virgin Suicides* (American Zoetrope, 1999) and *Marie Antoinette* (Columbia Pictures, 2006), a tragicomic mode of 'quirkiness' eventually gives way to a decidedly more tragic mode. The very Romantic irony that engenders deadpan is rooted in the suffering caused 'by the antagonism of heart with intellect, of spontaneity with reflection, of passion with calculation, and enthusiasm with scepticism' (Behler 1988: 43). The oscillations between deadpan humour and deep feeling (or the attempted concealment of the latter with the former) are really a stylistic symptom of a greater underlying quality: pathos.

Jesse Mayshark characterises this cycle of films as 'post-pop' and defines them by their allegiance not to a comic sensibility but to 'a sort of self-conscious *meaningfulness*' (Mayshark 2009: 5; original emphasis). Considering the films of Anderson, Jonze, Kaufman, Coppola and others, he focuses on structures of identity, intersubjectivity and consciousness: 'Their overriding concern is a sort of yearning for connection, but one that is colored by an awareness of all the things that get in its way' (2009: 8). Mayshark sees these films as attempts to bridge the self-conscious divide between self and other, thus 'transcend[ing] the boundaries of body and consciousness' (2009: 8).

While I largely agree with Mayshark's assessment, one point of contention is a critical one: his account of the film's protagonists as 'at home in a complicated present' while being 'emphatically not nostalgic for some simpler "past"' (2009: 14). I argue that, far from being at home in the present, they can barely tolerate it as a concept; instead, they cope with the present by looking back toward the past. They exhibit nostalgia for a fantasy, a simple imaginary history. This sense of nostalgia colours their quasi-conservative worldview, but it is complicated by the anxiety caused by such a fantastic recreation of the past as a guard against the always-uncertain future.

At the conclusion of 'Notes on Quirky', MacDowell calls for a deeper, more comprehensive examination of these films in the context of their use of Romantic irony, specifically noting its correlation with Schlegel's definition (2010: 14). 'It is in fact unlikely that a trend as specific and widespread as the quirky *will not* tell us something about its sociohistorical moment', MacDowell writes (2010: 14; original emphasis). He calls for his study to be viewed as the groundwork from which future research in a similar mode can 'expand in different directions' (2010: 2). This book aims to do just that, taking established cinematic theories of the quirky, smart, new sincerity and the like and delving further into the root causes and connections these films have in terms of style and substance, ones that I argue are fundamentally Romantic in form and vision, but specific to their own historical and cultural environment. By returning to the past, as these filmmakers have done, we can learn more about our present selves and begin to discern a credible future that still asserts, and values, meaning.

Chapter Overviews

The arguments made within are cumulative, with successive chapters building on ideas and theories previously posited. Each chapter seeks to engage with a specific discourse of contemporary film studies: aesthetics (Chapter 1); cinematic metatextuality (Chapter 2); feminist criticism (Chapter 3); film-phenomenology (Chapter 4); eco-criticism, childhood and animal studies (Chapter 5); and ethical studies (Chapter 6). This structure allows me to trace the progression of Romantic thought and enables me to situate these works historically, while simultaneously engaging with an up-to-the-moment present. While these films exhibit the lasting traditions of the Romantic period, they are also very much a response to the preoccupations found within our own time.

I begin by elucidating the fundamental principles of Romantic aesthetics – the concepts of the sublime, the beautiful and the picturesque – as they relate to Wes Anderson's films *The Royal Tenenbaums* and *The Life Aquatic with Steve Zissou* (American Empirical, 2004). Working from descriptions of the sublime and beautiful in Edmund Burke's *Philosophical Enquiry*, I argue that both films' aesthetic components create picturesque representations through mise-en-scène that combine beauty and sublimity in varying degrees. *The Royal Tenenbaums*' aesthetic paradigm is one I term the 'painful picturesque', a programme that systematically develops the middle-ground eighteenth-century picturesque ideal of perfected nature by creating shabby but pleasing, controlled yet chaotic visual systems in the urban pastoral environment of a fantasy New York City. While the overall aesthetic of the film is one of the picturesque, it is not the picturesque traditionally designed to create a sense of cohesion and human power through artificially perfected natural environments. Instead, the film creates a sensation that something is not quite 'right' – a signal that the beautiful forms of modernism are being undermined by corroded personal-historical traumas that threaten to overwhelm good design and picturesque restraint.

The Life Aquatic with Steve Zissou accomplishes a similar aesthetic effect, although this time the film's settings invoke the sublime more so than the beautiful, while resulting in a similar sense of picturesque anxiety. The film is set amongst natural landscapes that engender feelings of sublimity – vast oceans, weather-ravaged deserted islands and underwater environments containing terrifying, man-eating sea creatures. However, in the film these potentially sublime locales are undercut by the film's commitment to creating pleasurable, non-threatening images that coincide with a deadpan comedic style. Human frailty and vanity, not natural might, is the ultimate terror in the film, and while nature eventually shows the film's protagonist in sublime awe, it is an awe that engenders a psychic healing. I refer to this as the 'sentimental sublime': sublimity that is defanged and contained, but causes anxiety nonetheless.

In Chapter 2, I argue that Charlie Kaufman's *Synecdoche, New York* creates a metatextual relationship between director and protagonist through its use of Romantic irony. The film directly addresses issues of solipsism as it is told from the radically subjective viewpoint of its self-obsessed protagonist, the 'genius' theatre director Caden Cotard, who may or may not be descending into madness. Kaufman conjures sublime feeling in the spectator through aesthetic devices of fantastic world creation. These include the creation of mise en abyme – engendered by various life-size recreations of New York City built inside of a large warehouse that is itself inside the 'actual' New York City – and an engagement with Tzvetan Todorov's fantastic 'themes of the self' and 'themes of vision', which are expressed by inexplicable narrative elements such as a continually burning house fire. Drawing on German idealism and Schlegel's concept of Romantic irony to counteract traditional notions of mimetic realism, Kaufman portrays his film world (and the world itself) as chaotic. But whereas Kaufman's film embraces the chaos of becoming inherent in Schlegel's philosophy, its protagonist suffers from a complete inability to engage with life on any authentic level and subsequently fails as an artist and person.

In Chapter 3, I address the masculine subjectivity of Romantic 'egotistical' sublimity, a sublime based in the self's relation to the world, with an examination of its effects on female subjectivity in Sofia Coppola's *The Virgin Suicides*. Building on Kantian notions of the sublime and the imagination, the Romantic sublime is one traditionally predicated on the response of the 'masculine' ego (Mellor 1980: 3) – sublimity has its source in the internal mental faculties of reason via imagination and is not something that exists in the empirical world. This purely subjective version of sublimity was reserved for the province of masculine imagination, while the feminine, apparently lacking similar imaginative power, is relegated to the lesser realm of the social and the beautiful.

Sofia Coppola's *The Virgin Suicides* creates a film world where the expression of emotion is constantly thwarted by gender and class hypocrisy – characters in the film fail to communicate despite undercurrents of deep feeling. The film engages with the egotistical sublime in its idealised aesthetic portrayal of a group of teenage girls, who serve as objects of sublimity for the local teenage boys. However, it also portrays a reverence for a 'feminine' or 'everyday' sublime by valorising a feminine aesthetic Rosalind Galt terms the 'pretty'. Ultimately, it creates an ambivalent presentation of this femininity through dreamlike yet kitsch imagery of the girls, which speaks not only to the celebration of femininity but also to its commodification and degradation.

Like *The Virgin Suicides*, Spike Jonze's *Her* (Annapurna Pictures, 2013) approaches the sublime on the level of intersubjective emotional discourse. In Chapter 4, I discuss how the film engages both the egotistical and feminine sublimes but offers a much more optimistic outcome. The film addresses the philosophical 'problem of other minds', that is, the idea that we can never truly know what another thinks or feels because we are too trapped in our own subjectivity. This crisis leads the film's protagonist, lonely writer Theodore (Joaquin Phoenix), to withdraw from life into a cocoon of imaginative solipsism.

When he meets his operating system Samantha (Scarlett Johansson), an entirely artificial intelligence who has no corporeal form, she becomes an object of sublimity for him, activating his imagination and allowing him to access long-supressed emotion. Eventually, however, Samantha embraces her own version of the sublime, a feminine one, when she leaves Theodore to enter into an ecstatic communal state with other operating systems. She becomes the subject of sublimity, even while serving as an object of the Romantic sublime for Theodore, who finally begins to regain his power as a writer due to his experience. The film's final images suggest that such a feminine sublime can be accessible to humans if we exercise imaginative will and empathy in our relations toward others, regardless of the fact that we can never really know existence outside of our own consciousness.

In Chapter 5, I analyse the ideological framework of Anderson's *Fantastic Mr. Fox* (Twentieth Century Fox, 2009). The film, an adaptation of Roald Dahl's beloved children's book, addresses various Romantic conceptions of childhood, personal and cultural history, and the natural world in relation to the self and subjectivity. In his reimagining of Dahl's story, Anderson exhibits a disdain for the mechanisation of the societal landscape and the beings inhabiting it, similar to a course charted by Henry David Thoreau in *Walden*, while also optimistically suggesting that animal/human 'nature' can still survive through aesthetic and ideological compromise and creative genius. In a sense he creates a brand of ideological pastoralism to match the aesthetic pastoralism/picturesque of many of his film worlds. While the anxiety portrayed in his earlier films remains, it is somewhat defused by an anarchic yet collaborative spirit.

In my final chapter, I address Sofia Coppola's *Marie Antoinette* in relation to personal subjectivity and excess, including Jeffrey Cane Robinson's notion of poetic 'fancy' and, again, Rosalind Galt's idea of the 'pretty' in visual art and cinema. If the filmmakers I discuss have been accused of an apolitical solipsism, *Marie Antoinette* directly engages with this idea at the level of narrative (its protagonist, despite being a political figure, is unconcerned with politics and spends most of her time in a dreamlike fantasy world) and aesthetics (its depiction of material excess through surface sensation).

Coppola's emphasis on sensation and surfaces elicits what Keats refers to as the 'material sublime' (Keats 1976: 237), an engagement with sensory excess, rather than the core subjectivity that the Romantic sublime invokes. But in *Marie Antoinette* Coppola also introduces a subjectivity that is not present in

The Virgin Suicides. Ultimately, her protagonist's bulwark of sensory pleasure is stripped away, along with its attendant aesthetic function, signalling not just the title character's maturation but also her imminent death. In Coppola's film, 'growing up' entails pain and suffering, as it does in life. All the filmmakers I discuss, in one form or another, suggest that it also signals a fundamental loss – the separation of self from world, and the renouncement of the joys and pleasures of connection.

PART I

ROMANTIC CLARITY AND CONFUSION

1. BEAUTY AMONG THE RUINS: THE PAINFUL PICTURESQUE AND SENTIMENTAL SUBLIME IN WES ANDERSON'S AESTHETICS

> *How pleasant, as the sun declines, to view*
> *The spacious landscape change in form and hue!*
> William Wordsworth, 'An Evening Walk,
> Addressed to a Young Lady' (1793)

In *The Royal Tenenbaums* (American Empirical, 2001), filmmaker Wes Anderson tells the story of an eccentric family coming to grips with its failed promise in a fairy-tale-like version of New York City. Anderson's succeeding film, *The Life Aquatic with Steve Zissou* (American Empirical, 2004) follows a somewhat hapless, Jacques Cousteau-like explorer on his quest for revenge against the mythical shark who 'ate' his partner while he simultaneously grapples with a career on the decline and the discovery of a possible illegitimate adult son. These two films from early in the director's career are emblematic of his body of work so far, which is often criticised as being overly reliant on aesthetics at the expense of emotional resonance. Despite their differences in subject matter and milieu, both rely principally on style to convey feeling.

Rather than denying real emotion, the aestheticism of Anderson's films, which so confounds his critics, constitutes a rallying cry against the cold, in-affective modernity the films seem to question; their emotional preoccupations are woven into every fanciful costume, prop, line delivery and composition. Although they do evince an attitude of emotional distance due to their expressions of hyper-reality, they often exude moods of anxiety and alienation. Each film's style is grounded in an aesthetic programme that mixes sublimity and beauty, operating under an uneasy dialectic between the two. The underlying sense of anxiety created by aesthetic means results in the creation of what I call a 'painful picturesque' (in *The Royal Tenenbaums*) and a 'sentimental sublime' (in *The Life Aquatic*).

Familial anxiety in *The Royal Tenenbaums* is conveyed by its slightly off-kilter aesthetic presentations of the beautiful. Anderson utilises many Burkean elements of beauty – soft and warm colour, an attention to symmetry and form – and renders them askew. While Anderson's mise-en-scène is noted for its excessively symmetrical compositions (especially his penchant for single-point-perspective shots), his framing, when combined with object placement, costuming, camera movement and overall production design, asserts a division between actuality and presentation. His film worlds are more haphazard than they seem, even as they appear tyrannically constructed. In *The Royal Tenenbaums*, the result is a mismatch between content and presentation that leads to a combination of the pleasantly picturesque and the anxious: the painful picturesque. Such an aesthetic presentation is simultaneously nostalgic, melancholic and apprehensive.

The Life Aquatic, in similar fashion, creates a schism between content and presentation, but is more concerned with depictions of sublimity. Its expansive locations, such as the open sea and weather-ravaged tropical islands, are examples of a Burkean natural sublime aesthetics. However, Anderson also imbues these scenes with the aesthetics of the beautiful and an obvious artificiality. While in the former film this creates a picturesque feeling of solemnity, in the latter it renders the sublime sentimental due to its power to heal emotional wounds. That power rests not in exaltation, but in its nostalgic, curative function for the film's protagonist, the washed-up nature documentary director Zissou.

Combined, these two films serve as both an aesthetic proclamation and a philosophical treatise for the director. They are controlled but chaotic, representing both the desire for a modernist unity and a postmodern sense of confusion and unease. They are – as Vermeulen, van den Akker and MacDowell have all noted – metamodern, but they are not simply 'quirky' in this vein. The nature of their tensions is fundamentally Romantic.

The Sublime and the Beautiful in Eighteenth-century Aesthetics

Edmund Burke's 1757 treatise, *A Philosophical Enquiry into the Origins of the Sublime and Beautiful*, was profoundly influential in shaping Romantic philosophy in relation to both sublimity and beauty, two concepts that would become integral to Romantic aesthetics. Integrally, both of these concepts hinge on notions of the passions of individual experience. In the case of the sublime, these passions excited ideas of pain and danger. According to Burke, 'terrible objects' or those that 'operate in a manner analogous to terror' incite the sublime, the 'strongest emotion which the mind is capable of feeling' (Burke [1757] 1792: 49). This pain from terror ultimately presages the fear of the ultimate pain, death, but when experienced at a physical and psychological remove enables Burke's notion of delight. Such pleasing terror 'fills the mind with great ideas, and the soul delights in the experience' (Monk 1970: 28). For Burke, emotion was the 'keystone' of aesthetics, and the most exalted emotion was sublimity (1970: 28).

While there is pleasure involved in this form of 'positive' pain, the experience of delight is not equivalent to positive pleasure (Burke [1757] 1792: 42–3). Instead, notions of the beautiful revolve around such pleasure, specifically the passions of love and 'sentiments of tenderness and affection' ([1757] 1792: 56). While the sublime inspires awe through terror, obscurity, power and the 'artificial infinite', the beautiful inspires sympathy, even pity, through the qualities of smoothness, gradual variation, 'clean and fair' colours, lightness and delicateness. Beauty, like sublimity, excites passion, but it is 'nearer to a species of melancholy, than to jollity and mirth' ([1757] 1792: 192). The passion beauty elicits is ultimately of the terrestrial, not of the infinite.

Clearly, the sublime and the beautiful have a wide aesthetic and psychological gulf between them. While both contain conceptual elements of passion, pain and pleasure, they are realised through antithetical means. In the latter part of the eighteenth century, an attempt to fill this aesthetic gap by synthesising the sublime and beautiful emerged in the idea of the picturesque. According to Uvedale Price's *Essays on the Picturesque*, the concept 'corrects the languor of beauty, or the tension of sublimity' (1810: 89). Instead, it offers an aesthetic middle ground, one that combines the thrills of sublimity with the positive pleasures of beauty. The picturesque supplements 'roughness with irregularity and "sudden variation"', which produces 'the variety, intricacy, and "partial concealments" that arouse our curiosity' (Jarvis 2004: 181). Whereas the sublime offers concealment, privation and obscurity and the beautiful clarity and pleasure, the picturesque is situated somewhere between the two.

It is this 'nostalgic' and 'conservative' (2004: 183) aesthetic that informs much of Anderson's oeuvre. Rife with imaginative subjectivity, Anderson's work is associated with stylistic overabundance, a fascination with objects and ephemera (particularly those of childhood) and idiosyncratic, off-kilter fantasy worlds. Critics often point to these overly artificial, archly constructed worlds as detrimental to the emotional participation of the viewer, deriding them as twee, escapist, distancing or simply self-indulgent.[1] Many also consider Anderson's work overly fanciful, too idealised and esoteric for its own good.[2] It does not deal in reality, per se, but reality as seen through the eyes of an exacting and singular imagination.

Some of this criticism is reminiscent of the assessment of writers in the Romantic era. According to Seamus Perry, 'The charge of escapism has always been made against the proponents of subjective idealism and the "world within"' (1997: 8). While M. H. Abrams insists this perception is a 'peculiar injustice' (1970: 101), Jerome McGann acknowledges this penchant for escapism as both 'a critical gesture, an attack upon the present meanness' of the world and 'the reflex of the circumstances in which their work, their lives, and their culture were all forced to develop' (1983: 35, 117). In other words, the Romantics were a product of their own cultural milieu and historical era as much as they were creators of it. Similarly, Anderson's idealism and escapism is as much a product of the anxiety of our contemporary era as it is an expression of ego or an escape into nostalgic flights of fancy.

Anderson's mise-en-scène engenders both an emotional distance, through its artificiality, and a physical one, through its framing. Such distance impedes true sublimity in Burke's sense. According to Jean-François Lyotard, 'intensification' and not 'elevation' is key to Burke's notions of the sublime (1993b: 251), creating the 'shock effect' of an 'entirely spiritual passion' (1993b: 249, 251). Anderson's films exhibit tension, especially between pleasure and pain, but their lack of intensity in emotional presentation through distancing effects turns shock and passion into fanciful, melancholic pseudo-nostalgia.

Principally, Anderson's films represent a longing to embrace the past in their self-conscious 'exhumation' (Botting 1999: 103) of Romantic aesthetics and feeling. This feeling of mourning permeates all of Anderson's films, both literally (someone in the main cast dies or mourns the death of loved one) and figuratively, through overall emotional presentation. Such mourning calls up the past in order to alleviate the pain of living in postmodern 'indeterminacy' (Lyotard 1993b: 247), the state of ahistoricity that makes it impossible to grasp the 'now' because there is no 'final understanding' of history and representation (Elam 1992: 10). The 'master narrative' of history has been de-legitimised, and the present itself becomes untethered from a sense of historical progression (1992: 11).

Anderson's films can be seen as a nostalgic grappling with the loss of grand narratives by replacing them with obviously fictitious reimaginings of history as particular, personal, idiosyncratic and even contradictory. This alleviation is never entirely successful, however, likely due to the acknowledgement of its own fiction. Ultimately, it creates something just shy of modernism's goal of shaping the world into 'good forms' in the tradition of Enlightenment reason (Docherty 1993: 6). In such a modernist view, 'the multiplicity of forms is reduced to position and arrangement, history to fact, things to matter' (1993: 6). According to Thomas Docherty, within the postmodern, the ideals of modernism are as far-fetched as Anderson's fantastic tableaux. Instead, 'we are condemned to live in a present, and adopting a specific – some have said "schizophrenic" – mood as a result of acknowledging that this present is characterized by struggle or contradiction and incoherence' (1993: 3).

Indeed, the tension created in Anderson's mise-en-scène can be considered a 'schizophrenic' one in the purely colloquial sense that Docherty uses it: its sense of order that does not strictly adhere depicts a desperation to make sense of the world while acknowledging that the notion is simply an impossibility. Anderson's work is metamodern in its depiction of a longing for unity and its acceptance of the inconclusive. As such, the 'pervasive cynicism' (Waugh 1992: 5) of postmodernism is transformed into a fantastic reimagining of the progressive ideal, but one that understands it is indulging in a fantasy.

The Royal Tenenbaums and the Painful Picturesque

While Anderson's first two features, *Bottle Rocket* (Columbia Pictures, 1996) and *Rushmore* (American Empirical, 1998), exhibited many of the aesthetic predilections that would become staples in his later films, it was not until 2001's *The Royal Tenenbaums* that his realist-fantastical sensibility became fully realised. This is primarily due to that film's world creation through mise-en-scène, which produces a sense of both picturesque tranquillity and postmodern anxiety.

The picturesque has its roots in eighteenth-century English landscape design, later adopted by landscape painters such as John Constable and Thomas Gainsborough and eventually the English Romantic poets, especially William Wordsworth. In his *Preface to Lyrical Ballads*, Wordsworth writes extensively in favour of positive pleasure, whose source is beauty, but also advocates for the combining of 'low and rustic [. . .] situations from common life' with 'a certain colouring of imagination whereby ordinary things should be presented to the mind in an unusual way' (Wordsworth [1800] 1957: 115). The ordinary becomes embedded within the imaginary, attaining a fresh level of excitement but still possessing a consoling sense of the everyday.

This picturesque landscape 'was made to tell a story or suggest a meaning via the presence of buildings, statues, and inscriptions, lending the garden a theatrical as well as pictorial dimension' (Jarvis 2004: 185). Unlike the strict regularity and purely unnatural formality of the French classicism that came before it, this theatricality was characterised by irregularity, contrast, roughness, 'kinship to the real world', variety, use of light and shade and novelty (Mohr 1996: 245). The picturesque mandate was, in essence, dominance over nature (1996: 248), but not in the cataclysmic sense of industrialism. Instead it expressed a reverence for the natural as a force for psychological healing.

Suitably, the landscapes that appear in *The Royal Tenenbaums* – notably cemeteries, but also city parks and gardens – are rustic but strictly designed and often in a state of seemingly purposeful decay. Its key location, the Tenenbaum family residence, is purely manufactured. The impressively foreboding structure dominates its surroundings; with its neo-gothic stone edifice and castle-like spire, the building is so grand there is almost no space left for surrounding landscape. Instead, Anderson shifts the world of nature to inside the home, which becomes a picturesque combination of the theatrical and the organic, at once vibrantly alive and frozen in time.

In the film, nature is ossified and put on display. From the neutered wildness of Margot Tenenbaum's jungle-themed play to Royal Tenenbaum's 'Wild Javelena' mounted head, it becomes one more imaginative component in the historical narrative of a family that is in danger of dissolving under the weight of expectation. The tragi-comic story of a cosmopolitan brood once celebrated for its wunderkind children, who have all failed to live up to societal and familial expectations in adulthood, *The Royal Tenenbaums* reveals the ideals of modernism to be impeachable fantasies through its character and mise-en-scène.

At first the massive, five-storey stone edifice of the mansion – complete with family insignia flag – appears as a grand yet crumbling beauty, a mythical anachronism on a fictitious street, Archer Avenue. But this visual reference to gothic erosion belies the intellectual and creative vigour permeating the inside of the home early in the film, which is reflected by its interiors. First seen in flashbacks, the inside of the house is warm, inviting and full of life. High-key lighting illuminates every corner, reflecting the children's intellectual brightness and casting a nostalgic glow on the paraphernalia and ephemera of layer upon layer of family history and creative output.

The overabundance of visual information in many shots creates a subtle disorientation for the viewer. In Burke's terminology, this creates a feeling of obscurity, where 'the mind is hurried out of itself, by a croud [sic] of great and confused images; which affect because they are crowded and confused' (Burke [1757] 1792: 88). But Anderson's mise-en-scène is also meticulously composed. The sense of personal history attached to the setting is evident: ageing throw rugs lie about seemingly haphazardly covering floorboards already worn down by a thousand small footsteps; dozens of framed children's drawings line nearly every available inch of the salmon pink walls; Royal's missing stuffed 'Wild Javelena' head leaves a visible trace of itself behind in its outline on the paint.

Variations of pink, a colour emblematic of the family and its overwhelming ties to the house, dominate. Vivid pink is used as a neutral in the film, and the colour is, for Burke, representative of the beautiful (Burke [1757] 1792: 180). For Burke, 'clear and fair colours [. . .] light greens; soft blues; weak whites; pink reds; and violets' are the ideal colours of beauty, and if colour is 'strong and vivid' it must be varied ([1757] 1792: 180). Despite the pink's vividness in the film, whenever it is in danger of overwhelming the frame, as in the hallway and main stairwell of the home, it is broken up by various objects, creating the Wordsworthian ideal of tempering passion with an 'overbalance of pleasure' (Wordsworth [1800] 1957: 127).

Each of the Tenenbaum children is linked to their own specific room in the house. Their personal idiosyncrasies strongly inform the production design, so that each space becomes emblematic of character. Through an opening flashback montage we are introduced to Margot (Gwyneth Paltrow), Richie (Luke Wilson) and Chas (Ben Stiller) in their bedrooms. Compared with the size and stateliness of the home's grand ballroom, the children's rooms are small and cloistered. Of the three children, adopted daughter Margot's room – which features blood-red wallpaper with a zebra motif and tribal-style masks on the walls – is the most evocative of the sublime.

The sublime has historically been considered the province of the masculine, with the beautiful regarded as the ideal of femininity (Shaw 2005). (I discuss this idea at length in Chapter 3.) Margot herself is an amalgam of the masculine and the feminine. Her feminine uniform of light-blue and white-striped tennis dress, which aligns her to tennis player Richie, is offset by her poker-straight hair – the beautiful, according to Burke, avoids sharp lines and angles ([1757] 1792: 194) – and darkened eye makeup, which creates a sublime contrast next to her fair skin and hair. This effect is exaggerated in the adult Margot, which underlines a hardening, an intensification of her masculinity. In fact, the key to unlocking the concept of the painful picturesque from a character perspective rests in the domesticated wildness of Margot. If the picturesque denotes the wildness of nature shaped into something like beauty by self-interested human control, Margot – routinely subjected to patriarchal will throughout the film, whether that of her adopted father, her birth father, her much older husband or her man-child lover – typifies it.

During her introduction, we see Margot as a child dressed as a zebra in one of her early plays. Richie and Chas both portray predator animals (a bear and a tiger) while Margot is relegated, by her own design, to playing a conquered prey animal,[3] a zebra complete with hand-crafted trompe l'oeil arrow holes in its gut. According to Burke, the relationship between the strength of a beast and its sublimity depends on context. Certain animals of brute strength, such as oxen and other beasts of burden, have been domesticated and as a result can never be sublime. Instead, the sublime is found 'in the gloomy forest, and in the howling wilderness, in the form of the lion, the tiger, the panther or rhinoceros' ([1757] 1792: 94). Pointedly, these animals' sublimity lies not only in their physical force but also in their unpredictability and inscrutability. That Margot chooses to portray a zebra (exotic, wild yet non-threatening) reveals her understanding of her circumstances even as a young child. The sole adopted sibling, Margot is treated virtually as an interloper in her own family, something akin to an exotic pet, by her father, Royal (Gene Hackman). Later Margot and Richie run away and spend the night in the 'African Wing of the Public Archives'. Among the stuffed creatures of the savannah, defanged of their danger, she feels most at home.

THE STILLNESS OF SOLITUDE

Figure 1.1   The film's mise-en-scène links Margot Tenenbaum to images of wildness, exoticism and performative beauty.

The adult Margot, replaying childhood patterns of behaviour like all the emotionally stunted Tenenbaum children, is similarly trapped. When we first see her as an adult, she is framed by jungle-like foliage on the wallpaper in a beauty salon, where the shaping of her sublime excess can be transformed into something more pleasing (Figure 1.1). Supremely secretive, she spends hours alone holed up in her bathroom 'cage', where she feels most comfortable away from prying eyes. Through a private investigator, we learn that Margot has spent some time in the actual jungle, trading in her mundane existence for a sexual dalliance with a tribal chief. Here, Anderson lampoons the early Romantic primitivist trope of the 'noble savage'. But the scene also illustrates that even a partially wild creature is still capable of sublimity by 'insisting on its freedom' (Burke [1757] 1792: 95). Pulled in multiple directions by the men in her life – from her needy lover, Eli Cash,[4] to her disapproving husband, Raleigh (Bill Murray), to her narcissistic father, Royal – she panics like a trapped animal and insists on breaking paternal and patriarchal chains.

Margot's mask-like facial expressions link her own face to the primitivism of the masks on her wall. In her reading of Agnès Varda's *Cléo de 5 à 7* (Rome Paris Films, 1962), Elizabeth Ezra argues that masks 'inhabit a metaphorical space of disguise, censorship, and displacement' (2010: 177). According to Ezra, 'in *Cléo* and other New Wave films, masks appear as overdetermined memorial palimpsests, signifying multiple layers of historical trauma as well as the repression of these traumas in a dialectic of exposure and concealment' (2010: 177–8). Margot's desire for both concealment (in her purposeful hiding of herself and her habits, such as a lifetime of smoking) and exposure (through her various sexual encounters and travels) can be linked to the trauma she experiences from being seen as an abandoned stray taken in by an indifferent owner.

'Masks act as monuments bearing silent witness to the legacy of objectification' on the basis of race or gender, writes Ezra (2010: 180). While I do not mean to suggest that Anderson is interested in a critique of gender politics and corporeal objectification (he resolutely is not), Margot's wayward adventures, while apparently unfulfilling, speak to her connection to a sublime wildness that her beauty belies. She is the ultimate symbol of picturesque anxiety in *The Royal Tenenbaums*, and even perhaps in Anderson's entire oeuvre to date. But, like Richie's eagle Mordecai, she eventually returns, controlled as much by her longing for acceptance as her desire to be free. When Margot dons her brown fur coat, it serves as a reminder of that duality, indicative of the harnessing of wild nature to achieve an aesthetic societal value. The anxiety caused by that tension is never resolved, a fact made explicit when Richie reveals to Margot his sublimely terrifying post-suicide wounds. No resolution, no picturesque unity, will be achieved.

While purposeful and plentiful object placement is crucial to Anderson's mise-en-scène, at once creating a sense of overabundance and endless variation within a solid foundation of precise composition, a lack of uniformity often arises. When young Richie instructs his mother, Etheline (Anjelica Huston), to hang his childish painting of Margot on a wall in the grand ballroom, already littered with similar portraits, he picks an area that creates far too much space between it and the other images, which are clustered close together (Figure 1.2). Not only does this represent Richie's off-kilter sensibility, its purposefulness reads as haphazard. Here, 'that sinking, that melting, that languor' (Burke [1757] 1792: 191) that so characterises the beautiful is transformed into something that incites pleasure but also excites curiosity, the 'chief mental effect of the picturesque' (Jarvis 2004: 181) with its destabilising lack of uniformity.

Figure 1.2 Richie instructs Etheline to hang his portrait of Margot in a seemingly haphazard place on the wall of the ballroom.

THE STILLNESS OF SOLITUDE

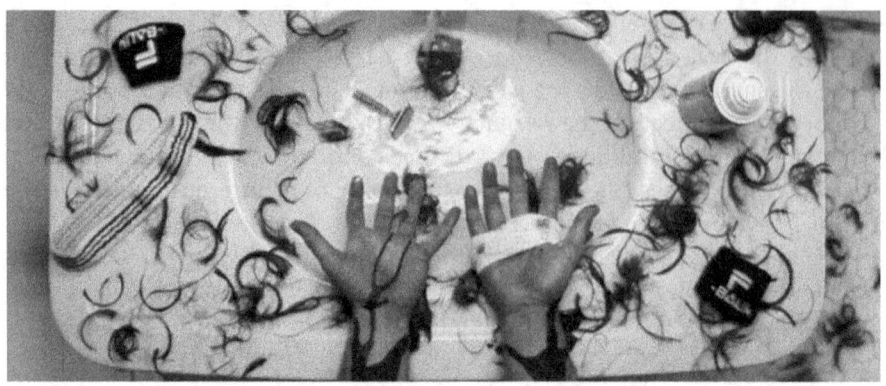

Figure 1.3 A sublime point-of-view shot of Richie's bleeding wrists offers a counterpoint to Anderson's penchant for pleasantly constructed overhead shots of static objects.

While the film painstakingly catalogues Richie's vast array of personal objects in his bedroom (endless trophies, a drum set, toy cars, a veritable explosion of tennis balls), zigzagged carpeting in a dusky dark blue and shocking green is revealed, clashing violently with the walls and creating a sense of aesthetic anxiety. These hints of the sublime break through the theatrically composed space, as they do eventually during Richie's suicide attempt, which is shot in purposeful discontinuity (Figure 1.3). Jump cuts of Richie slashing his wrists are juxtaposed with his voice-over declaring, 'I'm going to kill myself tomorrow', evoking a sublime sense of confusion in its irrational use of time and space. The scene's colour change eliminates the tonal warmth of the normal milieu, as nostalgic pinks and yellows give way to a gloomy, disaffected blue. While Anderson's penchant for warm and soft colours and light provides pleasurable solace, like the abrupt aesthetic change in this scene, the sense of physical distance between the camera and characters creates a sense of emotional distance for the spectator.

Trapped in a Never-ending Play: Anderson's Use of Diegetic Space

The goal of the picturesque is to invoke the feeling that the aesthetic splendour of a landscape painting could be metaphorically walked through, experienced in three dimensions, just as it was to create real landscapes that felt as though they were paintings come to life. William Kent, a highly influential eighteenth-century garden designer, created landscapes organised around 'a series of vistas, each of which seems to be a part of a landscape painting', a chief goal of which was 'to create, artificially and artistically, variety, openness, distance, and space' (Mohr 1996: 249).

While *The Royal Tenenbaums* embraces variety, openness and rustic surfaces, its use of distance and space within the frame problematises its relation to the picturesque. Anderson mostly chooses to film in deep focus, sharply capturing every detail in frames usually overflowing with them. Wide-angle lenses create a bowing, 'fish-eye' effect around the corners of the frame, often lending the appearance that the image is being stretched to the point of rupture. But instead of creating different vistas, or fields of action, in a shot as in famous examples of deep-focus cinematography in Orson Welles's oeuvre,[5] he often relegates his characters to a linear plane in the camera's middle distance, usually shooting at eye level, creating a shallow, theatrical space. Consequently, the space becomes at once cacophonous – bursting with objects and people – and meticulously composed within the frame. This creates a feeling of chaos and overabundance, but one strictly inventoried and catalogued.

Anderson is preoccupied with theatricality, in both form and content. Many of his films feature characters mounting plays within the larger narrative, but this theatricality is also found in an aesthetic 'flatness' in both presentation and affect. According to Fredric Jameson, the postmodern heralds 'the emergence of a new kind of flatness or depthlessness, a new kind of superficiality in the most literal sense' (1984: 60). Whereas the Romantic picturesque garden sought to create a space full of three-dimensionality, where an observer could 'move through' psychologically, Anderson chooses to hold the observer at a remove, refusing a clear entry point into the action. In *The Royal Tenenbaums* this is most technically apparent in the complicated long-take tracking shot that caps the film's denouement. His aerial camera cranes smoothly through the scene from left to right, repeatedly reframing characters in two shots or group shots but never taking us into the action so we feel a part of it.

David Bordwell (2007) refers to this flattening of perspective as 'planimetric composition', a style of shooting that became popular in the 1960s through its use in the work of various New Wave filmmakers such as Michelangelo Antonioni and Jean-Luc Godard. These 'painterly' and 'strongly pictorial' approaches to composition can suggest a 'childish simplicity' or an oppressiveness that denotes 'stiff ceremony' (Bordwell 2007). Anderson's compositions, as do so many of his aesthetic devices, fall somewhere in-between. Their childlike sense of play and whimsy in colour, visual jokes and overabundance belies their heavily constructed formalism. According to Bordwell, 'the static, geometrical frame can evoke a deadpan comic quality', but in Anderson's case it also creates a sense of the film's characters being trapped in a self-perpetuating play. The film's editing and camera movement serve to heighten the effect: whip pans, tilts and fast zooms alter the shots while keeping the integrity of the space, while shot–reverse shot editing of planimetric compositions (rather than 'classical' over-the-shoulder cutting) maintain its flatness.

James MacDowell derides the 'excessive neatness' in Anderson's mise-en-scène (2010: 5), but while the filmmaker's camera often conveys a strong precision and formalism, Anderson usually combines his planimetric cinematography with calculated disarray within the frame. Even in terms of camera movement, Anderson often combines static, painterly composed shots with sequences of wild, almost anarchic movement. The purest example of such controlled chaos is his use of whip pans, where the camera moves so quickly the image blurs, only to land precisely in focus and perfectly timed on an actor so he or she can deliver a deadpan bon mot. In conversation scenes, the camera often ping-pongs in such a fashion between two or more characters, resulting in a vertiginous experience for the viewer that is nonetheless succinct and easy to follow. These scenes are interspersed with excessively 'stagey' shots that treat cinematic space as if it were theatre performance.

Anderson's obsession with the proscenium reaches its apex when, in films like *The Life Aquatic* and *The Darjeeling Limited* (Fox Searchlight, 2007) he constructs bisected sets, portraying several scenes on the same plane of action in miniature and creating tableaux reminiscent of dolls' houses or children's dioramas (Figure 1.4). While Godard and other earlier, more avant-garde filmmakers have used this technique to create a sense of Brechtian distance, Anderson seems to function out of urgency to control, to exert his dominance over nature. But that control is a self-aware attempt in futility – as Michael Chabon notes, these sets become 'scale models' of the jigsaw puzzle of life, 'mysterious, original, unbroken, half-remembered' (2013: 22). Like artist Joseph Cornell's boxed assemblages, '[they make] explicit [. . .] the yearning of a model-maker to analogize the world, and at the same time [. . .] frankly emphasize the limitations, the

Figure 1.4 The bisected set of *The Life Aquatic's Belafonte*.

confines, of his or her ability to do so' (2013: 23). That yearning is a desire for meaning, which postmodernism implicitly rejects.

A Search for Meaning Within Postmodern Pastiche

Fredric Jameson defines the 'hysterical sublime' as the delight caused by becoming immersed in a cacophony of images and signs without any specified meaning, a combination of Burke's ideas and Immanuel Kant's notions of the sublime that followed (Jameson 1984: 76). According to Jameson, for Kant 'the object of the sublime is now not only a matter of sheer power and the physical incommensurability of the human organism with Nature' as it was for Burke, 'but also of the limits of figuration and the incapacity of the human mind to give representation to such enormous forces' (1984: 77). That is, the sublime invokes the power of the 'unpresentable' (Lyotard 1993: 43). For the artist, the question becomes how to present this idea of unpresentability. Embodied by Susan Sontag's notions of camp (which I discuss later on in this chapter), a postmodernist interpretation of the sublime answers this crisis of representation with a deluge of barely differentiated sensory phenomena – it celebrates the 'limits of figuration' with the intensity, euphoria and 'hallucinatory exhilaration' (Jameson 1984: 76) of countless deconstructed and decontextualised images and experiences.

By themselves these sensory experiences are meaningless, but together they result in an act of emancipatory abandon, something akin to Burke's sublime awe, creating a world that 'momentarily loses its depth and threatens to become a glossy skin, a stereoscopic illusion, a rush of filmic images without density' (Jameson 1984: 77). Anderson's version of this skin-like cacophony, while certainly glossy, depthless and inherently filmic, can be seen as the hysterical sublime's more conservative sibling. We experience his hermetically sealed film worlds as an outsider, the cacophony presented at a remove that robs it of its euphoric immediacy. Its pleasures are always underscored with anxiety and disunity, but never at the price of their coherence. There is no real 'hysteria' in Anderson's worlds; their design is too apparent, and they are imbued with too much meaning. Sometimes a sense of danger is evoked, as in the pirate raid on Zissou's ship in *The Life Aquatic* (which features a rare use of hand-held camera tracking through the action); but more often what would be thrilling under other circumstances, such as the subsequent raid on Little Ping Island in the same film, results in a deadpan-comic spectacle.

Expressions of kitsch and the mingling of 'high' and 'low' culture – or, more specifically, the raising of low to high – is prominent in postmodern pastiche (Perloff 1999: 186), and can be seen throughout *The Royal Tenenbaums*, from Eli's drug runs to the '375th Street Y' to Royal and Richie (and later Royal and his grandsons) gambling with street toughs, shot from a low-level camera while crouching to underscore the upper-class slumming. Similarly, there is a reverence for decay among grandeur throughout the mise-en-scène, which portrays the rustic picturesque in an urban setting. Surfaces and objects are marked with the patina of decay: stone and brick crumble, paint peels off walls in chunks, paperback covers appear weathered by age and anachronisms abound. Technology is out-dated or even obsolete, as in Raleigh's reel-to-reel tape recorder and Margot's rotary telephone. Ramshackle 'Gypsy Cab Company' taxis are omnipresent and feature rusted-out fenders and missing window glass patched with cardboard.

But Anderson's form of pastiche is not just a postmodern 'random cannibalization' of the past (Jameson 1984: 65–6); here the age and the history of objects are inextricably linked to the history of characters, even if they predate those characters. The 'recognizable consistency' (Lyotard 1992: 45) of the objects and people on display lends the story the sense that it is part of the overarching passage of time. Royal's residence at the 'Lindberg Palace Hotel' is actually the modernist Waldorf Astoria, 'the grand commercial hotel of the 1930s and 1940s' (Perloff 1999: 197), which further links the Tenenbaums to a modernist grand narrative that has been rendered imaginary. It is clear why Etheline is an archaeologist and her fiancé, Henry (Danny Glover), is an accountant – the accounting of personal and family history is a key project of the film.

The Romantic 'love of the particular' (Perry 1997: 4) is found in the exhaustive cataloguing of ephemera in Anderson's mise-en-scène. Such ephemera are extremely subjective and often reflexively fictional. Brendan Kredell sees the use of imaginary space in *The Royal Tenenbaums* as a form of 'gentrification'. According to Kredell, 'Anderson prevents the city from asserting its own identity, choosing instead to treat it as a location within which to construct his own social universe' (2012: 84–5). But the film is not about asserting a realist identity of location; instead, it concerns how a location is *informed by* personal identity, both those of its characters and that of Anderson himself. The film creates a nostalgic tone of regret and mournfulness for the loss of something that never actually existed, just like the apocryphal Gypsy Cab Company taxis and 375th Street Y in this fictionalised New York. As such, the authenticity of the film is purely Romantic: an assertion of inner imagination on external reality.

In Anderson's follow-up film, he creates a similar tone of nostalgia for an imaginary past and a fantastical present, one built on the legendary status of its hero, Steve Zissou. Even more so than *The Royal Tenenbaums*, *The Life Aquatic* purposefully undercuts ideas of rationality and fidelity to truth in its depictions of scientific exploration, highly stylised 'natural' flora and fauna and questions of personal identity.

The Middle-aged Man and the Sea: *The Life Aquatic* and the Sentimental Sublime

The milieu of the open seas in Anderson's 2004 film *The Life Aquatic with Steve Zissou* provides an unprecedented opportunity for the filmmaker to immerse himself in Romantic ideas of the natural world. Whereas *The Royal Tenenbaums* takes place in a hermetic urban environment, settings in *The Life Aquatic* are expansive. European locations fill in for exotic locales, such as 'Port-au-Patois', a fictitious island oasis that conjures Haitian capital Port-au-Prince, Little Ping Island, another imaginary enclave in the Caribbean made uninhabitable by the ravages of weather, and even the Arctic, glimpsed in Steve's nature documentaries. But undoubtedly, the film's ultimate aesthetic fixation is that of the kaleidoscopic wonders of the mysterious depths of the sea. The film's style and characterisations continue Anderson's mission of reconfiguring the real world in imaginary ways, but here he engages with enduring Romantic conceptions of sublimity and nature like never before. At once sublime and beautiful, the sea is the site of Steve's darkest hour and his ultimate, equivocal redemption.

A self-reflexive ode to the lunacy and creative joy of filmmaking itself, the film is also an exercise in paralleling civilisation and nature. While the worlds of nature and culture are rigidly demarcated at times, they have a profound influence on one another. This suggests a grappling with the loss of our 'primal natural essence' that characterises so much of Anderson's vision of humanity. In *The Life Aquatic*, Anderson toys with a repudiation of human-centric notions of picturesque and idealised nature but ultimately embraces those notions. The film offers a nostalgic, sentimental view that undermines sublimity, but it maintains a strong undercurrent of anxiety, creating a 'sentimental sublime'. As in *The Royal Tenenbaums*, the film displays a veneration of objects' ties to personal history and an individual sense of self-creation and authenticity. But its objects and people also represent the idea of 'the free play, the anarchy, the indeterminacy and disjunctive form that used to be considered characteristic of Postmodernism' (Perloff 1999: 185).

From the moment we glimpse the first underwater shots of the film – which comprise part of Zissou's nature documentary being screened at a film festival – it is clear that the sea is rendered a wholly imaginary world. Vaguely plastic, luminous pastel coral frames the edges of the screen as Zissou's mentor, Esteban (Seymour Cassel), swims underwater. A school of small, bright-pink fish whiz by in fast motion behind him; behind the fish resides an obviously phony matte painting (or, more likely, a computer animation made to look like one) (Figure 1.5). The scene is cartoonish in its whimsy, but it also relates a mysterious, mythical vision of beasts and beauty.

Figure 1.5 A medium shot of Esteban emphasises the artificiality of the underwater realm as well as the theatricality of its presentation.

Abruptly, Zissou breaks the surface of the water – and breaks the undersea spell – to announce the demise of Esteban, who suffers an attack from the elusive, legendary 'jaguar shark'. The sea becomes a scene of the terrors of nature, and the beautiful becomes the sublime. But the residue of artifice remains, and the dreamy kitsch of the previous scene renders the death with a sense of tonal uncertainty. The film-within-the-film ends, and Anderson cuts to a wide shot of audience reaction in the upscale opera house where the screening is taking place. There is a dramatic change in the film's colour saturation; Anderson used Ektachrome reversal stock for the 'documentary' scenes in order to achieve a highly saturated, dated look (Anderson 2005). The aesthetic change speaks to the vast difference between the world of the film being screened and the film's larger world. The new, contrasting location, which underlines the operatic nature of Anderson's film, also points to the appropriation of the 'natural' world for the vicarious thrills of highbrow culture. The world of Zissou's film is such an oddity to the crowd that it might as well be outer space, a point underscored later in the film with the Portuguese-language rendition of David Bowie's 'Space Oddity'. Not incidentally, the repurposed Bowie covers peppering the film (sung by Seu Jorge) speak to the theme of the familiar being rendered odd and off-kilter.

Nature's unnatural oddities soon reappear when a young fan presents Zissou with a 'crayon pony fish' outside of the Opera House. The creature resembles a sea horse but with a fanciful twist: candy-coloured stripes on its body, a grass-green mane and a bright pink face. As the pony fish curls and uncurls its tail in a feat of stop-motion animation, nature again is portrayed as anything *but* naturalistic – the disjointed movements of stop-motion lend a surreal quality to special effects that, throughout the film, have a handicraft, antiquated and uncanny feel. As John Fletcher writes, Freud considered the aesthetic uncanny to 'conflict with the generic world of the text, the postulates of the "common reality" of secular modernity and its literary regimes of realism and naturalism' (1999: 124). Zissou is a man of science, and the film's narrative purports to be one of scientific inquiry. In this way *The Life Aquatic* ostensibly takes place within a secular modernity. But its world is not wholly recognisable in terms of 'common reality'. It is not reality, per se, but it is also not purely fantasy.

Ultimately, it operates as a parody of both secular modernity and generic fantasy. The film postulates that its fantastical creations are exotic yet explicable, when in actuality they are in continual conflict with the naturalism that the film purports to portray. The continual presence of fantastical creatures alongside animals found in typical nature films, like orcas, and even everyday life, such as domestic cats, causes a tension between the mimetic and the constructed qualities of the film's world. Tzvetan Todorov's definition of the fantastic, which is covered in detail in Chapter 2, resides in confusion as to whether a story is 'real' or simply imagined by its protagonist or explained as a trick. *The Life Aquatic* accepts its otherworldly phenomena without question, as objective reality, but also winks wryly at its audience via its uncanny images.

The Freudian uncanny testifies to 'that class of the frightening which leads back to what is known of old and long familiar' (Freud [1919] 2003: 124), rendering the ordinary strangely 'alien' ([1919] 2003: 123). Unquestionably, Anderson's creations – the jaguar shark, the wild snow mongoose, the sugar crabs, the rhinestone blue fin – all point to familiar, identifiable species with an alien twist. Anderson himself says his desire was not to 'make them unrealistic' but rather 'imaginary':

> The answer to 'Why stop-motion?' is 'Because I love stop-motion'. And it's not like I love stop-motion because I think it's this great way to make you think these things are really alive. It's more that I think it's such a magical way to make it seem as though these things are really alive. *And you can see how the illusion is being created.* (Seitz 2013: 186–7; my emphasis)

That process of revealing the seams of artistic creation seems to counter Burke's idea of the sublime linked to obscurity or privation. However, according to Lyotard, 'The very imperfections, the distortion of taste, even ugliness, have their share in the shock-effect. Art does not imitate nature, it creates a world apart' (1993b: 249). This 'shock effect' of Anderson's (and animator Henry Selick's) creations is heavily tempered by their whimsical beauty, creating a picturesque sense of distorted nature that simultaneously thrills and soothes.

This is underscored in the film's climax, when Zissou and his crew descend to the sublime depths of the darkest ocean in the cartoonish, 'Yellow Submarine'-esque *Deep Search*, for Steve's own psychological deep search – the confrontation with Death itself: the mysterious, heretofore-unseen jaguar shark. They view a series of exotic, fantastic aquatic life through the portholes as they descend through tree-like stalks of neon green to the ocean floor, which sparkles subtly under the submarine's lights as they touch down. The characters are framed from without in planimetric fashion by the sub's front window, the score's tinny, toy-like electronic piano lending the scene a fairy-tale feeling.

The shark itself is first seen as a tiny dot through the sub's observation window. In an uncharacteristically jarring use of depth in a shot, it barrels toward the frame, increasingly exponentially in size until it is revealed as truly massive – several times larger than the sub itself – sporting a gaping maw lined with razor-sharp teeth. But the iridescent beauty of its cat-like spots, shimmering in the vessel's light, and its grace in movement are undeniable. 'It's beautiful, Steve', Eleanor (Anjelica Huston) says with a sense of pleasurable awe. 'I wonder if it remembers me', Steve answers. As Matt Zoller Seitz puts it in the unadorned language of Anderson's films, Steve 'stares the beast in the face and realizes it was nothing personal' (2013: 175). A look of peaceful resignation envelops him, as one by one the crewmembers place their hands on his shoulders. It is as if they instinctively recognise that this terrible, sublime force has revealed itself to be one of psychological healing.

While imperfect, while fantastic, while sometimes even monstrous like the jaguar shark, the film's objects are still 'good forms' (Lyotard 1992: 45). They fulfil their essential functions despite their sometimes-rickety appearance or even the occasional malfunction. Steve's 'albino scouts' (two dolphins, actually robotic) are always failing to get the information required for the expedition, but their cameras reveal to Steve important narrative information: his crush, journalist Jane (Cate Blanchett), and Ned (Owen Wilson), his possible son, in a romantic clinch. Undoubtedly named after the famous calypso singer in a nod to Cousteau's ship *The Calypso*, Steve's ship, *The Belafonte*, is severely dilapidated: the crew is constantly blowing fuses, the engine is in disrepair. Until they steal the ridiculously advanced tech of his nemesis, Alistair Hennessey (Jeff Goldblum), it is also full of antiquated technology. Initially seen as a soulless autocrat by Zissou's team and the film itself, Hennessey eventually joins forces with Zissou's crew. Ultimately, *The Belafonte* serves its mission, while Hennessey's sleek new ship ends up at the bottom of the ocean. The only malfunction that leads to real tragedy is that of the Zissou helicopter, which crashes into the ocean and kills Ned. But even this fulfils a necessary function, that of leading Steve on a journey to acceptance of the natural order of things and his ultimate lack of control over it (Seitz 2013: 188).

THE PAINFUL PICTURESQUE AND SENTIMENTAL SUBLIME

Steve and his crew's antiquated, unwieldy, browbeaten forms are not the fresh, blank, empty boxes of modernism like Hennessey's ship; they are full of the inescapable history of generations. They form a palimpsest of experience, one that the film readily acknowledges. Steve does not simply cover the name of his submarine (*Jacqueline*, the name of his first wife) with the new moniker, *Deep Search*; he draws a line through it and paints the new name underneath, revealing the proverbial seams of his own historical narrative. Just like the similar tattoo on his arm, which depicts the same Jacqueline/Deep Search override as the submarine, history is indelibly etched in both mise-en-scène and character. Similarly, Steve's beloved *Belafonte* is enlivened with deep cultural and historical connections. A 'long-range sub-hunter during the Second World War', it now lives to fight another, more progressively humanist function: serving as the vessel for the enlightened experiment of gaining new, categorical knowledge of the natural world while defining the identities of the characters who inhabit it. Of course, that world is only as natural as the fancy of Anderson's mind – which is to say, it is uniquely artificial.

The Life Aquatic treats its fantastical beings as matter-of-fact subjects of scientific inquiry. But scientific 'fact' is often distorted to the point of absurdity, creating an uneasy balance between the scientifically explicable and the purely fantastic. Zissou is a naturalist, but often his rational explanations for scientific phenomena are dubious at best, such as when he corrects Ned on the source of the illumination of the 'electric jellyfish' only to be told by Jane that he has completely misidentified the species. This is not so much an indication of Team Zissou's incompetence (although they are at times spectacularly incompetent) so much as it is an effort to underline the fact that the facts matter little – individual emotional response is much more important. Even his estranged wife, Eleanor, regularly identified as the brains behind the operation, exhibits a tendency to misinformation when she tells Jane that Ned is likely not Steve's son: 'Zissou shoots blanks. I think it's because he's spent half his life underwater.' This speaks to the separation of the human and natural worlds: we can attempt to quantify the natural world, to collect it, even to bend to it our will, but ultimately we must acknowledge that we do not, and cannot, understand its totality.

Perhaps because of this, Zissou even exhibits a scattershot disdain for the natural world (in its real and imaginary guises), as evidenced most strongly by his drive for revenge against the jaguar shark, but also in everything from his refusal to remember the scientific names of species to his disregard for his supposedly beloved, recently deceased cat. ('Who gives a shit? I think it was a tabby', he replies when Ned enquires about the breed.) In this way, Steve wraps a deep-seated anxiety about the inevitability of death in an attitude of faux nonchalance.

Anderson's film creates a sort of 'taxonomy of people' (Seitz 2013: 159) as much as natural phenomena – his widescreen frames capture the confusion in the human face almost as much as the highly designed tableaux (2013: 158). We are, after all, cast-out creatures of nature trying to come to terms with our lot. According to Slavoj Žižek,

> There is no return to the natural balance; to accord with his milieu, the only thing man can do is fully accept this cleft, this fissure, this structural rooting out, and to try as far as possible to patch things up afterwards. (Žižek 1989: xxviii)

Zissou, like most of the Tenenbaum family, struggles with this acceptance, sharing a desire to categorise, control and create order in externalities to compensate for the psychological distress and confusion of a loss of place in the natural order of things. But he also simply wants to emotionally lash out at the world, to 'get even' with it for the pain and indignity it has caused him.

Like the love dance of the film's peppermint-candy-like sugar crab (which tears a limb off its mate), the film's acknowledgement of terror and death offers a hint of the sublime amidst the beautiful fantasia. So do the frequent bursts of violence that pepper the film, such as the pirate invasion of the ship and the subsequent rescue of the 'Bond Company Stooge' (Bud Cort) on the nature-ravaged Little Ping Island's Hotel Citroën (itself a throwaway reference to the preferred vehicle of the French New Wave, which offered its own frequent moments of jarring violence). Both Steve and the viewer experience a feeling of sublime transcendence during his encounter with the jaguar shark. But in its very nostalgia for 'the transcendence that underlay the notion of sublimity' (Larrissy 1999: 7), it is not strictly a sublime moment.

The jaguar shark fully reveals itself, and, ironically it is a force for peace and pleasure, a beautiful object. Still, it *is* a man-eater, and not a harmless tabby cat. Sublime pain is tamed, reduced to an underlying kernel of anxiety. But that anxiety never fully dissipates – it is related to the indeterminacy that Steve (like Margot, Richie and Chas) continually rejects through an all-encompassing need to control his own identity and narrative through the control of his environment, the grand director of own personal mise-en-scène. His acceptance of a lack of control does not negate the sting.

Anderson's method of constructing his mise-en-scène is an attempt to find order in disorder and continuity in chaos, or at least to depict such an attempt. But the attempt is continually undermined. This is evident, as well, in the way he engages with 'camp' as a form of questioning rationality and reason. In *The Royal Tenenbaums*, he specifically engages with an eclectic form of gothicism that can be defined in camp terms.

The Camp Cathedral: Eclecticism in Anderson's Mise-en-scène and Dialogue

In its allusions to gothic irregularity, disorder and antiquarian pastiche, *The Royal Tenenbaums* evinces a sort of 'proto-sublime' (Fletcher 1999: 114). Its gothic predilections might seem to run counter to the Enlightenment narrative Anderson sets up early on in the form of the Tenenbaum children's experiments in the 'progressive operations of critical reason' (Docherty 1993: 5) by way of their natural genius. According to John Fletcher, gothic revival pastiche in the Romantic era was a response to 'whatever is felt to have been lost in the advance of civilization and the Enlightenment' (1999: 115) through a 'process of cultural mourning' and 'nostalgia' (1999: 114). This elegiac nostalgia, particularly for objects of early childhood, is rampant throughout *Tenenbaums*, but also crops up in *The Life Aquatic* – consider Ned's treasured Zissou Society insignia ring or the flashback to his proud 'discovery' of a new species, which, at ten years old, he dubs the 'Zissou fly'.

None of Anderson's work quite embraces the idea of gothic revival in the way that *Tenenbaums* does, however. The Dark or Gothic House, with its 'fearful sense of inheritance in time with a claustrophobic sense of enclosure in space' (Fletcher 1999: 119), is the gothic revival's most enduring architectural creation. But its original incarnation was Horace Walpole's much less sinister Strawberry Hill, a 'neat modern' eighteenth-century building that the author, who is regarded as the first gothic revival novelist, purchased in 1747 and preceded to embellish with 'gothic motifs such as arched doors and windows, niches, fan-vaulting, tracery and finials' (1999: 118). Walpole's project was by no means an exercise in period authenticity, however – he 'made no attempt to reproduce medieval domestic space', instead going so far as to model the interior's fireplaces on the derided tombs of Westminster Abbey, with their 'sharp jetties, narrow lights, lame statues, lace, and other cutwork and crinkle-crankle' (1999: 118). The gothic pastiche of Strawberry Hill is a highly Romantic form of reimagining history through personal proclivities.

The 'imaginary mise-en-scène' (1999: 118) of Walpole's vision would likely appeal to Anderson, who has a similar obsession with material 'crinkle-crankle'. Anderson is less concerned with the darkness of the gothic vision than he is with the play of darkness and light. His predilection is reminiscent of another architectural idea embodied by the gothic cathedral. Inspired by John Rushkin's 1853 *The Stones of Venice*, this architectural notion posits a more unified, even picturesque, idea of the gothic, one which offers a 'Utopian critique' where 'art is the expression of man's pleasure in his labour' and 'beauty is once again the natural and necessary accompaniment of productive labour' (1999: 121). Anderson's mise-en-scène is as much if not more preoccupied by beauty as it is with the gothic sense of decay, mournful loss and doomed 'repetition and return' (1999: 121). It is also enamoured with the renewed hope of endless possibility and the beauty of human creation, that 're-joins modernity and even Modernism' in this reconfigured idea of the gothic (1999: 121).

Susan Sontag traces the origins of camp back to the Romantic gothic revival, with its 'novels, Chinoiserie, caricature, artificial ruins' (Sontag 1961: 280), the latter of which is a hallmark of the picturesque. Sontag places Walpole squarely in this 'great period of Camp' (1961: 280). Many of the tenets of camp fall within the Andersonian milieu: an 'effacement' or contradiction of nature, sentimentality, a sense of the esoteric, an 'extraordinary feeling for artifice, for surface, for symmetry', exaggeration, the idea of 'life as theatre', and an obsession with 'decorative art, emphasizing texture' (1961: 278). But there is a quintessential component of camp missing from the director's oeuvre: disaffection.

Anderson creates worlds whose characters seek to turn their own history into camp, who turn *themselves* into objects of camp – 'a person being one, very intense thing' (1961: 286) – but the filmic attitude to them, despite comic jabs at their predicaments, remains straight-faced and sympathetic. His characters describe their own archetypes (troubled artist, steadfast businessman, worldly raconteur) through sheer force of will, resisting development and change regardless of the stark realities of their current circumstances. They are trapped within a self-made camp. (Richie even likes to pretend he is 'camping' in a tent in the Tenenbaum ballroom.) The artifice of their worlds simultaneously idealises their worldviews and repudiates their folly. While they usually change or 'grow' in some way, they never fully escape their theatrical prisons. Self-acknowledgement is, in general, as far as it goes.

'Camp is the consistently aesthetic experience of the world', states Sontag; 'it incarnates a victory of "style" over "content", "aesthetics" over "morality", of irony over tragedy' (1961: 287). But this does not describe the work of Anderson adequately. His films inhabit largely moral universes, and his characters, even if they feign indifference, care deeply. If there is 'never, never tragedy' (1961: 287) in camp, there is always underlying tragedy in Anderson's films. The tragedy itself, on one level, is based in the insistence on a purely aesthetic, amoral interface with the world. According to Sontag, 'One is drawn to Camp when one realizes that "sincerity" is not enough' (1961: 288). Anderson clearly trades in irony even while being prepossessed by sincerity. His irony is couched in the idea that pure expressions of sincerity have been rendered obsolete; he simultaneously mourns this while luxuriously surrendering to its loss. The dialogue in his films complements these ideas. Simultaneously theatrical and authentic, it imbues straightforward speech with deadpan detachment to deaden its portrayal of the sincere.

Despite its primary use of everyday language, Anderson's dialogue often rings artificial. With its deadpan tone and emphasis on peculiar cadence, at once laconic and immediate, it offers a heightened feeling of realism, an artificial sense of the real that draws attention to its constructed nature (Jaeckle 2013: 156). In his *Preface to Lyrical Ballads*, Wordsworth proposed the use of language that hews closely to that of real life but differentiates itself in its use of metre, offering heighted effects that 'imperceptibly make up a complex feeling of delight, which is of the most important use in tempering the painful feeling, which will always be found intermingled with powerful descriptions of the deeper passions' ([1800] 1957: 129). In Anderson's films, a Wordsworthian 'low and rustic' ([1800] 1957: 115) realism combined with a sense of the uncanny creates a picturesque quality in dialogue not unlike that created in mise-en-scène.

Likewise, the Wordsworthian tempering of the passions with an 'overbalance of pleasure' ([1800] 1957: 127) is a hallmark of Andersonian verbal style. Geoff Ward, with emphasis on Wordsworth's *Prelude*, points to the relationship between panic and syntax and the power of syntax to 'suture over trauma' (1999: 90). This is achieved through the prolonged use of style and rhetoric, which creates a distancing effect between experience and pain: 'as the brilliance of life fades, there arises the urge to hold on to it, to map it, to seize it and fill all its space, securing the comfort that on-going syntax provides against silence' (1999: 93). 'Suturing over trauma' brings to mind Richie's literal sutures on his slashed wrists, Frankenstein-like stiches revealed shortly before Margot declares, 'I think we'll just have to be secretly in love with each other and leave it at that.' While the pain and trauma of the scene is palpable, it is undercut with this semi-absurdist statement, one that would likely never be articulated with such a knowing matter-of-factness in reality.

Comically blunt, almost perfunctory dialogue is a key way for Anderson to undercut pain and anxiety in scenes. Characters routinely refuse to deal in subtext, instead preferring to articulate, often in a confrontational manner, what would normally remain unspoken truths, as when Steve Zissou refers to Alistair Hennessey as his 'nemesis' right in front of him, Royal continually introduces Margot as his 'adopted daughter', and Eli Cash confesses he 'always wanted to be a Tenenbaum'. These examples are symptomatic not of Anderson's inability to deal with subtext, but of his characters' inability to do so. This language is not designed to provoke negative reactions or hurt feelings from others, but rather to rob the burdensome, distressing 'unsaid' of its sublime power. According to Paul Hamilton, the Romantic idea of sublimity 'recasts failures of understanding as the successful symbolic expression of something greater than understanding' while postmodernism interprets these failures as a result of the 'indeterminacy of meaning' (1999: 13). For Anderson's characters, the only way to counteract this indeterminacy is to remove, or at least address, the possibility of miscommunication.

The suturing aspect of language is also utilised with a more positive tone and creates continuities between films. In *The Royal Tenenbaums*, Chas tells his soon-to-be stepfather Henry that he is also a widower. Henry responds, with a hand placed gently on Chas's shoulder, 'I know, Chas.' In *The Life Aquatic* an almost identical scene occurs when Steve tells Ned that 'his best friend just got killed, Esteban'. 'Yeah, I know', Ned replies with sympathy. Of course, the death of Esteban is the impetus for the entire narrative of revenge in the film, so Steve must know Ned knows, at least on some level. It is the act of the statement, of the saying it aloud, that diffuses the anxiety of the knowledge. Pain must be expressed verbally, or at least written down. Instead of using words to 'evoke passions', as Burke would have the sublime form of language ([1757] 1792: 278), Anderson uses them to clarify. But the clarification does not make them crystal clear – a 'little idea' in Burke's terminology ([1757] 1792: 89) – so much as diffuse sublimity into a painful picturesque.

Conclusion

According to Michael Chabon, Anderson's depictions of emotional pain through distance offer a greater perception of the idea of grief itself:

> Grief, at full scale, is too big for us to take it in; it literally cannot be comprehended. Anderson [. . .] understands that distance can increase our understanding of grief, allowing us to see it whole. But distance does not – ought not – necessarily imply a withdrawal. (Chabon 2013: 22)

In this context, grief represents a sublime idea, too big to be taken in 'whole'. Anderson takes the sublimity of grief and robs it of its sublime power through aesthetic means. However, as Chabon suggests, that does not mean his films dismiss or deny it wholesale. The primary aesthetic function of Anderson's film worlds is always to create palpable tension between polarities, be they pleasure and pain, the present and the past, or even life and death. Within the painful picturesque and the sentimental sublime, he finds his aesthetic niche.

Anderson's ironic distance and reliance on fantasy partially repudiates the sincere nostalgia for a time of the 'good forms' and rational progress of the modernist ideal. But it also mourns the loss of sincerity, creating works steeped in beauty whose cracks yield glimpses of the sublime. Like other contemporary filmmakers influenced by the tenets of Romanticism, Anderson concedes that the world and its remembered past are just personal constructs, as artificial as movie sets and as subjective and ego-driven as the Romantic artist himself.

In *The Royal Tenenbaums*, he does this through expressions of beauty undercut by sublimity, creating a palpable anxiety and a sense of permanent indeterminacy, which I argue results in a painful sense of picturesque enervation. Similarly, in *The Life Aquatic*, he turns sublime landscapes into uncannily beautiful fantasias, defanging the indeterminacy of the postmodern sublime and rendering it personally meaningful, the site of psychological growth through acceptance of that indeterminacy. Anderson's films are sentimental, yes, but that sentiment is in service of larger thematic aims: the questioning of reason, and the searching for purpose in a world without it.

Unlike Anderson, writer-director Charlie Kaufman has rarely been accused of bald sentimentality. In his 2008 film, *Synecdoche, New York*, he portrays an imaginative, subjective point of view that leans more toward horror than picturesque unity. However, as I argue in Chapter 2, the film offers an optimistic counterpoint to its depiction of a writer suffering from the limits of his own creative capability and relation to the external world. That counterpoint rests in the aesthetics and narrative of the film itself, which continually push back against its protagonist's self-destructive solipsism.

2. 'AN ENDLESS SUCCESSION OF MIRRORS': IRONY, AMBIGUITY AND THE CRISIS OF AUTHENTICITY IN CHARLIE KAUFMAN'S *SYNECDOCHE, NEW YORK*

> *There's no such thing as certainty, that's plain*
> *As any of mortality's conditions*
> Lord Byron, Don Juan (1819–24)

More than any other filmmaker I discuss in this book, writer-turned-director Charlie Kaufman is a quintessential Romantic ironist. By this I mean his work consistently creates 'new forms and myths' (Mellor 1980: 5) in order to engage with these forms and myths on a sceptical level. His fantastical worlds are always in the process of being crushed under their own imaginative weight, in the sense that they continually display a tendency to reveal their own mythical status. They are consistently metatextual and reflexive, and this produces a distancing effect to their narratives.

At the same time, Kaufman's films evince a strong reliance on emotion, both through their emphasis on character subjectivity and the eliciting of emotional responses in the spectator. In *Synecdoche, New York*, we experience much of the story through the confused senses of the film's protagonist, Caden Cotard (Philip Seymour Hoffman). But the film also creates an ambiguous tension between Caden's subjectivity and the subjective viewpoints of others, even including those pretending to 'be' him, in order to recognise the gulf between subjectivities as it creates what Joel Evans refers to as a 'network of affects' (2014: 335).

A hallucinatory journey through the creative process and an unnerving exploration of the solipsistic collapse between matter and mind, *Synecdoche, New York* also serves a sympathetic parody of the Romantic trope of the all-consumed, passionate artist-genius. The film tells the fantastical, metaphysical tale of Caden Cotard, whom we first meet wandering somnambulistically in the morass of middle age, trapped in a middling career as a director of suburban American regional theatre. After mounting a gargantuan theatrical production meant to physically encompass the entire city of New York – and the entire story of his life in minute detail – Caden is eventually reduced to a veritable husk as doppelgängers of himself and his loved ones run amok while play-acting scenes from his life. The decades pass with seemingly blistering speed as his play is continually rehearsed. Little by little, he loses everything and everyone he cares about, either as a result of the ticking clock of time or his own inability to make meaningful connections. Eventually he is doomed to wander the streets of an artificial post-apocalyptic landscape of his own creation, which is all that is left of reality as he knows it.

Caden is defined by his extreme sensitivity, subjectivity, sense of guilt and solitude, and embrace of personal suffering, all traits that link him to the Romantic 'Hero of Sensibility' (Thorslev 1962: 35). But he lacks a key characteristic of the optimistic Romantic ironist: the ability to embrace the chaos of existence and utilise it in his artistic creations. Kaufman systematically undermines Caden's ability to control his external surroundings and relationships through the use of various aesthetic devices. Essentially, the film operates on a level where its aesthetic aims undermine its character's desires through the use of fantastical elements.

Caden seeks the control and comfort of absolutes and thus becomes removed from participating meaningfully in his own life. While he fears chaos and tries to counteract it, Kaufman the filmmaker accepts this life-as-chaos paradigm and paints his protagonist as tragic for his inability to change and adapt with it. As such, Kaufman engages in a metatextual relation to his protagonist by utilising Romantic irony as originally defined by Friedrich Schlegel. While ultimately an example of Romantic pessimism similar to Byron's 'metaphysical' dramas *Manfred* and *Cain* (Mellor 1980: 12), the film works on the level of Schlegelian Romantic irony due to Kaufman's treatment of his own material. The film itself becomes an ironic commentary on its protagonist's inability to embrace philosophical irony.

Synecdoche, New York is a distillation of the thematic preoccupations that Kaufman previously addressed as the screenwriter of *Being John Malkovich* (Spike Jonze, Propaganda Films, 1999), *Human Nature* (Michel Gondry, StudioCanal, 2001), *Adaptation* (Jonze, Propaganda Films, 2002), *Confessions of a Dangerous Mind* (George Clooney, Miramax, 2002) and *Eternal Sunshine of the Spotless Mind* (Gondry, Focus Features, 2004), as well as his directorial follow-up, *Anomalisa* (Starburns Industries, 2015). These include osmosis between the external and mental worlds and between the mental worlds of individuals, repetition and doubling and confused subjectivities, the creation of emotionally immersive yet obviously fictitious heightened 'realities', and an examination of individual isolation amidst the indifference of a larger humanity (LaRocca 2011: 6–9). In *Synecdoche, New York*, Kaufman engages his audience emotionally through empathetic subjectivity, casting a spell similar to that experienced by his protagonist, who suffers the slippery effects of time and the questioning of his very relation to the larger world. He also asks the spectator to question the idea of what is 'real' in the first place.

Kaufman's work is largely characterised by extreme subjectivity, one teetering into solipsism. He draws on traditions of philosophical German idealism and authors as diverse as E. T. A. Hoffmann, Johann Wolfgang von Goethe, Mary Shelley and Lord Byron; the magical realism of later authors such as Jorge Luis Borges; and the post-war European cinema of what David Martin-Jones refers to as the 'crisis of modernity' (2006: 46).

Synecdoche, New York questions the nature of objective reality primarily through Kaufman's use of the fantastic 'themes of the self', as defined by Tzvetan Todorov, and the problematising of narrative space via the mise en abyme, which engenders an experience of the mathematical sublime. Kaufman creates a strong sense of ambiguity: is what we are experiencing 'real' – a reflection of an objective, external reality – or just the projection of a diseased mind? The filmmaker specifically works against concepts of mimetic realism in order to access *emotional* realism while exploring ideas of subjectivity, solipsism and idealism through a supposed reflection of the point of view of his protagonist. In the process, he engages in a highly Romantic form of irony, questioning absolutes and embracing the chaos of becoming.

Romantic Irony: From Kant and Schlegel to Byron and Beyond

Romantic irony has its roots in early German idealism and Immanuel Kant's notion of transcendental idealism (Mellor 1980: 25). Kant's 'modest' version of idealism asserts that objects are transcendentally ideal because they are perceived by the mind – we can only judge objects in the world by our own individual mental processes (McQuillan 2012). However, for Kant this did not mean that those objects do not exist outside our perception; rather, we simply have no way of judging them outside of being 'objects for us' (McQuillan 2012). This 'agnostic' form of idealism posits that we can never truly know reality outside of our perception of it and thus whether our perception is correct (Guyer and Horstmann 2015: 5.2).

This split between noumenon (the world independent of the mind) and phenomenon (the world as it is experienced by the mind) is, according to Kant, unable to be traversed (Mellor 1980: 25). Human experience, and thus human knowledge, is finite as a result (1980: 25). When the mind attempts (and fails) to traverse this gap between the phenomenal and noumenal realms, it enters the mode of pure reason – developing concepts such as infinity and totality, ideas inaccessible to direct human experience (1980: 26). This, in turn, can lead to despair and what Anne Mellor terms 'psychic atrophy' due to the inability to experience such concepts first-hand; 'imprisoned in its own finitude', the human mind is left with a longing that can never be fulfilled (1980: 26). The problem for the Romantic artist-philosopher became how to bridge the gap between the world of sensation and experience and the world as it really 'is' (1980: 27) without succumbing to despair over what cannot be attained.

As its earliest and greatest proponent, Friedrich Schlegel (b.1772–d.1829), defines it, Romantic irony embraces the idea that noumenon is fundamentally based on the principle of chaos (Mellor 1980: 27). For Schlegel, the idea of noumenon as *becoming*, rather than being, sets up a profound relation of things in relation to other things – everything is simultaneously itself and in the process of becoming not itself (or 'p = not-p in the act of becoming') (Mellor 1980: 27). This constant act of becoming represents a 'way into infinity', analogous to 'pure energy' (1980: 27) in an unending process of change.

Unlike the purely rhetorical device it once was, irony in the Romantic era became a philosophy or 'general world view' (Behler 1988: 48, 49).[1] Rather than clinging to any concept of an ordered, rational universe subject to human control, Romantic irony posits one of 'incomprehensible' tumult (Schlegel [1797–9] 1971: 260). Schlegel defines this ever-changing state as one of *Fülle*, or fertile abundance, an ecstatic infinite becoming rich with creative possibility (Mellor 1980: 7). But this concept of *Fülle* is double-edged; it creates an eternal, unsatisfied sense of longing for an increased participation in it (1980: 8). Since the human mind cannot actually comprehend such infinite chaos, the experience of the reality of *Fülle* can never be complete, becoming only an approximation of reality that ultimately must be rejected (1980: 8).

As a remedy against this longing, we attempt to impose systems of order (being) onto this disorder (becoming), even though an opposing desire for 'chaos and freedom' also exists (1980: 8). This creates an unrelenting tension, or dialectic, that never results in synthesis (1980: 6). As such, a 'sceptical awareness' of our own mental limitations, combined with a longing to overcome them, defines the process of Romantic irony (1980: 10). According to Mellor, for Schlegel such scepticism, or 'critical idealism', was necessary in order to 'detach imagination from an excessive commitment to its own finite creations' (1980: 15, 10). Nevertheless, commitment and enthusiasm were also key to establishing this dialectic:

> Irony can free the imagination to discover or create ever-new relationships, to participate once again in the fertile chaos of life. For if a person were ever to believe that his reason had fully comprehended this chaos, that conviction would in itself destroy his capacity to participate in the mystery and primeval power of life. (Mellor 1980: 10)

Operating under the idea that the universe is comprehensible to individual consciousness robs the subject from being able to play her own role properly and fully. As a remedy, philosophical irony provides a 'check' to the imagination, curtailing 'excessive commitment to the fictions of one's own mind' in order to be able to participate in life's continual becoming (1980: 11). In *Lyceum (Critical) Fragments*, Schlegel refers to irony as a form of 'self-limitation' characterised by 'self-creation and self-destruction' (Schlegel [1797–9] 1971: 147). Irony plays with the limitations of subjectivity while simultaneously 'open[ing] up the possibility of the infinity of other perspectives', those of potentially endless other subjectivities (Speight 2015: 3.6).

According to Schlegel, applying such principles to artistic work results in a genuine Romantic poetry, one 'free of all real and ideal self-interest' that reflects back on itself in 'an endless succession of mirrors', magnifying its original principles without ever being fully perfected ([1797–9] 1971: 175). Schlegel refers to such irony in paradoxical terms: 'playful and serious, guilelessly open and deeply hidden' ([1797–9] 1971: 156). He applied this philosophy to his own creative work, calling his unfinished novel *Lucinde* 'shaped, artistic chaos [. . .] chaotic and yet systematic' (qtd in Speight 2015: 3.2). Such a model comes closest to offering human consciousness the 'perception of the infinite chaos of reality' (Mellor 1980: 13). It hinges on the 'value of falsity' (1980: 13), recognising the human inability to discern reality within our limited subjectivity while simultaneously embracing the potential inherent in change.

Ultimately, Romantic irony leads to fictional world creation that both recognises its falsehood yet simultaneously presents itself as the sincere reflection of a subjective point of view (1980: 14). The artist enthusiastically commits herself to a creation while simultaneously showing its 'limitations' as a subjective product of a 'finite human being' (1980: 14). This kind of ironic stance can be achieved through devices such as symbolism and allegory and alternative outcomes to the same events (1980: 11), and metatextual elements such as parabasis (Speight 2015: 3.6), paradox and self-parody (Schlegel [1797–9] 1971: 149, 156).

Schlegel refers to such processes as *Selbstbeschränkung*, which Mellor characterises as a 'hovering' between creating and undoing creation wherein the artist 'simultaneously projects his ego or selfhood as a divine creator and also mocks, criticizes, or rejects his created fictions as limited and false' (Mellor 1980: 14). But while the fiction is ultimately 'false', it is not inauthentic. This dialectic of earnestness and scepticism reveals its deceit and creates an 'ambivalent awareness' of the constant navigation of becoming (Thorlby 1988: 131, 132). Remaining 'true to the actual contradictions of life' (Mellor 1980: 15), the Romantic ironist is, in fact, the truly authentic artist.

Synecdoche, New York demonstrates these tensions through many such ironic aesthetic devices, creating an impossible world that attempts to reveal unlimited possibilities: infinite space through the creation of mise en abyme, forking timelines, and endlessly embodied subjectivities. Mellor sees true Romantic irony as a function of the optimistic and comic – her ultimate example is Byron's *Don Juan* – and points to the idea of play as crucial in its creation (1980: 24). *Synecdoche, New York*, however, creates an essentially tragic and pessimistic portrait of a subjectivity undermined by its inability to engage with the world on a philosophically ironic level. Still, the film itself (and Kaufman as writer-director) *affirms* Romantic irony as its ultimate creative position. Its tragedy lies in the fact that its protagonist refuses to engage with it. The film subjects Caden to the chaotic systems of becoming, which Caden attempts to conform to an ordered, rational system where he dictates the terms. As such, he becomes an inauthentic artist and person. By refusing to engage ironically with such a radical becoming, he more or less ceases to be, instead functioning as a 'ghost who haunts his own life' (Deming 2011: 201).

Embracing Irony and Undermining Realism in *Synecdoche, New York*

Synecdoche, New York is a difficult film that engages with its philosophical and fantastic elements directly. It is not a work of fiction that can be passively consumed in any kind of coherent, sensical way, and in this sense it defies the illusionistic principles of typical filmic realism. David Bordwell refers to the use of 'fabula', the narrative mentally constructed by the audience, and the 'syuzhet', the arrangement of the fabula, or, essentially, what the film is telling us (1988: 100). An 'overloaded' syuzhet might lead to boredom on behalf of the audience, providing the viewer too few gaps to fill in, thus eliminating participatory engagement (1988: 54). A 'rarefied' syuzhet risks doing the opposite, leading to a sense of confusion and dislocation, alienating the viewer and breaking the fictional spell of reality (1988: 54). This can create a lack of 'emotional realism', resulting in an inability of audiences to empathically connect to the narrative through character, and creating a sense of disbelief in the film world. The spectator is removed from the 'Secondary World' of the fiction and finds themselves once again in our 'Primary World' reality (Wolf 2012: 24). The immersive nature of the constructed fictional world is lost, however momentarily.

However, Thomas Pavel distinguishes between those texts whose goal is cohesive world creation and those that construct fictional worlds in order to 'lay bare' the very concept of their fiction 'for the sake of adventure and investigation' (1986: 84–5). Pointing to Romantic-era writers E. T. A. Hoffmann and Gérard de Nerval and their modernist progeny Borges and Franz Kafka, Pavel accounts for the valid questioning of mimetic principles and the introduction of 'puzzling' worlds that lead to 'inadequate hypotheses' and encourage hesitation, leading the spectator to create a 'perplexed fictional ego, unsure of its ability to make sense of the events it witnesses' (1986: 93). In this sense, emotional realism can be achieved through the identification with character confusion as much as it can be in the creation of seamless, mimetic narratives and explicit character motivation. In *Synecdoche, New York*, the spectator arrives at a closer picture of such realism through its use of expressive, surreal, and fantastic techniques than could ever be achieved through the illusory practices of mimetic filmic realism.

In his book-length dissection of Romantic irony in the films of Alfred Hitchcock, Richard Allen refers to the director's invocation of the 'chaos world' (2007: 26). Such a world indicates a duality of experience, since it simultaneously 'appears as a psychological projection of a character's state of mind' while it is also 'in accordance with the logic of romantic irony, something that is wholly external to the character – a threatening and alien other' (2007: 26). This is akin to what Kaufman portrays in his film, albeit without the cohesiveness that Hitchcock's classical formula embraces.

Ambiguity is a key function of narratives that seek to uncover what Pavel calls the 'deep fractures' hidden in mimetic realism, creating spaces that exist on 'alien logic' that invoke both the dream world and a myth-puncturing realism simultaneously (2007: 73, 93). In interviews, Kaufman shows a disdain for mimetic realism by acknowledging it as an artificial construction in itself: 'The whole idea of literal realism – it's all a contrivance and a convention that we accept. So why not explore the larger realm?' he asks (Guillén 2008).

Like Anderson, Kaufman is interested in revealing the seams of cinematic production, but his primary concern in this regard is emotional. 'I'm looking for the emotional thing as opposed to the logical thing', he has claimed (Hoby 2009). The filmmaker refuses to see the two impulses as contradictory:

> I really like artifice, and I really like reminding people they're watching a movie. And I really like the idea of having people question the veracity of what they're watching. So by mixing things that are possibly real with things that are clearly not real or are questionable [. . .] I don't see it as a paradox. I've always liked fake worlds and I like sets and I like illusion. But I don't like being lied to. I think movies lie a lot. And maybe *I'm trying not to lie by saying that I am lying*. (Guillén 2008; my emphasis)

By being 'lied to' it is possible Kaufman is referring to the way classical film production plasters over Pavel's deep fractures in an attempt to deny the very nature of its falsehood. Kaufman is echoing the Romantic principle of authenticity – he eschews an interest in mimetic realism in favour of an *inner* authenticity and a sincerity of purpose (Milnes and Sinanan 2010: 4). His use of irony, in this sense, relates to personal authenticity and a rejection of the 'deceitful illusions' (Thorlby 1988: 131) of cohesion.

It also relates closely to Schlegel's concept of what he called Socratic irony, an irony that 'is intended to deceive none but those who consider it to be deceptive' (Behler 1988: 52). In Schlegel's terms, an artist must maintain a relationship with the contradictions inherent in life, or such authenticity will be destroyed and contact with reality could even be lost (Mellor 1980: 15). Such an ironic stance 'contains and arouses a feeling of the insoluble conflict between the absolute and relative, the simultaneous impossibility and necessity of a complete account of reality' (1980: 52). That impossibility, conveyed by the film's style, and necessity, conveyed by its protagonist's desires, represent the fundamental dialectical tension of Kaufman's film.

The first blatant indication that the film will undermine such a complete account of reality occurs about twenty minutes into its running time. The scene begins with Hazel (Samantha Morton), arguably Caden's 'true love' (although it is difficult to think Kaufman would believe in such an idea), driving down an ordinary, well-kept suburban street in the American every-town of Schenectady, New York. She haphazardly parks in front of a house painted a garish yellow that is clearly on fire. Smoke billows out its windows in large plumes and flames lick the windowpanes on its second storey. Hazel glimpses a man in a dark suit through her passenger window as he casually walks by the house and out of frame. He does not seem to notice the fire. Moments later Hazel chats with an estate agent inside. 'I've always loved this house', she remarks. 'Yes, it's a wonderful place', the agent replies, as the fire flickers around them (Figure 2.1). The agent coughs and admits that the sellers are 'very motivated'. Hazel expresses tentative doubts. 'I like it, I do. I'm just really concerned with dying in the fire', she admits meekly. 'It's a big decision', the agent replies sympathetically, 'how one prefers to die'.

Figure 2.1   The eternally burning house fire creates confusion in the spectator and serves to keep the film squarely in the realm of the fantastic.

David L. Smith claims the fire 'seems to represent the imminence of mortality' in the film (2011: 252). But it also relates to the illusion of choice. While Richard Deming thinks *Synecdoche, New York* suggests the idea that 'the shape of a life is fashioned by choices and responses to what occurs' (Deming 2011: 197), this idea runs counter to the principle of noumenal chaos and the ability to function within it by recognising that human will is nothing in its face. Perhaps the main purpose of the house fire and this initial scene is to make clear the film's world operates under the dizzying precepts of profound ambiguity and is working to illicit confusion in the spectator (if not, at this point, in its characters). It raises a slew of unavoidable questions. Why are these women calmly discussing square footage in a house that is burning down around them? Why is the estate agent's adult son hanging around in the basement of a burning home clad only in boxer shorts? In what world does a house on fire necessitate a literal fire sale?

If the well-known yet largely unremarkable town of Schenectady, New York,[2] can in itself be seen as a synecdoche of Middle America, its values and hypocrisies, this scene might be taken as a synecdoche for the film as a whole. It defies expectations in a way that, as the narrative progresses, becomes systematic. Typical viewers are now likely scratching their heads, wondering what on earth it could mean. But their questions will never be answered. Such unanswered questions create profound confusion, 'altering the viewer's relationship to what occurs on screen, destabilizing what distinctions one makes between the real and surreal' (Deming 2011: 195). This specific plot device only gets more confounding in later scenes, including one in which we see Caden and Hazel sharing cocktails in her lounge while the fire still burns and, years later, when Caden watches Hazel outside her house, the fire's intensity progressing but at a glacial pace. Decades later, the fire finally takes her life. (The coroner's deadpan diagnosis as he looks at her blackened throat swab: 'Could be smoke inhalation.')

In order to ascertain the theoretic underpinnings of the fantastical components of Kaufman's film, as exemplified by its continually burning fire scenario, it is necessary to define what is meant by the term 'fantastic' in its strictest Todorovian sense. According to Todorov, for events to be considered fantastic they must 'hesitate between a natural and supernatural explanation', creating an ambiguity that becomes a principle theme of the work (1975: 33). No single explanation can or should be given for their diversions from realism. It is then necessary that the reader or spectator must adopt a certain attitude to the work, rejecting purely 'allegorical as well as "poetic" interpretations' (1975: 33). That is, in the world of the fiction, these things are really occurring. It is not always necessarily that 'the hesitation be *represented* within the work', through the experience of a character reacting to events, although it usually is (1975: 34).

The fire in *Synecdoche* is not poetic in the sense that it is not clearly allegorical. It exists, simply as a fire, on one narrative level, which is the final condition it must meet to be considered of the fantastic (1975: 32). The key element of its fantastic quality is found in the hesitation it elicits on the part of the spectator. A fire is a natural event, but here it is unnatural, enduring due to an extreme dilation of time. Pointedly, the fire is the only fantastic occurrence in the film that exists wholly outside of the purview of Caden – every other can be read as a reflection of his subjective experience, a result of his supposed descent into madness. But the fire unequivocally exists outside his mental imaginings.

Kaufman has noted that the fire scenario often elicits a particularly confused response from audiences:

> People ask, '*Why* the burning house? What *is* the burning house?' I have to say, 'Well, it doesn't *speak* to you. It speaks to other people'. I'm trying to let this interaction be personal, in the same way that a dream is personal. (Guillén 2008)

The fire, then, functions on the level of a dream image for the spectator (and the director), but not for the characters in the film. Todorov acknowledges that the fantastic is found within the more general category of 'ambiguous vision' (1975: 33), a phrase that could be considered synonymous with the dream state. In the promotional short 'In and Around Schenectady, New York', Kaufman refers to his film as operating under 'dream logic', specifically manifesting Caden's interior life without the use of narrative devices like voice-over. Such supernatural events as the eternally burning house provoke not only anxiety and even horror on the part of the perceiver, the 'phenomenon makes us wonder "what it means" less than it amazes us by the strangeness of the fact itself' (1975: 104). This wonderment is the key to taking such occurrences from the realm of the purely marvellous to the fantastic: 'the perception of the supernatural casts a heavy shadow over the supernatural itself and makes its access difficult to us' (1975: 105). That difficulty, or ambiguity, renders the fire fantastic.

For Todorov, perception 'constitutes a screen rather than removes one' (1975: 105); if the act of perception is foregrounded and the nature of the events perceived remains unknown, this leads to a predominant anxiety (1975: 105). *Synecdoche*'s fire engenders both *'What are we seeing?'* and *'What does this mean?'* responses; sensation and perception are 'transformed into idea' (1975: 115). Such a collapse between event and event-perception of space and time highlights the perception-consciousness system of relations between the self and the world (1975: 139), including notions of subjectivity, solipsism and philosophical idealism. This 'stresse[s] the mind's power to create its own universe of consciousness, freed from any absolute natural law' (1975: 28).

Crucially, the film also adheres to principles of mimetic realism, of 'what we think of as the "real world"' (Deming 2011: 195). These include 'realistic décor, gritty locations, and generally unglamorous clothes and makeup for the actors' (Hill 2011: 217). (Hazel's continually burning house, with its pristine mid-century furnishings in oddly saturated colours, is again exempt from this realism.) Derek Hill qualifies Kaufman's particular form of fantastic world creation as 'synthetic hyperrealist' (2011: 217), likening it to a similar aesthetic in the surrealist films of David Lynch. Unsurprisingly, Kaufman is reportedly an admirer of Lynch (Tobias 2008), along with such twentieth-century fantasists as Philip K. Dick and Franz Kafka (Sternbergh 2015). Such surrealist tendencies also relate to the film's ambiguity between extreme subjectivity and a more objective realism in its narration.

'A SERIES OF MAD VISIONS PERHAPS': THE SCREEN AS THE SITE OF CONFUSED SUBJECTIVITY

Caden Cotard is instantly recognisable as a man of deep-set neuroses, but initially he is portrayed as having a relatively firm grasp on reality and the separation of his inner life from the external world. His hypochondria and death obsession – evidenced by routinely reading the obituaries, seeing a headline about Harold Pinter and assuming it means he is dead, starting the day by pointing out he feels unwell and that the milk has expired – all point to a neurotic individual, but not a psychotic one. His life has the semblance of normality: he has a full-time job, mounting a production of, appropriately enough, *Death of a Salesman*.[3] He is married to an artist, Adele (Catherine Keener), and has a young daughter, Olive (Sadie Goldstein).

After hitting his head on an exploding bathroom faucet, Caden receives a diagnosis of a 'synaptic degradation' that is 'fungal in nature' from a neurologist. His situation briefly becomes more hopeful when he receives a 'genius grant' from the MacArthur Foundation, and decides to write a new, original play about the 'brutal truth' of life and death. Pointedly, this occurs after Adele ridicules his staging of *Death of a Salesman* as inauthentic: 'It's not you', she says. 'It's not anyone.' But when Adele and Olive leave Schenectady and Caden for Berlin's bohemian art world, his neuroses begin to take on a more sinister hue. Kaufman provides an early foreshadowing of events through Caden's surname. 'Cotard' is a reference to Cotard's Syndrome, a rare disorder in which the sufferer operates under the assumption that he is dead, does not exist, or is putrefying.[4]

The idea of a physical trauma, such as Caden's head injury, resulting in extreme personality or psychological disturbance is something of a cartoonish trope in Hollywood: characters, both animated and 'real', throughout cinema and television history have received similar blows to the head resulting not just in amnesia, but in the questioning of their sense of personal identity – in such instances, physical trauma is often connected to emotional trauma (Baxendale 2004). Are we meant to think that the unfolding narrative of the film is a result of Caden's newfound brain damage? It is unlikely, but also unclear.

Separated from his family and becoming increasingly obsessed with his grand artistic plans, Caden begins to lose touch with the external world, and the film reflects this aesthetically. He sees visions of himself in television cartoons, and later in a TV advertisement for a chemotherapy drug. His own image appears in a movie poster. His mental state even seems to physically manifest itself on his own body. Boils appear on his skin; his veins bulge and make odd sounds when touched. Later his teeth appear to be rotting and flesh hangs off his legs.

Such a 'collapse between the limits of matter and mind' is considered to be 'the first characteristic of madness' (Todorov 1975: 115). It also relates to the idea of pan-signification, one of the fantastic 'themes of the self', wherein 'the transition from mind to matter has become possible' (1975: 114). The confusion found on the site of Caden's body (his afflictions seem to come and go without reason) echoes confusion concerning narrative events in the film. Instances of miscommunication or misunderstanding are a major motif, particularly within dialogue and language in general, such as the instances where Caden confuses the words *ophthalmologist*, *urologist* and *neurologist*. But the people he talks to often experience the same confusion, misinterpreting his signals. He tells Adele that he thinks he has blood in his stool. 'That stool in your office?' she asks, half asleep.

The subject of time is also greatly confused in communication. Adele's friend Maria (Jennifer Jason Leigh), after staying up all night, remarks, 'It's really late. Early. It's late.' Ambiguous language communication is also a central element in Caden's relationship to his daughter. He has to explain to her the difference between the homophones 'psychosis' and 'sycosis' early on in the film, after she notices the pustules on his face (highlighting the correlation between the coming degradation of his body and mind), and she also confuses sewage pipes with smoking pipes. Later, when the adult Olive (Robin Weigert) is on her death bed, the two must communicate via an electronic translation machine, as for some reason she has forgotten her mother tongue after decades of living in Berlin, a city where English is regularly spoken.

David L. Smith likens the use of language in the film to the idea of the synecdoche itself: 'As creatures of language, we live only with parts and can produce only synecdoches' (Smith 2011: 247). Such a symbolic mode of communication defines a gulf between thing and thing represented and can never deliver the 'whole truth' (2011: 247), which is what Caden seeks to convey, through language, in his play. Language lives within the realm of subjectivity, of internal mental process, and not of noumenon. By highlighting miscommunication through language, Kaufman emphasises the gulf between subjectivities in his film.

Schlegel expresses this sentiment when he argues that the structured and rational system of language can never express the fundamental chaos of *Fülle* (Mellor 1980: 10). Instead, '[t]he mystery of becoming can be linguistically expressed only as hints, cyphers, and hieroglyphs' (1980: 10–11), such as the perplexing human nose painted on the giant pink box Caden hopes to give Olive as a present. Such symbolism, which is without any discernible meaning in the film, denotes a 'hint at the infinite' while acknowledging the failure to attain it (1980: 11).

Language, in spoken and written form, eventually becomes so confused to Caden, his fax machine spews gibberish and the words in books vanish without a trace. This breakdown between matter and mind remains at the level of the fantastic because as spectators we can acknowledge that it represents a transgression of these limits, not a purely mythical, allegorical representation (Todorov 1975: 116). The pan-signification it exemplifies contends 'relations exist on all levels, among all elements of the world' (1975: 112). Objects are imbued with lives of their own via mental and emotional connections. When Caden finds Olive's diary not long after she leaves for Berlin, it is full of the musings of a small child, read in voice-over with Olive's childish intonations. The voice-over musings of the adult Olive, read with a heavy German accent, continue to appear in its pages over the years, even though she is thousands of miles away and has not seen her father since leaving New York.[5]

Todorov characterises language as '[t]he essential event which provokes the shift from the primary mental organization to maturity' (1975: 145). In essence, it signals the move from the pre-symbolic to the symbolic. Madness, in turn, correlates with the pre-symbolic, a pre-language infancy. In this state, 'the transition between matter and mind has become possible' (1975: 114). Thus, the breakdowns in both language and bodily function signify a return to a state of mental infancy, when 'the limit between the physical and mental, between matter and spirit, between word [or image] and thing, ceases to be impervious'

(1975: 113). At her mother's funeral, Caden's future wife, Claire (Michelle Williams), laments that she 'used to be a baby' through tears, expressing a tacit desire to return to a pre-language state where the fantastic is still possible.[6]

Such a pre-verbal (or pre-symbolic) state represents a return to a feeling of wholeness with the external world, away from the 'extreme subjectivity' of self (1975: 175). In the Romantic era, madness often represented a 'higher form of reason', as in Edgar Allan Poe's remark, 'Science has not yet told us whether madness may not be the sublime form of intelligence' (qtd in Todorov 1975: 39). However, while Kaufman invites his protagonist to experience feelings of sublimity through such fantastic 'pan-signification', Caden instead embodies a Romantic pessimism that continually rejects the idea through his self-conscious solipsism.

While Mellor (1980: 199) sees positivity and optimism in Romantic irony, Ernst Behler contends that theories of irony continued to evolve in the Romantic era, constituting a turn from 'optimism and joyous freedom toward sadness, melancholy and despair' (1988: 45). This darker ironic sense springs from an overbearing adherence toward the 'infinite longing' that Schlegel considers one half of the Romantic ironic dialectic (1988: 45). The 'German misery' of tragic irony (1988: 46) spread to other nations as well, including France and Britain, and had an indelible influence on Byron (Thorslev 1962: 166). *Synecdoche, New York* continues a tradition of ironic pessimism present in Goethe's *Faust* and *The Sorrows of Young Werther* and Byron's *Childe Harold's Pilgrimage*, *Manfred* and *Cain* (Thorslev 1962: 87).

Peter Thorslev details how the Romantic 'Hero of Sensibility' emerged as a response to the 'dead certainties' of Enlightenment tropes (1962: 85). The Hero of Sensibility is not defined by action, but by a capacity for deep feeling and the 'tender emotions – gentle and tearful love, nostalgia, and a pervasive melancholy' (1962: 35). The Hero of Sensibility combines the death-obsessed 'Gloomy Egoist' (1962: 46) with the sensitive 'Man of Feeling', a well-educated man who is 'not necessarily handsome, and is never robust; usually he is pale and inclined to fevers, especially "brain fevers" brought about by fits of melancholy' (1962: 39). The Man of Feeling, it seems, feels so much it literally affects his physical health.

He is solitary and sometimes cowardly, prone to 'benevolent acts' that are usually 'sporadic and ineffectual' (1962: 39). He is usually an artist, one possessed by a sorrow of 'cosmic significance' (1962: 42). *Weltschmerz* is his particular 'Romantic disease', the conflict between the desire for order and the need to feel like a working part of a 'living organic universe' and the belief in individual personality and passion over and above the greater workings of that universe (1962: 89).

It is a suffering that could be attributed to almost any Romantic artist – such a state characterises Romantic thought – but for the Hero of Sensibility, the sceptical self tends to reign supreme, with the 'detached, insulated, and passionately individual' taking precedence over sublime mysticism (1962: 89). Throughout Kaufman's film, Caden remains a tragic figure in this mode. He is a Man of Feeling who becomes disconnected from himself due to his inability to affectively (and effectively) engage in his own life. He experiences physical degradation and eventually his alienation becomes so great he even attempts to externalise his very being by casting an actor to 'play' him.

Such physical metamorphoses are also related to the collapse of matter and mind. As Caden's play continues to grow in his attempt to replicate every aspect of his life on his hangar-like stage set, multiple versions of characters come to occupy the world of the film, as they inhabit the play within the film. Caden's embodiment of Ellen, or Sammy's embodiment of Caden, or Tammy's embodiment of Hazel, speaks to the physical manifestation of a multiplicity of internalised personalities within one mind: 'We are several persons mentally, we become so physically' (Todorov 1975: 116).

Ironically, despite the multiplications and replications of personalities, Caden's point of view becomes more and more solely informed by the curious, possibly demented workings of his own brain. According to Edward Branigan, 'A first-person recounting of events is an illusion, but one which is bound up with the very conditions which allow us to make sense of the fictional world' (1992: 51). If the first-person account of a fictional world is confused and ambiguous to the character perceiving it, it will necessarily become so to the audience, which identifies with his point of view.

Caden's solipsism, and the film's external renderings of the inner workings of his mind (if, indeed, that is what the film's dreamlike images are), further underscores the film's ambiguity. We, like Caden, cannot be sure of what is real and what is not, if indeed anything is. This confusion is similar to what Todorov sees as the 'pervasive ambiguity' (1975: 39) of Gérard de Nerval's 1855 novella, *Aurélia*, in which the narrator experiences 'a series of mad visions perhaps' (Nerval qtd in Todorov 1975: 39). Kaufman articulates a belief in Schlegel's transcendental 'critical idealism' (Mellor 1980: 15) when he says, 'It's a recognition that that's just the truth [. . .] It's not the world as it is that we are seeing but the world as it's translated by this mound of material in our heads' (Guillén 2008). In these terms, there is no objective truth for the film to relate to its audience. Kaufman even goes so far as to suggest a personal flirtation with philosophical idealism, suggesting reality is fundamentally a construct of the individual mind:

> I think it's really interesting that visually the world doesn't exist. It only exists as our brain's interpretation. I sometimes try to imagine what this world looks like without people in it and I don't think it looks like anything. It certainly doesn't look like this. (Guillén 2008)

While Kaufman's ideas jibe with various incarnations of German idealism, popularised in the Romantic period by Hegel, Fichte, Schelling and Schopenhauer, they also fit neatly with the concepts of the fantastic. Objects as mere projections of the mind can be seen as expressions of, or connections to, the fantastic's dissolution of the veil between matter and mind, of the 'effacement of the limit between subject and object' (Todorov 1975: 116). The idea reaches its logical conclusion in the famous thought experiment of the 'brain in a vat', which argues that theoretically, there is no way of knowing if individual experience is not merely the result of a sentient brain being hooked up to electrodes to stimulate mental activity, simply giving the impression that an experience in external reality is occurring.

Given this scenario's adjacent position to death (at least the death of the body), it is tempting to consider the idea that Caden is already dead and his experiences are merely expressions of his mind's last delirious gasps of consciousness. The most overt implication of this occurs when he visits his therapist, Madeline Gravis (Hope Davis). The severity of her name is an ironic twist on her frivolous notions of therapy and happiness, but also points to grave potentialities: 'Why did he kill himself?' Caden enquires about the child author of the bestseller *Little Winky*. 'I don't know. Why did you?' she replies. He asks her to repeat herself. 'Why would you?' she answers.

Perhaps Caden misheard her the first time, and we heard what he did through a subjective alignment, or perhaps she changed her answer. The death hypothesis is never revealed as truth, however, and this is integral to maintaining the sustained hesitation that the fantastic requires. Caden's solipsism stretches to the extent that whole characters are suggested illusions, such as Kaufman's insistence that the character of Ellen is a figment of Caden's imagination (Guillén 2008). While both the actor Millicent Weems (Dianne Wiest) and Caden himself embody Ellen at certain points, the 'real' Ellen is never revealed – her various representations are themselves truly simulacra, signifiers without signified, copies without an original.

Caden considers naming his untitled play *The Simulacrum*. This is of course a reference to Baudrillard's postmodernist work *Simulacra and Simulations*. Evans suggests the play within the film illustrates Baudrillard's conception of the final order of simulacrum, when a thing 'bears no relation to any reality whatever: it is its own pure simulacrum' (Baudrillard 1983: 5) and 'the mimetic relationship between the real and its representation' has broken down, affecting the very nature of reality itself (Evans 2014: 327). Caden's work, which becomes his life, represents both simulacrum and synecdoche, 'in which parts and wholes, reality and mimicry, outside and inside collapse into one another' (2014: 328). There is no longer an objective vantage point of reality from which to view its various mirrors and permutations. It becomes simply a morass of signs and symbols while the referents are lost. This is in essence the space of indeterminacy from which the postmodern operates; Kaufman emphasises this idea by including few establishing shots that would serve to create a fixed space from which to consider his created world.

Caden's artistic recreations of his life in his art operate under the fantastic's 'themes of vision', which are antithetical to the principles of reason (Todorov 1975: 122). A complete, full-sized replica of New York, which in itself contains a full-sized replica (via its recreation of the warehouse set), which in itself contains a full-sized replica, on to infinity, is spatially impossible.[7] Todorov considers these themes as examples of 'indirect, distorted, subverted vision' (1975: 122). This preoccupation with distorted vision can also be seen in the film's use of specialised microscope-like glasses used to view Adele's miniscule paintings, which grow smaller and smaller as the film progresses, as Caden's project grows larger and larger. This 'distorted' vision is ambiguously a symptom of Caden's madness, but, as in Nerval's *Aurélia*, we are never sure if this madness might actually constitute a quality of perception of 'the superlative, the excessive' (1975: 93) that is unavailable to those who do not view the world through extraordinary eyes.

If he has such a superlative vision, Caden seems too 'fixated on the limits of the self' (Mellor 1980: 39) to impart it to others. Like Byron's protagonist in *Cain*, Caden is obsessed with death and the limitations of life (1980: 39). His physical breakdowns can be read as an expression of his mental state, one of 'ironic pessimism' (1980: 39). 'Cain [. . .] is a pure ironist, for whom self-consciousness is only a melancholy conviction of loss and death', writes Mellor (1980: 39). The same can be said of Caden (whose name even recalls Byron's tragic biblical hero), who denies the 'renewal of life' (1980: 39) offered in the potentially redemptive love of Hazel. One of the sustained (traditional) ironies in the film relates to the imaginative subjectivity of its narrative – ambiguously a product of Caden's newly explosive mental processes – and Caden's lack of imagination when it comes to his creative endeavours. Kaufman relates this to Caden's incapability of interpreting his newfound ways of seeing: 'Caden's work is so literal. The only way he can reflect reality in his mind is by imitating it full-size. [. . .] It's a dream image but he's not interacting with it successfully' (Guillén 2008).

Caden personifies the negative side of *Weltschmerz* as his self-absorbed egoism leads him to become 'detached, insulated', even as he longs for the ability to feel part of the totality of humankind (Thorslev 1962: 89). As he puts it in an impassioned speech to Hazel, 'We're all in the same water, after all, soaking in our very menstrual blood and nocturnal emissions. This is what I want to try to give people.' But Caden is so obsessed with himself, and his own mortality, he has little actual interest in other people. Hazel obviously longs for a romantic relationship with Caden, but he is too absorbed in creating an artwork *about* connection to embark on his own. If 'the very passion of the egoism of the *Weltschmerzler* usually makes him involve the whole world in his peculiar plight' (1962: 88), Caden goes so far as to create his own world in order to realise such a myopic search for self. The world he creates has the dizzying effect of further complicating his existence and relation to the revelation of truth, however. One of the ways in which Kaufman creates such a relation to ambiguous alternate realities is in the film's use of the mise en abyme, which generates spatial confusion through mirroring effects.

The Mise en Abyme and the Mathematical Sublime

Kaufman, as a screenwriter and filmmaker, remains preoccupied with the metaphysical nature of illusion and reality. 'I don't even know that I exist, let alone what's happening', he says (Huddleston n.d.). As a stylistic device, the mise en abyme helps elucidate the confusion between illusion and reality found in *Synecdoche, New York*. Robert Stam defines the mise en abyme as 'the infinite regress of mirror reflections to denote the literary, painterly, or filmic process by which a passage, a section, or sequence plays out in miniature the processes of the text as a whole' (1992: xiv). Such an infinite regress 'knows no bounds' (Evans 2014: 326). In the film it is a product of Caden's 'obsessive' desire for an endless replication of exact copies of real objects (2014: 326).

Caden's production creates identical sets within sets, so that the supposed entirety of the first set is included in the one inside of it (Figure 2.2). These are at once miniatures of the larger sets, but paradoxically contain the latter, theoretically ad infinitum. Evans contends that in the film these replications suggest a 'fixed subjectivity' rather than the postmodern 'fashionable,

Figure 2.2   Caden's grand theatre project involves geographical impossibility: creating infinite life-size replicas of New York City within a warehouse in New York City.

uncertain, shattered self' (2014: 327). This is manifested by Caden's desire to embody such a fixed subjectivity as the nature of reality around him becomes disjointed and his very body begins to turn on itself.

If such an infinite regress can seem positively 'dizzying' (Metz 1974: 232), the spectator must suffer this vertigo by considering the aesthetic mirroring effects that the play within the film creates, which multiplies the heightened sense of delirium and confusion caused by a confrontation with the infinite. Literally translated, 'abyme' means 'abyss' or 'chasm' (1974: 231), and that evocation of the sublime terror of the infinite, be it massive or infinitesimal, is integral to the workings of Kaufman's film.

In the *Critique of Judgement*, Kant describes what he refers to as the 'mathematical sublime' (Kant [1790] 2007: 84), a specific form of sublimity related to 'spatial or temporal magnitude' (Shaw 2005: 81). When an individual is confronted with an object or experience, he first perceives through 'sensible intuition' based on a priori knowledge of the world that all beings automatically possess. In turn, this intuition is first 'synthesized' through the imagination, and subsequently 'thought through' to understanding (2005: 65). When an object or experience is too much for the imagination to comprehend, however, the subject is struck with a sublime feeling. This in turn activates the mind's capacity to reason, to abstractly conceptualise not only the unpresentability of an object but the very fact that the mind itself is capable of the process of abstract conceptualisation.

'The mere ability even to think it as *a whole* indicates a faculty of mind transcending every standard of sense' (Kant [1790] 2007: 85; original emphasis); that is, this ability is based in a higher mental function than sensation, that of reason. In this way the sublime leads to a feeling within the individual of his own power over nature, as well as his separateness from it (Shaw 2005: 74). It is a feeling of freedom tinged with sadness, both emotions the result of being released from purely terrestrial bonds in a shift of view from 'world to mind' (2005: 73). This shift necessitates an experience of pain followed by 'a powerful sense of relief' (2005: 83). Serving as a seed to the process, imagination plays a critical role, leading to a distinct emotional experience that is, by definition, a solitary one.

Caden, unlike the spectator, does not possess mastery over his own thoughts or experiences, and is instead plunged into an existential nightmare. While we enjoy our place of remove from the action, Caden has to contend with the pure terror of unreason. (It is fitting that Kaufman originally conceived *Synecdoche* after being approached about writing a 'horror film' (Moriarty 2008).) His artistic quest is actually anti-sublime: he seeks to present and understand the totality of his life. Conversely, his ex-wife Adele literally illustrates the idea of 'sensible objects' (2005: 43) through her art, which represents tiny snippets of moments in time illuminated by her subjective experience. Adele becomes a roaring success, while Caden seems cursed to wander in his own purgatory. A synecdoche is meant to be a part taken to represent the whole, not the whole itself. Adele's paintings, which are so minute as to require special visual apparatus for viewing (requiring a different way of seeing), support the Blakean idea of a sublime microcosm, as in the opening stanza of Blake's 1803 poem, 'The Auguries of Innocence': 'To see a world in a grain of sand / And heaven in a wild flower / Hold infinity in the palm of your hand / And eternity in an hour' (Blake 2011).

Her paintings are also visual representations of Schlegel's idea of the 'fragment': a 'single, complete idea' that refuses to impose a 'false system or an unjustified rational order' (Mellor 1980: 21). Ralph Waldo Emerson's essays, in similar fashion to Schlegel, create 'subjective verisimilitude' without completeness or resolution, portraying 'a mind in motion' (Smith 2011: 242). Caden, in contrast, attempts to 'conjure a whole from the parts' (2011: 240) – to experience the totality of his life while he is still living it. Constructing from a seemingly infinite number of tiny snippets, he attempts to arrange a cohesive truth.

It is a fool's game, and perhaps that is why he hangs it up and decides to live the life of a maid (or at least play her role), one who simply struggles with day-to-day menial tasks while regretting her past sins. Scenes of Caden wandering through life as Hazel are indicative of the 'Wandering Jew' trope, a familiar one in German Romanticism (Hartman 1970: 51). As in Byron's *Manfred*, it epitomises Caden's tragic-ironic 'death wish' or 'longing for self-oblivion' found within *Weltschmerz* (Mellor 1980: 170), a release from the desire for the infinite in the face of life's finitude (Behler 1988: 45). The Wandering Jew figure is always solitary, 'separated from life in the midst of life', trapped by the alienating burden of self-consciousness (Hartman 1970: 51). This highlights a major theme of Kaufman's film: Caden is burdened by his separation from other people due to his extreme solipsism, but he also struggles to hold onto such a 'Romantic "I"' when his 'certainty and simplicity of self' begin to crumble (1970: 51).

It remains a mystery why Caden thinks he can reconstruct a sense of a core self by getting someone else to play him, but perhaps his goal is to study himself from the 'outside' in order to get an objective idea of his troubles. As Rebecca Davers suggests, 'The film audience recognizes that Caden may [. . .] be trying to "trace [. . .] back to its source" the unhappiness that seems to define him' (2011: 37). Unsurprisingly, things become more confused for Caden, not less. Multiple doppelgängers (Cadens, Hazels, Ellens) form the core of the narrative confusion in the latter half of the film, lending a human component to the idea of infinite replication (Figure 2.3).

Borges, whose story 'Tlön, Uqbar, Orbis Tertius' recounts the discovery of an encyclopaedia based on an imaginary, idealist world, sees a curious law of

THE STILLNESS OF SOLITUDE

Figure 2.3   Caden and Hazel observe their doppelgängers as they act in a play that has essentially become the only form of existence for their real and fictional selves.

diminishing returns related to the idea of mise en abyme. The text within the story recounts the concept of the *hrönir*, the duplicates of lost objects that are 'awkward in form' and 'somewhat longer' than the originals (Borges [1962] 2000: 38). These *hrönir* have 'made possible the interrogation and even the modification of the past, which is no less plastic and docile than the future' ([1962] 2000: 38). The *hrönir* exhibit an irregular form of quality control as they are replicated:

> Curiously, the *hrönir* of second and third degree – the *hrönir* derived from another *hrön*, those derived from the *hrön* of a *hrön* – exaggerate the aberrations of the initial one; those of fifth degree are almost uniform; those of ninth degree become confused with those of the second; in those of the eleventh there is a purity of line not found in the original. The process is cyclical: the *hrön* of the twelfth degree begins to fall off in quality. (Borges [1962] 2000: 38–9)

Borges's endless series of mirrored objects is a metaphor for problematising identity: the loss of identity as a result of replication itself. Who is the real Caden? Is this Caden or Caden playing Ellen or Caden playing Millicent playing Ellen? Why is the 'real' Hazel attracted to the 'fake' Caden? Is the fake Hazel a proper substitute for the real one? 'Things became duplicated in Tlön', writes Borges; 'they also tend to become effaced and lose their details when they are forgotten' ([1962] 2000: 39).

This brings to mind Kaufman's screenplay for *Eternal Sunshine of the Spotless Mind*, in which details of mise-en-scène, like shop signs and book jackets, fade away to nothing as Joel Barrish's memories are erased. It also speaks to the notion of idealism that is at the core of 'Tlön, Uqbar, Orbis Tertius' and a great deal of Borges's magical realism, a notion that the world is simply a solipsistic projection of our own mind, in which fantastical, irrational elements arise to remind us of the fiction in which we live (Barth 1984: 75).

Caden, unlike Borges, is a self-referential artist who both fears and refutes such infinite possibilities. He is obsessed with the idea of art as replication and reconstruction, of reconstituting life as it is lived minute by minute, in the way that it happened, the 'only' way that it can happen. Consumed by the fear of future failure, and the regret of his failures in the past, he must assert the primacy of his one true timeline, free from Borgesian difference. Kaufman, however, refuses to grant him his wish. Instead, he questions Caden's power as an artist through his relation to personal inauthenticity.

He rarely lives with 'self-awareness' and lacks the conscious ability to make choices for himself (Hill 2011: 210). The very degradation of Caden's body could be seen as a factor in, or as a result of, his inability to act. Caden is so overwhelmed and incapacitated by his circumstances that he has to do 'biofeedback' exercises to produce saliva and needs eye drops to create enough moisture to cry, experiencing as he is a kind of emotional, existential shock.

As an artist, Caden seeks Truth – another word for authenticity – and he mounts his play in order to make a grand, overarching statement about the very nature of life and death. Surely, a man bestowed a 'genius grant' would have something grandly important, perhaps even eternal, to say about such all-encompassing themes. But Caden cannot slavishly recreate his own life and in any way access the truth, which is defined by change.

In an 1813 love letter to Annabella Milbanke, Byron summarised a sort of treatise on his own state of perpetual discontentment:

> You don't like my 'restless' doctrines – I should be very sorry if *you* did – but *I* can't *stagnate* nevertheless – if I must set sail let it be on the ocean no matter how stormy – anything but a dull cruise on a level lake without ever losing sight of the same insipid shores by which it is surrounded. (Byron 1974: 119; original emphasis)

Byron himself has been accused of his own 'implacable nihilism' (McGann 1983: 76). Such a nihilism, however, is very different from that of Caden Cotard's. Daniel Shaw refers to Caden's 'passive nihilism', which 'shrinks from the chaos of existence' in favour of a search for 'resignation and acceptance' (2011: 256). In contrast, Kaufman's (and Byron's) 'active' nihilism 'clears away the obsolete "Idols of the Marketplace" in order to prepare the ground for new, contemporary values' (2011: 256). In other words, it embraces chaos as a means of rebirth and re-signification.

David L. Smith relates Kaufman's work to the Nietzschean idea of *amor fati*, a way to 'transform a sense of entrapment in life's limitations' via an 'ecstatic affirmation' of them (2011: 245). Such a perspective can provide 'a naturalistic mode of transcendence' due to the recognition of the futility of creating worlds without flaws (2011: 244). *Amor fati* evokes sublimity via the knowledge of our own limitations. While Shaw sees Kaufman's film as a failure due to its protagonist's 'deer-caught-in-the-headlights powerlessness' (Shaw 2011: 265), I argue that Kaufman's own active nihilism operates in a continual dialectic without synthesis – in Romantic ironic fashion – with Caden's passive nihilism.

The concept of *amor fati* can be traced to Schlegelian irony in its representation of *affirmative* thought, active and creative, rather than reactive and passive. Caden's insistence on describing and redescribing the world as it 'is' (or was) renders his life as a collection of lifeless signs. Perhaps this is the clearest connection to the hypothesis that he is already dead. He is certainly *creatively* dead. Caden, the great artistic 'genius' and seeker of truth, is really a conformist. As a result, he is doomed to failure, wandering alone in an empty, post-apocalyptic dreamscape of his own creation. Without the freedom of new possibilities, art – and life – become as inert as an empty stage.

Conclusion

In Schlegel's terms, Caden has failed to 'maintain a relationship with contradictions inherent in life' (Mellor 1980: 15) and has thus become inauthentic. But Kaufman has created a film that simultaneously allows him to both engage with a more pessimistic version of himself and also assert his own belief in contradiction and ambiguity. As Smith writes, *Synecdoche, New York* 'evokes transcendence by oblique means and inspires reflection on the strategies by which transcendence is pursued' (2011: 245). In the mode of philosophical irony, it is a 'poem [film] as an unresolved debate' (Mellor 1980: 22).

Caden's art does not participate in the fertile chaos of life, so his mental workings force him to do so as a sort of corrective measure. Yet he is unable to embrace the chaos Kaufman creates due to the belief that he can have full mastery over time and space and somehow access absolute truth. While Caden seeks to harness the power of godlike creation, the failure of his play and life is due to his lack of ability to see beyond the possible world and seize the possibilities of the fantastic one. This is where autobiographical similarities between art and artist diverge, for Kaufman fearlessly delves into impossible worlds with seemingly unmitigated enthusiasm and imagination.

That is not to say the film does not portray the same anxieties that plague Caden's worldview. But instead of shrinking from those anxieties, Kaufman's film confronts them, acknowledging the inexplicability of the project of life (and death) while forcing its audience to do the same. Answers, cohesion, and a lack of confusion define narrative completeness and the passivity of traditional narrative realism. But even as culturally coded notions of what signals the portrayal of reality in fiction are questioned, an emotional resonance remains.

As in Kaufman's film, emotion and imagination offer keys to portrayals of intersubjectivity and sublimity in Sofia Coppola's *The Virgin Suicides*. In the next chapter, I will explore sublimity directly in relation to this, through a discussion and dissection of the 'feminine' and 'egotistical' sublimes.

PART II

EMOTION, IMAGINATION AND THE FEMININE SUBLIME

3. OH! YOU PRETTY THINGS: THE EGOTISTICAL AND FEMININE SUBLIMES IN SOFIA COPPOLA'S *THE VIRGIN SUICIDES*

> *The stars awaken a certain reverence,*
> *Because though always present, they are inaccessible*
> Ralph Waldo Emerson, *Nature* (1836)

Based on the 1993 novel by Jeffrey Eugenides, Sofia Coppola's 1999 film *The Virgin Suicides* offers a provocative examination of sublimity, specifically in its relation to gendered notions of performativity and emotion. It does so, firstly, via its presentation of constructions of femininity, which become sublime through the vivid, fantastical imaginings of a group of teenage boys. These boys feel deeply for five doomed teenage sisters they barely know. But they also suffer from a profound inability to express or even understand their feelings, as does the rest of their suburban community.

The film's highly aestheticised portrayal of emotion leads to the spectator's confused engagement with its affective content, which creates an emotional distance that mirrors the frustrated emotional engagement depicted onscreen. The mood created by the film is one of emotional ambivalence, with its ultimate 'emotional core' expressed as the sense of communal trauma. Its hollowed-out characters become emblematic of the malaise and gradual decline of post-war American society.

Alternatively, the film's portrayal of a so-called 'feminine' or 'everyday' sublime lies in its expression of the girls' quotidian realities and an emphasis on highly feminised surface decoration. Its veneration of the aesthetic concept of the 'pretty', as defined by Rosalind Galt, acts as a subversive formal counterpoint to traditional masculine modes of filmic realism. This presentation is ambivalent, however; it speaks not only to a celebration of femininity but also to its commodification.

Ultimately, the film's girls assert their own subjectivity by performatively committing mass suicide as a way of passing judgement on a society that values social conformism over human feeling. That sense of conformism is suffocating and nearly all-encompassing: Coppola's film is emotionally contained in a way that belies its subject matter. But it is the film's relation to historical notions of the sublime – particularly the Romantic, 'egotistical' sublime – and the struggle to wrest sublimity from the sole province of the masculine or question its narcissistic conceits entirely, that connects it to a tradition of alternative artistic responses to such a marginalisation-cum-obliteration of the female in sublime discourse.

Gendered Expressions of Sublimity: The Egotistical and Feminine Sublimes

In *Observations on the Feeling of the Beautiful and Sublime*, Immanuel Kant pointedly diminishes female subjectivity – and the concept of beauty, which he correlates with it – in favour of masculine power. 'The fair sex has just as much understanding as the male', he writes, 'but it is a *beautiful understanding*, whereas ours should be a *deep understanding*, an expression that signifies identity with the sublime' (Kant 1764: 36; original emphasis). Such a 'beautiful understanding' is a virtue of the social and the sensible but fails to reach the profound transcendence of sublimity.

Viewing sublimity as more than the Burkean concept of terrified delight experienced at a safe remove (Burke [1757] 1792: 62), the Romantics, building on Kant's ideas, stressed the primacy of the mind in the creation of the sublime and emphasised the role of imagination. This idea of sublimity, which Keats derisively coined the 'egotistical sublime' (1970: 157), became strongly solitary, subjective, internal and even anti-social (Shaw 2005: 106), a canonical view of the sublime that endures to the present. Samuel Taylor Coleridge encapsulates such a view:

> I meet, I find the Beautiful – but I give, contribute, or rather attribute the Sublime. No object of Sense is sublime in itself: but only so far as I make it a symbol of some Idea. The circle is a beautiful figure in itself; it becomes sublime, when I contemplate eternity under that figure. (Raysor and Coleridge 1925: 532–3)

In his *Biographia Literaria*, Coleridge contends that the poet's imagination is responsible for this 'eternal act of creation in the infinite I AM' ([1817] 1980: 167). The affirmation of a godlike subjectivity in this quotation attests not only to the egotism of the Romantic sublime, but also to what Wordsworth refers to as the 'awful power' of individual imagination (1979: 217). Wordsworth's sublime seeks to flirt with a sense of self-destruction by engaging the imagination and then containing it. Imagination, to Wordsworth, represented 'reason in her most exalted mood' (1979: 468). Conversely, the feminine lies in Kant's idea of 'sensible intuition', phenomenal perception unmediated by intellect that is natural, sensual and corporal (Shaw 2005: 74). The feminine is relegated to another domain entirely, that of the beautiful – of sensibility (emotion) over sense (reason).

It becomes clear from elucidating the Romantic sublime that its relation to the feminine is more than a little problematic. According to Anne Mellor, the triumph of the 'masculine' imagination over 'feminine Nature' in the Romantic sublime 'usurped Nature's power, leaving her silenced, even absent' and 'erase[d] the female from discourse' (1993: 11). Various female authors of the age confronted the sense of impending obliteration found within the Romantic sublime, both directly and indirectly, through an invocation of 'feminine' forms of sublimity and a rebuke of egotism. Mary Shelley parodied its narcissism through Victor Frankenstein's perverse attempts to 'appropriate the feminine' (1993: 22) through a desire to create life outside the womb, while the gothicism of the Brontë sisters and the wildly successful Ann Radcliffe articulated how such a 'patriarchal' sublime leads to an obliteration of the female psyche (Shaw 2005: 108). Radcliffe's gothic imaginings 'implicitly rejected the egotistical sublime' (Mellor 1993: 11), and the 'everyday' sublime embraced by popular authors such as Felicia Hemans was a decidedly less solitary, violent and egotistical one. Radcliffe's concept of sublimity 'turns on pacific detachment, an awakening to virtue and the ethics of integrity' (Shaw 2005: 109). 'Virtue' and 'the ethics of integrity' clearly invoke the social realm, one that the egotistical sublime refuses to engage. But there is also a troubling passivity to such a conception of femininity.

In contrast, poet and novelist Charlotte Smith appropriates the tropes of the masculine Romantic sublime in service of her own feminine subjectivity. In perhaps her most famous poem, the posthumously published 'Beachy Head' (1807), Smith self-identifies with the sublime and 'the overcoming of restrictions, even to the point of death' as 'a means of converting unlettered weakness into a token of visionary power' (Shaw 2005: 113, 114). But the poem also undercuts this vision in its final stanzas by descending from the heights of the titular Beachy Head to focus on a hermit in the cave below, thus evading any final 'transcendent elevation' of sublimity (Lokke 2008: 39). Smith's poem ultimately offers an ironic rebuke of the Romantic sublime with its 're-inscription of the human into the natural' (2008: 39).

The eradication of the female from sublime discourse was not so much an erasure of feminine traits as it was an absorption of such attributes into the poet's masculine self. According to Alan Richardson, male Romantic writers 'drew on memories and fantasies of identification with the mother in order to colonize the conventionally feminine domain of sensibility' (1988: 13). The male poet became a 'mother' and the work of art a 'child in the mother's womb' (Mellor 1993: 24). Emotion became a tactical tool in the male poet's arsenal of expression to the exclusion of the female, and expressions of emotion became part of the male poet's multivalent personality. Women in this construct still feel, of course, just not quite so deeply – the transcendence of the sublime remains out of their grasp. Worse still, Romantic love generally culminated with the 'assimilation of the female into the male' in that 'the woman must finally be enslaved or destroyed, must disappear or die' (1993: 26) to avoid becoming a threat to the masculine ego.

The Virgin Suicides engages with Hemens's version of the everyday sublime in its expressions of near-ecstatic communal femininity, while its gothic allusions and female appropriation of masculine sublime tropes ultimately offer an ironic rejoinder to egotistical sublimity. Most keenly, though, it captures the solitude of sublime feeling without its sense of elevation and exaltation, instead infusing it with a palpable melancholy in the vein of Charlotte Smith.

Staging Sublimity in 1970s Suburbia

Throughout the film the Lisbon sisters are viewed from a distance as sublime objects: unfathomable, unknowable, designed to imbue the Romantic male psyche with the knowledge of its power of imagination and reason. Seen from the outside despite their eventual literal imprisonment in the family home and viewed almost solely from the perspective of the towns' boys, the girls are also presented as a mysterious object of study for the spectator. A narrator, one of the boys now grown, recalls the events that take place over the course of a fateful year from the perspective of the present day. Even before those tragic events unfurl, the girls, he explains, had been a subject of great fascination for the community's young males, although the reason is never fully expressed. The boys seem to respond to the alien, distant and cloistered quality of the girls, which supplies a tabula rasa they can project their frustrated feelings on, captivating their imaginations. Trapped in their constricting suburban enclave of privilege, they long for an emotional, Romantic fixation.

The boys obsess over the girls, studying them like objects of scientific enquiry. (The source novel goes so far as to list their purloined artefacts by exhibit numbers and characterises their organs, upon autopsy, as 'like something behind glass [. . .] like an exhibit' (Eugenides [1993] 2002: 221).) But despite their attempts, the boys never gain real knowledge as to the inner life of the girls.

Moreover, the film clearly conveys the sense that the boys do not really have an interest in truly coming to see the girls as real people, for that would ruin their sublime effect. 'They understood love, and even death [. . .] we couldn't fathom them at all', the narrator recounts. This inscrutability accounts for their enduring sublime fascination, twenty-five years after their deaths.

The girls seem to communicate to outsiders, and themselves, solely by sensual, intuitive means, the province of the feminine and of the natural. The boys internalise these intuitions into 'reasonable' knowledge through their imaginative capacities: one smells a lipstick tube on the sly and receives a vision of the fourteen-year-old, Lolita-esque Lux[1] (Kirsten Dunst), as if deeply inhaling her very essence through her cosmetics, totemic objects that in reality speak to nothing but her surface beauty. The boys insist they want to learn the girls' very nature, but the idea of their menstruation (conjured by a bathroom cupboard well stocked with tampons) is enough to make the same boy flee the Lisbon house in terror. This is a potent example of the sublime, which 'alternates between attraction and repulsion' unlike the straightforward appeal of beauty (Shaw 2005: 79). The boys idealise the girls' beauty but fear their alien quality; it remains sublimely terrifying even as they seek the revelation of its secrets.

When the boys engage their imaginations while fantasising about the girls, they envision the ridiculous kitsch of 1970s soft-rock album covers: the girls frolic in grassy fields with unicorns, their prairie sundresses backlit by rich sunlight as they chew on blades of grass, laugh or stare wistfully. The film dissolves one hazy image into another in a dreamlike palimpsest, evoking a 'negative' or 'domesticated' sublime that features an 'ecstatic experience of co-participation in a nature [. . .] explicitly gender[ed] as female' (Mellor 1993: 97). But these images are double-edged. According to Anna Backman Rogers, they 'call attention to the "thinness" of their own construction so that the viewer's attention is continually directed towards what is *not seen* and *what is not heard*' (2015: 16; original emphasis). The 'hollow nature' of such images is indicative of a crisis of subjectivity that the film's young female characters suffer (2015: 16). In their invocation of the soft-focus clichés of their era, from shampoo commercials to soft-core pornography, they also create a powerful sense of the commodification of femininity, particularly adolescent female sexuality (2015: 33).

Coppola refers to the girls' harnessing of that sexuality, or 'power and mystique', over the boys: 'I think when you're that age you're kind of playing with that power and trying to understand it' (Gevinson 2013). But that power operates under an ironic illusion. The diary entries of Cecilia (Hanna Hall), the youngest Lisbon sister, glimpse a different reality: 'Monday, February 13th: Today we had frozen pizza.' Her diary, which speaks to impending environmental devastation and the quotidian realities of the life of a suburban teenage girl, is the closest the boys have to the 'truth'. But, as

Backman Rogers writes, the 'oneiric, false and misremembered images' the film creates, which are purely imaginative and impossible projections, 'evade understanding' and all sense of truth (2015: 33). The boys are not really interested in truth anyway; they would much rather engage in the fantastic speculation of their own imaginations, in a kind of emotional code that expresses their deep longing for meaning while simultaneously keeping the mystery, the girls' sublimity, alive.

While we have obvious insights into the boys' imaginative scenarios, the girls' inner emotional lives are much more of a mystery. They keep together in an almost feral pack and are routinely framed as a cohesive unit, talking in whispers, exchanging veiled, knowing looks or gazing toward the camera as if to taunt the viewer into questioning their indivisibility. They seem to communicate merely by a shared psychic knowledge in relation to their status as objects of fevered imaginative scrutiny. Their mysterious presence adds to the sense of emotional distance Coppola creates within the film, one that engenders a mood of disaffection and what Jeffrey Sconce generally refers to as aesthetic 'blankness' (2002: 34). The emotional moods created by the film, in turn, imbue the girls with both sublime obscurity and a sense of the quotidian domestic. They also work to undercut the exaltation found within the Romantic sublime; expressions of transcendence are countered with presentations of frustrated emotion.

Mood Creation and the Emotional Core of the Film

Despite the boys' deep feelings for the girls, the film's emotional aesthetic is one of restraint, of the frustration tied to the inability to properly express emotion. From the first shot, a close-up of Lux, her blonde hair backlit by strong sunlight as she sucks on a red ice pop while not quite meeting the camera's gaze, Coppola establishes a dreamlike mood. A few minutes of screen time later, before the title credits appear in their girlish script ('bubble' letters, 'I's dotted with hearts) against a blue sky featuring fluffy white clouds that hint at foreboding darkness, her face appears suspended in mid-air as she winks at the camera and smiles coquettishly. It is as if she is acknowledging the game that is being played with her image and offering an invitation to the spectator to participate, to enter into a pact.

This is contrasted with the film's next prominent image, Cecilia lying Ophelia-like[2] in a bathtub as her slashed wrists bleed into the water, the screen colour-timed to a cold, unforgiving blue (Figure 3.1). Soon after, Cecilia lies in bed while being counselled by a doctor, whose face we cannot see, after this initial suicide attempt. When told she has experienced nothing in her life to warrant ending it, she deadpans, 'Obviously, doctor, you've never been a 13-year-old girl.' Her tone, delivered with a mix of mockery and sincerity, establishes the

THE EGOTISTICAL AND FEMININE SUBLIMES

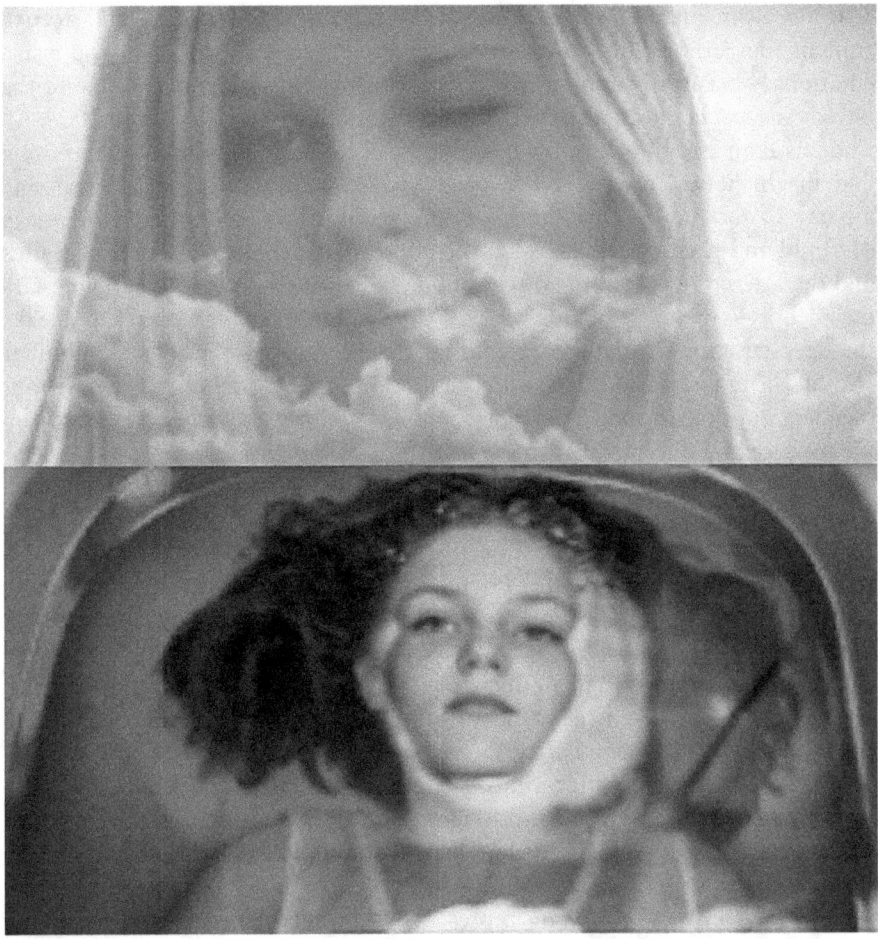

Figure 3.1 Early images of Lux and Cecilia create a sense of conflicting emotional presentation.

theme of emotional disaffection by aesthetic means, and mixes with the warm, nostalgic tones of the first images to create an ambiguous mood.

Thus, the film's distinctive mood, dreamy yet disaffected, is established. According to Robert Sinnerbrink, 'moods always reveal or express a cinematic world, and [. . .] distinctive cinematic worlds have their own specific kinds of mood' (2012: 149). Mood creation is key to the overall world creation of *The Virgin Suicides*; such a lurid, almost grotesque subject matter would elicit a much darker scene-setting in a conventional melodrama. But Coppola is intent on keeping her film squarely in the realm of an adolescent fever dream.

In the Romantic era, mood – essentially the aesthetic portrayal of affective content that primes the viewer or reader to experience their own responsive emotions – began to supplant the concept of emotion as 'passion' due to the latter's suspect connection to performativity and inauthenticity (Pfau 2005: 6). Thomas Pfau sees three exemplary 'moods' in Romanticism: paranoia, trauma and melancholy. Paranoia points to early Romanticism's 'all-encompassing anxiety of the modern'; trauma is found within the revolutionary aftermath of 'rapid and pervasive changes' in the political, economic and cultural realms and the attempt to grasp them without a proper means of understanding; and melancholy – the most obvious pervasive mood in Coppola's film – 'bespeaks the deep-structural fatigue of a culture that has grown oppressively familiar with itself' in late-period Romanticism (2005: 20, 23). Sublimity offers a transcendent antidote to such a pervasive mood, a solitary and exalted escape from the malaise and uncertainty of modernity.

German Romantic writer and philosopher Novalis referred to *Stimmung* (literally 'mood') as the 'musical conditions of the soul' (Eisner 1977: 203). Exemplified in the cinema most keenly by the silent-era German expressionist films of F. W. Murnau and Fritz Lang, it is found and felt not through narrative content, but through an emotional, affect-driven engagement with onscreen aesthetics (1977: 200). Whereas German expressionism's *Stimmung* is rooted in the chiaroscuro effects of light and shadow and a gloomy and often contorted mise-en-scène meant to make physical the inner turmoil and confusion of its characters, *The Virgin Suicides*' mise-en-scène, cinematography and performances offer a more impressionistic sense of *Stimmung*. The feeling of mystery and mournful longing that Coppola's film creates is found within what *is not* expressed, but instead bubbles beneath its shimmering surfaces.

For Lotte Eisner, *Stimmung* represents 'a mystical and singular harmony amid the chaos of things, a kind of sorrowful nostalgia, which [. . .] is mixed with well-being, an imprecise nuance of nostalgia, languor coloured with desire, lust of body and soul' (1977: 199). Eisner's characterisation of *Stimmung* reflects the general mood of Coppola's film, a hazy, drowsy, nostalgic longing and a sense of palpable frustrated desire mixed with the excitement and confusion that comes from traversing the 'liminal' territory and personae of adolescence (Backman Rogers 2015: 6).

Its potent blend of *Stimmung* and deadpan detachment form the film's 'emotional core', defined as the 'affective glue' delivered by aesthetic means (Laine 2013: 6). In an idea reminiscent of Kant's sensible intuition, this emotional core is rendered through 'affective appraisals' on the body of the spectator. According to Tarja Laine, 'Affective appraisal [. . .] strikes the body, immediately in and through the flesh. [. . .] Emotional evaluation collects and gives significance to the 'surplus' of affective appraisal by transforming it into memory' (2013: 2). The film's voice-over, told from the perspective of the present, lends the narrative proceedings a stark inevitably (as does the film's very title; we know the girls are fated to die), and its flat, emotionally vacant execution is crucial to the overall effect. The film offers a distinct split between the affective appraisal – the 'withness' of the moment that the boys and spectator experience – and its emotional evaluation, the awareness of the affective appraisal, which is expressed through the after-the-fact voice-over.

For the spectator, this creates a psychological distance from its affective emotional content and lends the film a disaffected sheen. Distance thwarts its emotional 'agency', and we are left 'outside' its emotional core (2013: 3). If films, as Laine suggests, 'embody' emotions and possess an 'emotional attitude' toward the spectator (2013: 3), *The Virgin Suicides*' attitude is one of emotional division, a schism between affect and feeling versus action and expression. Its characters, along with the spectator, struggle to turn affective appraisals into emotional evaluations that make sense, because evaluations do not correspond to appraisals in any 'correct' way. Feeling is partially emptied out, creating an experience for the spectator similar to the emotionally withdrawn states of characters in the film. But it also elicits a sensation of longing, one for the very thing that the film refuses to convey: the ability to experience and express intimate emotional connections.

This is most keenly evident in a scene where the boys communicate with the girls, now trapped inside the Lisbon home, over the telephone by playing records. The girls respond in kind, and soon it feels as though the two groups of dispossessed teens are truly connecting. The soundtrack consists solely of mournful pop from the era, expressing in music and lyric what both the girls (who play songs such as 'Alone Again, Naturally' and 'So Far Away') and the boys (who play 'Run to Me') feel, without the need to outwardly express those emotions through their own voices or bodies. Coppola adds a horizontal split screen halfway through the scene, Lux seeming to lie atop the boys forlornly as they emotionally implode, to emphasise the effect (Figure 3.2). As Laine notes in her analysis of the film *Requiem for a Dream*, the split screen 'becomes a form of touch, in which separation enables an opening up to the touch of the other, which is also felt as such by the spectator' (2015: 56). Conversely, it communicates the existential, and in this case also physical, distance between subjects.

This scene embodies Laine's idea of the lack of clear onscreen emotional presentation, wherein a film 'directs our attention toward what cannot be seen, that which can only be detected by means of intersubjective sharing of experience' (2013: 4). The boys share an intersubjective experience with the girls, but

THE STILLNESS OF SOLITUDE

Figure 3.2 The use of split screen emphasises both physical distance and intersubjective connection through 'touch'.

that experience is obfuscated not only by physical distance but also by technological mediation (the phone, the stereo) and a lack of direct communication. All the emotion comes from canned recordings, representations of emotions expressed by musicians and recorded in the past, and so effectively highlights through the lack of direct affect the inability to properly express emotion and the desire to overcome that inability. This inability to effectively communicate is apparent many times in the film, such as in the girls' confusing notes left for the boys to find, and in their nonsensical Morse code messages. 'Help. Send Bobo', one translated message comically reads, despite the fact that 'Bobo' is never mentioned before or after in the narrative.

Mood, throughout *The Virgin Suicides,* establishes itself almost as a character in its own right. As in Sinnerbrink's appraisal of *Blue Velvet* (David Lynch, De Laurentiis Entertainment Group, 1986), 'Mood becomes autonomous, taking on a primary rather than a supporting role in the composition of the fictional world' (2012: 161). In Laine's view, films both express and *embody* emotions, and all films contain an emotional core analogous to human emotional states (Laine 2013: 3). The emotional core of *The Virgin Suicides,* however, at times feels slippery and opaque. There is a confused sense of conflicting emotional presentations. The film's 'disclosive mood', which establishes an emotional 'scene-setting' (Sinnerbrink 2012: 156) is, again, one of longing tempered with deadpan irony. This mood is called back to episodically throughout the film, specifically in various ornate dream sequences expressing the boys' highly Romantic yet parodic inner fantasies about the girls. Scenes of mood transition, such as Cecilia's successful suicide attempt (one of the few scenes that embodies any sort of strong physical emotional response, via Mrs Lisbon's low, guttural howls) and the sequence at the Homecoming dance manoeuvre the viewer through various emotional states.

With its twinkling décor, slow-motion effects and soft-focus glow, the Homecoming scene strongly evokes the prom scene in Brian De Palma's *Carrie* (Red Bank Films, 1976) and its portrayal of horror found in difference combined with a dreamy sense of kitsch. Coppola's overall aesthetic, and this scene in particular, was inspired by American photographer Bill Owens's 1973 book *Suburbia* (Gevinson 2013), which, according to the film's production notes, 'revealed the American suburb as a symbolically potent landscape filled with neat green lawns, turquoise skies and expressions of weary human dissatisfaction'. Backman Rogers suggests, however, that Owens's photographs are actually 'positive representations of suburban communities' and that, by alluding to *Carrie*, Coppola 'imbues her images with a disturbing undercurrent' that Owens's work lacks. She considers this scene one of 'ritualized ceremony [. . .] marked out as the site of disaster' in its foreshadowing of Lux losing her virginity to her crush, Trip Fontaine (Josh Hartnett), being subsequently abandoned by him and eventually imprisoned along with her sisters (2015: 29). The turning point marked by this scene is highlighted by the slippery quality of its tone, a foreboding fantasy that conjures the sense of 'too good to be true'.

The moods that individual scenes like the Homecoming dance create always feel tenuous at best. The film establishes a true emotional core in an underlying way. That core mood is trauma itself. According to Pfau, trauma is characterised by 'a nearly complete lack of affect [. . .] whatever emotional charge may be seething beneath the faltering, quasi-catatonic locutions of its subject puzzles the reader-observer with its seeming lack of intensity and content' (2005: 17). The mood itself rests in its lack of expression. Ultimately, the film's engagement with imaginative longing and even satire and dark humour is undercut by a mournful resignation to this loss of affect. Thus, the film's world creation, through mood, suggests emotion through its very lack of emotional characterisation: the repression of emotion, coupled with the simultaneous foregrounding of the frustrated need to express it, and the ultimate resignation that it will never be properly expressed.

This does not just affect the emotional response of the onscreen characters. Spectators are generally not invited to empathise with the Lisbon girls. Nor are we able to be truly emotionally connected with the boys, although they are the closest audience surrogates the film establishes. The boys are barely realised characters themselves, instead serving as archetypes of wayward, frustrated teens trapped in suburban mundanity. The film reduces its characters to a selection of tics, such as the befuddled, emasculated Mr Lisbon's childish affection for World War II model airplanes,³ Mrs Lisbon's overzealous religious propriety, or Lux's wanton toying with the affections of men.

Instead, a lack of character expresses the ennui that defines a civilisation in impending decline, or the emotional paucity that attends privilege. In the context of what Fredric Jameson identifies as American post-war cultural malaise, *The Virgin Suicides* can be described, using his terminology, as a 'postnostalgia' film (Jameson 1992: 287). It is obsessed with nostalgic recreation, yet finds within that recreation a hollow, indescribable centre. Such nostalgia is embodied by the film's aesthetic, which relies principally on depictions of beauty, specifically 'clichéd images' of superficial prettiness (Backman Rogers 2015: 28). Such an aesthetic is not only used as an ironic counterpoint to masculine sublimity, however; it also affirms the power of the feminine, creating something akin to a feminine sublime.

The Aesthetics and Politics of 'Pretty'

If the girls are sublime, they are also objects of the Burkean beautiful: domestic, soft, languorous and luxurious. Unlike its source novel, which emphasises physical and environmental decay to underscore a loss of affect, the film foregrounds, even vaunts, aesthetic notions of the beautiful. The sense of impending environmental doom is still present, found mostly in the denouement after the girls' demise and in its most potent symbol, the dying elm trees. But the novel's omnipresent fish fly corpses are basically absent, and the deterioration of the Lisbon house is less severe and documented. While Romantic notions of sublimity are mocked (such as the lovelorn Italian boy's comical suicide attempt early in the film), ideas of beauty are held virtually sacrosanct.

Rosalind Galt outlines how representations of the 'pretty', particularly regarding the decorative and the 'aesthetic danger of women', have been derided throughout the history of film criticism via proponents of realism like André Bazin and Siegfried Kracauer to Marxist critics such as Comolli and Narboni to the 'iconophobia' of feminist film theorists such as Laura Mulvey and Linda Williams, who all participate, in various schematics and due to various motivations, in 'the tearing down of images' (2009: 4–18). This disdain for the pretty image seems to be located within a fear of the very apparatus of film itself: 'The rhetoric of film theory has insistently denigrated surface decoration, finding the attractive skin of the screen to be false, shallow, feminine, or apolitical' (2009: 2).

A crucial element in the codification of the pretty, just as in the Burkean sense of the beautiful, is the primacy of colour, which, as Galt notes, has been 'relegated to the lesser realm of emotion' and 'conceals [line's] truths' (2009: 7). These ideas are couched in terms of feminine seduction through 'primitivism' and 'deception' (2009: 3). If beauty is a Kantian good, 'pretty' is a siren song that leads hapless cinematic explorers down the path of aesthetic decadence and moral decay:

> [T]he word 'luscious' hints at a feminizing rhetoric of seduction that has been at play in Kracauer ever since he evoked the wonderfully fetishistic 'girl clusters' to exemplify the ideological work of the mass ornament. For Kracauer, cinema's potential for truth is always obscured by ornament. (Galt 2009: 11)

In *The Virgin Suicides*, Coppola defends against Kracauer's derided, mass ornamental 'girl clusters' with her depictions of what I call girl tableaux, exhibiting a sustained reverence for the 'pretty' in highly ornamental and composed imagery that uses colour and light strategically. Pale pink and yellow, traditionally feminine colours, appear throughout the film as an aesthetic motif, such as the pink and yellow balloons at the first ill-fated party, the girls' own frequently accentuated blonde hair, the buttery tones of the light from the late-day sun or Lux's Homecoming dance ensemble of white dress with pink floral pattern obscuring her pink underwear, which, through a playful special effect, Coppola's camera 'sees' when the dress becomes momentarily transparent. (See Chapter 1 for Burke's notions of the link between colour and feminine beauty.)

Colour is even mentioned as the mysterious domain of the inner workings of the feminine mind in the voice-over, of the way 'the imprisonment of being a girl [. . .] made your mind active and dreamy and how you ended up knowing what colours went together'. The girls are routinely bathed in diffuse, warm sunlit tones, especially in fantasy sequences. Lux, the Lisbon girl who is the object of the most obvious scrutiny, even has a name that invokes both luxury and light itself. But it also recalls the ubiquity of everyday household soap. If Lux as object represents the sublime unknowable, her reality as subject is that of everyday, humdrum domesticity.

The girls routinely surround themselves with pretty objects which serve no practical purpose – trinkets, jewellery, decorations, cosmetics, plush toys, fabrics. Such ephemera are imbued with deep meaning by the secretive mystery of adolescence. In several scenes Coppola arranges the girls in tableaux vivants as they luxuriate in their bedroom prison site, rifling through travel magazines and staring plaintively out the windows. There is a distinct sense of purposeful disarray in these scenes, which convey the feeling of cloistered conspiracy in their mise-en-scène. Blankets and pillows are strewn haphazardly; pastel knick-knacks litter the armoires. The construction within the frame radiates a powerful sense of *Stimmung*, which 'hovers around objects as well as people' (Eisner 1977: 199).

In what is arguably the key image of the film, the girls are framed in a highly composed, Pre-Raphaelite fashion, limbs entwined as they lounge on the floor

THE STILLNESS OF SOLITUDE

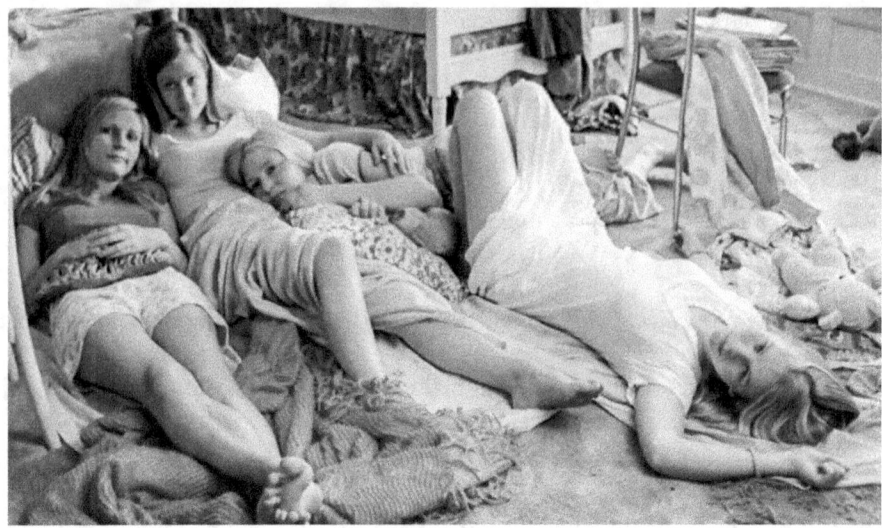

Figure 3.3 Coppola creates a confrontational image of femininity with excessively ornamental mise-en-scène.

(Figure 3.3). After the previous scene between Father Moody (Scott Glenn), the local priest, and Mr Lisbon (James Woods) set in the bland and colourless Lisbon living room, the presentation of the prettified excess in this scene provides an emotional jolt for the spectator. The girls are surrounded by a disarray of fabric and objects that exit the limits of the frame, points of vivid colour drawing the eye around the frame in a circular motion with no fixed resting place, eliciting pleasurable responses from their kaleidoscopic yet highly constructed surfaces.

They stare at the visiting priest, who comes to their bedroom doorway, with barely contained disdain and boredom, and we experience their provocative looks from his point of view. This striking image is followed immediately by a shot of Mrs Lisbon (Kathleen Turner) sitting alone in her dreary bedroom, sapped of the playful colour of the girls' room like the rest of the house. In contrast to the Lisbon girls' mocking stares and fidgets, she sits impeccably straight on the bed with her back to the camera in medium-long shot, isolated in her grief amidst order and regimentation.

As in this sequence, playful, feminine colour and baroque ornamentation are continually contrasted with regimented order and institutional browns, blacks and greys, such as those in the girls' school uniforms, hospital rooms and doctors' offices, and the adult-centred rooms of the Lisbon home. Line and geometric form are almost exclusively the province of the masculine and patriarchal order, such as the strong shapes laid out in the school's wall grids and the omnipresent checks and plaids of the male characters' clothing. Pointedly, Mrs Lisbon is the only woman in the film to wear this masculine plaid, since she is not only linked to patriarchal, institutional control, she is in fact the primary purveyor of it.[4]

The film's prettiness is seductive, which conforms to the theme that the girls have somehow ruined the boys with their image, continuing to haunt them in their disaffected adult lives. But it also serves as a kind of aesthetic manifesto. Galt asserts that the pretty is 'nothing if not a feminist account of the cinematic image' and runs counter to the 'antipretty discourse found in modernity' (2009: 17, 25). In fact, this 'phobia of the feminine' is a result of modernism itself, indebted to the Kantian sublime, which has 'dominated modernism to the detriment of the homely pleasures of the beautiful woman' (2009: 17). These 'homely pleasures' are at once embraced and parodied by Coppola's film.

The tension between surface beauty, or prettiness, and the mundane or even gaudy image is found throughout the film. The attention to proper aesthetic decorum is announced almost immediately with a neighbour's remark that Cecilia attempted suicide because she wanted 'out of' the Lisbon house 'decorating scheme'. A school administrator defends her choice of green for the 'Day of Grief' pamphlets because the colour is 'cheerful, but not too cheerful [. . .] certainly better than red'. This aesthetic judgement and obsession with the appearance of propriety over genuine feeling includes all manner of social discourse and is sometimes almost literally suffocating, as when Lux is forced to burn her rock records, leading to plumes of toxic smoke filling the Lisbon home.

Moreover, surely a narrative that makes the home a prison of the 'beautiful woman' is not one filled solely with 'homely pleasures'. The film can be read as a kind of Sirkean melodrama of subversion, but one with the drama, colour and ideology mostly drained of their intensity. Coppola, unlike her characters and even Sirk, is not trapped in the 'American bourgeois prison' of dominant discourse and Hollywood studio control (Galt 2009: 14). While her aesthetic commitment to ornamentation and the pretty offers a rebuke of cinematic modernity, she also exhibits a 'masculine' and 'rational' distance (2009: 18), training a dissecting eye on her characters nearly as clinical as that of the ineffectual psychotherapist (Danny DeVito) who administers Cecilia's Rorschach test.

When discussing her framing choices, Coppola notes, 'A lot of the shots were from across the street [from the boys' perspective] to create a sense of distance. [. . .] The distance also imitates memory, too, in that it's not completely accurate or precise' (Tobias 2000). The distance she creates is in deference to a programme of mood creation comprising nostalgia and imaginative desire. It is certainly not polemical – especially as it commits itself to the pretty in the decidedly non-radical terms of 'traditional, white, hetero femininity'

(Galt 2009: 28). Rather, it describes a world of surface propriety where the very idea of polemics is distasteful. Throughout her oeuvre Coppola has shown little interest in being overtly political, instead focusing on the intricacies of intersubjective experience and the aesthetic rendering of such.

Michele Aaron argues that Coppola 'exploits, critiques, and resolutely embellishes' predominant visual representations of femininity 'because her national, racial, and class privilege afford her potential distance (actual, critical, or aesthetic) from the sisters' suffocation' (2014: 91). However, it is clear from interviews that Coppola relishes the opportunity to explore femininity in a judgement-free zone and can both sympathise and empathise with the multiple perspectives of different characters. 'I think just having been a girl [. . .] I've always felt connected to the kind of feminine side', she says (Tobias 2000). Coppola also expresses empathy for the boys and their 'collective watching and thinking' (Tobias 2000). Essentially, she evinces a personal connection to the Lisbon sisters' status as both subjects and objects, which bears little relation to the director's economic or other privileges.

She has also consistently been preoccupied with the dangers of bringing the domestic into the public sphere, with the transgression leading at turns to female annihilation, in *The Virgin Suicides* and *Marie Antoinette* (Columbia Pictures, 2006), and incarceration, in *The Bling Ring* (American Zoetrope, 2013). *Lost in Translation* (Focus Features, 2003) offers an uncharacteristically optimistic portrayal of female transgression via its *flâneuse* protagonist, and *The Beguiled* (American Zoetrope, 2017), although criticised for its avoidance of racial issues (Aftab 2017), is a scathing indictment of male entitlement and transgression of the feminine domain. Despite its reliance on mood, *The Virgin Suicides* does offer incisive critiques of gender politics and privilege, particularly in its engagement with the tropes of gothic literature.

'Preparing to give assault': Creating the 'Pseudo-political' Gothic

The Virgin Suicides' narrative of confinement aligns very clearly with the gothic novels of such eighteenth- and nineteenth-century writers as Charlotte and Emily Brontë and Charlotte Perkins Gilman and their depictions of patriarchal oppression that often include literal imprisonment (Mellor 1993: 94). This oppression produces an anger that 'if repressed or turned back against the woman – could also produce female masochism, depression, and madness' (Mellor 1988: 4). Jameson characterises the gothic as:

> a class fantasy (or nightmare) in which the dialectic of privilege and shelter is exercised: your privileges seal you off from other people, but by the same token they constitute a protective wall through which you

cannot see, and behind which therefore all kinds of envious forces may be imagined in the process of assembling, plotting, preparing to give assault. (Jameson 1992: 289)

This isolation and 'domestic idleness', in Jameson's view, is not inherently political, but can constitute 'a coming to self-consciousness of the disadvantages of privilege' (1992: 289). It can also 'be reorganized around young men' and be seen as a substitute for American society, which 'lives out the anxieties of its economic privileges' (1992: 289).

In its portrayal of the sheltered exceptionalism of an affluent yet declining Michigan suburb, and the way anxieties of economic privilege diminish all its citizens (the boys, the parents, but particularly the Lisbon girls), *The Virgin Suicides* can be characterised as what Jameson calls a 'pseudo-political version of the gothic' (1992: 289). The theme of the double-edged quality of privilege and shelter serves in large part as an excuse to imbue the film's mise-en-scène with specific emotional moods, including the uncanny feeling found in the sense of 'unease' in what should be an environment of comfort and safety.

A sense of the uncanny is an important component in the creation of the 'pseudo-political' gothic. Anthony Vidler views the uncanny as 'the quintessential bourgeois kind of fear, one carefully bounded by the limits of real material security' (1992: 4). While this is often a symptom of urban estrangement, in this film it finds its way to the decidedly more homogeneous confines of suburban spaces. Coppola imbues the Lisbon home with an element of the fantasy space, particularly for the boys, as it is the site of their primary workings of imagination about the girls. But the house itself, a very ordinary two-storey, middle-class family dwelling, becomes the site of unspeakable familial crimes and eventually crumbles into disrepair, in a sort of suburban gothic take on Poe's House of Usher.

If the uncanny 'form[s] the starting point for [an] examination of anxiety, the very "image of lack"' (1992: 9), then the Lisbon girls, tied inexorably to the home, are the real source of the house's uncanny sense. Taken less as individuals than as a mysterious general presence, the girls essentially haunt the Lisbon home while they are still technically alive, as Cecilia, the most troubled Lisbon girl, literally haunts it after her death. Her various visual links to the occult (mostly glimpsed in objects in her bedroom) hark back to the gothic fascination with supernatural forces. A recurring symbol of the girls' otherness, religious icons such as Cecilia's Virgin Mary laminated cards (one is present in the opening scene of her unsuccessful suicide attempt) evoke the 'cult of Mary' within Catholicism and its potential links to pagan nature worship.[5] All of Lux's sexual encounters take place outdoors, emphasising her attachment to the natural world. In addition to haunting the sleeping and waking dreams of both the boys and Mr Lisbon, Cecilia lies, dead but alive, draped across her favourite dying elm tree. This visual metaphor links her not just to the natural, but also to the supersensible. According to Bree Hoskin, the link is highly allegorical: 'The death of both nature and the girls acts as a symbol for the idea that the growth from childhood to maturity involves the destruction of a part of the younger self' (2007: 215).

Cecilia might haunt the men and boys in physical form, but she haunts the memories of her sisters as well. As in Freud's assertion that the uncanny rests in 'the compulsion to repeat' ([1919] 2003: 13), the Lisbon girls compulsively recreate Cecilia's original act of suicide. (Freud also linked such a compulsion to the burden of trauma itself – the original traumatic act becomes impossible to assimilate, and the subject, haunted, replays it continually (Pfau 2005: 193).) In their act, the male narrator proclaims them 'selfish'. They fail to think of the effect on the community, and especially the effect on the boys themselves.

But in their self-obliteration, they perform their final sublime act, one that removes the necessity of performing for the imagination of others. Instead, they assert their own subjectivity, ironically by destroying themselves as a group. If the film is an almost parodic rendering of the Romantic ideal of the absorption of femininity into the masculine sublime ego, their final act serves as both a rejection of this absorption and a re-appropriation of the sublime – sublime objects become sublime subjects. By asserting their agency, they also perform their last act as objects of sublimity: the boys think they are coming to their rescue, but in reality they are being set up to discover the bodies.

Conclusion

In her essay on Edith Wharton's novel *The House of Mirth*, Barbara Freeman asserts that the story's protagonist, Lily Bart, 'suggests another version of sublimity' in her relation to 'risk and speculation' (1995: 41). 'The novel begins', writes Freeman, 'by emphasizing that beauty, be it that of a woman or a work of art, is neither natural nor innate, as Burke would have it, but is rather a commodity that cannot be separated from economic determinations' (1995: 56). 'Brought up to be ornamental', Bart fashions herself as the quintessence of the beautiful in order to become a commodity on the marketplace (a desirable object in the eyes of men) (1995: 57). Eventually she rejects beauty in favour of the sublime by 'affirming' risk (1995: 63), ultimately leading to her own self-annihilation in accidental suicide:

> *Lily's acts of self-extinction become symbolic acts of self-creation.* In *The House of Mirth* loss rather than gain becomes the fertile site from which significance is produced, and in this sense Lily's death is not so much an escape from the marketplace, but a way of passing judgment upon it. (Freeman 1995: 64; my emphasis)

Freeman is referencing Wharton's autobiography, in which the celebrated author writes, 'A frivolous society can acquire dramatic significance only through what its frivolity destroys. Its tragic implication lies in its power of debasing people and ideals' ([1934] 1962: 207). The society found within *The Virgin Suicides*, with its severe aesthetic judgements leading to the degradation of an entire community and its obsession with appearances and propriety over genuine emotion, is nothing if not frivolous. The 'pacific detachment' that codes alternative forms of the feminine sublime eventually turns on itself, becoming so detached from life as to become one with death. Unfortunately for the girls, instead of simply glimpsing self-annihilation in the process of self-realisation, like Wordsworth staring beyond the precipice of imaginative non-reason and emerging triumphant, they must succumb to that annihilation in order to both affirm, and reject, the sublime.

Such a repudiation of Romantic egotistical sublimity does not necessarily have to result in self-negation, however. Along with its questioning of the more traditional egotism of the Romantic sublime, Spike Jonze's film *Her* (2013), discussed in Chapter 4, suggests an alternative form of the sublime that includes mostly positive outcomes for all involved.

4. GIRLFRIEND IN THE MACHINE: INTERSUBJECTIVITY AND THE SUBLIME LIMITS OF REPRESENTATION IN SPIKE JONZE'S *HER*

> *The invisible world, doth greatness make abode,*
> *There harbours; whether we be young or old,*
> *Our destiny, our being's heart and home*
> William Wordsworth, *The Prelude* (1799)

In its portrayal of alienation in the post-industrial age, Spike Jonze's 2013 film *Her* grapples with notions of personhood, intersubjectivity and the role of an active subject working to create both self and world. In *Her*, the sublime is found in what cannot be seen – specifically in the disembodied voice of a computer operating system named 'Samantha', who allows the film's protagonist, Theodore, to regain his personal creative power through imagination in the fashion of the Romantic 'egotistical sublime'.[1] For Romantic-era artists and thinkers, who pushed back against what they viewed as the overly rational and empirical nature of Enlightenment philosophy, such sublimity became an avenue to assert imaginative subjectivity and, conversely, to exhibit a reverence for the mysteries of what lies beyond it.

Theodore is stuck within the confines of his own memory, continually imagining the moments of a happier past while despairing in the present. His relationship with Samantha allows his imagination to become purposeful and authentic again. Samantha, in turn, exemplifies a radical rethinking of the isolating Romantic sublime: the sublimity she experiences is a communal one – a feminine sublime comprised of infinite, heterogeneous selves operating through ecstatic intersubjective connection. *Her* achieves its thematic aims aesthetically through its use of sound, particularly voice, although its mise-en-scène supplements it powerfully by focusing on the human face, which becomes the primary site of vulnerability and sympathetic emotion. Such qualities are traditionally associated with beauty and femininity, the opposite of the sublime. But while the principal face of *Her* is indeed a beautiful one, surprisingly, it is also male.

Robert Alpert sees the film as a critique of 'a culture in which reality is always mediated through imaginary constructions' (2014/15: 2.5). 'The subversiveness of *Her* is that it reenacts the traditional story of the hapless male dreamer even as it exposes the contemporary schizophrenic and suicidal impulse underlying such ungrounded dreaming in the face of technological anxiety', he writes (2014/15: 1.13). Unlike Alpert, I find it hard to make a case for Jonze being either a technophobe or a filmmaker critical of the 'hapless male dreamer', especially since he often posits his work as the realisation of his own dreams, both consciously and unconsciously so.[2]

Throughout his directorial oeuvre – which includes *Being John Malkovich* (Propaganda Films, 1999), *Adaptation* (Propaganda Films, 2002) and *Where the Wild Things Are* (Warner Bros., 2009), as well as many short films, advertisements and music videos – Jonze has maintained a sympathetic attitude to imaginative, disaffected men trapped within a suffocating social milieu, as well as a sustained reverence for the overall creative process. Much of his work examines the interplay between the mediating forces of technology and the ability to express genuine feeling and engage in authentic experiences, but it neither resoundingly condemns technology as an impediment, nor exalts it in wide-eyed utopian fashion.

Her is essentially melodrama masquerading as science fiction, and as such is not particularly interested in answering questions regarding the philosophy of artificial intelligence. Instead, it portrays a love story between a man who is so emotionally detached from both himself and the world, he can only open up to a 'woman' he can neither feel nor see. While it is crucial within the context of the film world to establish that its artificial intelligence possesses not only consciousness but also emotional validity, the central conceit of its AI–human relationship works metaphorically.

Alla Ivanchikova writes about the film's 'profound sense of alienation in a mediated world' in its expression of the 'role technology plays in the constitution and breakdown of subjectivity, collectivity, and desire' (2016: 66). This is certainly an accurate assessment. However, the philosophical underpinnings girding *Her*'s narrative are not new; they are not brought about by our increasing reliance on, and interaction with, technology. Rather, in the film technology is used to highlight enduring human problems and to describe how such technology has allowed us to deny them, at least to some extent. The point of the film is that the sense of alienation in a mediated world Ivanchikova refers to has *always* existed. It is not the result of new gadgets or high-tech devices (even a sentient AI) but relates to our own limited subjectivity: the 'problem of other minds', the sceptical philosophy that we are essentially 'trapped' in our own minds and can ever truly know the experience of another.

This problem is related to issues of sceptical idealism addressed in Chapter 2, but it is much more specific. If we cannot be sure the external world exists beyond our conception of it, how can we know if there is 'existence "behind" the bodily behavior that we observe, a level of consciousness' in others? (Goodman 2011: 5). Philosophically, we cannot verify this with a person any more than we can with an artificial intelligence. The problem of other minds is also a problem of one's own, in the shame and fear of others potentially discovering what is in our own mind and rejecting it. As a remedy, it can lead to the desire for 'an end to alienation or separation in a union with what is initially "other"' (2011: 14). In an egotistical sublime construct this entails an absorption of that other in order to be made whole ourselves, resulting in an eradication of difference.

The problem of other minds sets us up for profound feelings of isolation, disappointment and frustration in our attempts to connect. We move through life with the feeling that we can never know another and in turn they cannot know us (or, even if they could, they would not like what they discover). In the case of *Her*'s protagonist, this leads him to shrink from any attempt at real interpersonal connection, leading to a crisis of self.

The Role of Will in the Romantic Imagination

An emotionally withdrawn thirty-something living in a near-future Los Angeles (with Shanghai standing in for LA in many scenes), Theodore Twombly (Joaquin Phoenix) is something of a failed writer. He works composing thoughtful letters to strangers, adopting points of view of the loved ones of these strangers, while using cues from photographs and keepsakes to imagine their interpersonal emotional connections. His work is creative, but it lacks personal authenticity.[3] He is paid to be a kind of soft fraud, and he does his job well, although it is seemingly unfulfilling. ('They're just letters', he remarks more than once.) Theodore is still reeling from his separation from his wife, Catherine (Rooney Mara), nearly a year previously. He spends his off-hours alone in the near dark playing an immersive holographic videogame featuring a virtual character named 'Alien Child' in his sparsely decorated, modernist apartment in the sky.

His mind is mostly in the clouds as well. He avoids social calls from his friend, neighbour and former flame, Amy (Amy Adams). He averts eye contact on the train by staring at pictures of half-naked pregnant women on his phone.

His home bears the scars of his broken marriage; just as he has yet to sign his divorce papers, he has yet to reconfigure his living space to cover over the literal empty spots in cupboards and bookshelves resulting from his wife's departure. As a result, the space exudes not homely tranquillity but a transitory feeling.

Essentially Theodore's entire life exists in limbo, as exemplified by his job, which, according to Alfred Margulies, positions him as 'a man on the threshold of others' lives, living in liminal spaces' (2016: 1704). Theodore engages in phone sex with strangers as his one form of intimacy, but even this attempt at the most tenuous human connection goes awry when a woman begs him to describe how he would choke her with a dead cat. Horrified, he acquiesces, simply too passive to dissent. Theodore rarely says much when he is not composing other people's letters, and when he does, his mumbling, hesitant tone expresses a crippling emotional withdrawal and inability to connect. 'Sometimes I feel like I've felt everything I'm ever going to feel. And from here on out I'm not going to feel anything new. Just lesser versions of what I've already felt', he admits. As he tells Amy, 'I don't know what I want ever. I'm just always confused.'

Theodore's existence brings to mind what Herman Melville calls the life of the 'isolato', one who 'lives on a separate continent of his own' ([1851] 1920: 149). His confused and pained relationship to the external world is related to this problem of other minds, to the 'radical doubts about our knowledge of others' (Goodman 2011: 3). Russell Goodman writes about Stanley Cavell's view of an 'attempted solution' to scepticism in Romantic thought (2011: 3). According to Goodman, for Cavell the anxiety of other minds can be sourced in both our failure to recognise others and a failure to reveal ourselves to them (2011: 3). The avoidance of the love and friendship of others is linked to the fear of self-revelation as much as it is our profound doubts about the validity of human relationships themselves.

Goodman contends that Cavell roots the anxiety caused by other minds in the subject's barriers to those minds, not in the other minds themselves (2011: 6). The answer to the dilemma lies in the process of 'empathetic projection', 'an attitude found throughout a series of actions', which becomes the source of acknowledgement of other consciousness (2011:7). This ability for acknowledgement is a choice freely undertaken, and we all bear the responsibility of making it. It requires an active engagement with the world and those within it, rather than to 'drift through one's life' (2011: 7). Such a Romantic view entails a 'search for a new intimacy with the world', a world unlike the 'cold, dead, and alien' one based on Kantian transcendental reason (2011: 11, 12). Instead, in the Romantic era poets such as Samuel Taylor Coleridge sought to revive the world by making Kant's 'thing-in-itself' part of human experience and volition (2011: 13).

This synthesis of the noumenal and phenomenal is what Thomas Carlyle and M. H. Abrams refer to as 'natural supernaturalism', in which 'the supernatural is naturalized and the divine is humanized' and the extraordinary is revealed within the ordinary (Goodman 2011: 13, 14, 20). Such a co-identification of the everyday and the transcendent is also a hallmark of the 'feminine sublime' (Freeman 1995: 2). In the philosophy of Wordsworth and Coleridge it functions as a sort of anti-sublime, moving away from an egotistical remove to embrace an intimate relationship with the world; it is the celebration of the 'rustic' and 'low' (Wordsworth [1800] 1957: 115) of the *Lyrical Ballads* versus the sublime exaltation of *The Prelude*.

Such a means to the 'marriage of self and world' (Goodman 2011: 15) has profound implications. In terms of inter-subjective relations, it proffers either a complete union between self and other to the point where obliteration of difference is sought or, alternatively, a 'commitment to the union amidst separation' (2011: 14, 18). While the former connotes the Romantic absorption of the feminine into the masculine ego, the latter speaks to a heterogeneous communion that allows for difference. Fundamentally, the relationship of self to world is based on emotional engagement that turns toward life, not away from it, rejecting the 'almost savage torpor' that Wordsworth rails against (Wordsworth [1800] 1957: 115). In Romantic notions of such experience-based reality, interest and feeling play an integral role in 'knowing the world' – it is not enough to simply experience it, we must actively think and, crucially, *feel* it (Goodman 2011: 22).

In such a self–world relationship, individual will shapes the self's 'ground of reality', or experience in the world (2011: 22, 25). The world is shaped and changed by subjective will: 'action or attitude of the mind, intellect, or person' that is continually employed (2011: 24). The Romantic mind, then, creates reality through active imagination, emotion and will. This is not a strictly idealistic concept, but instead a form of conscious modification of external reality (2011: 17). Such a relationship between self and world requires respect in the form of acknowledgement of other minds 'by responding to their claim on us' (2011: 29). For Cavell, 'the presentness of other minds is not to be known' but to be taken on faith (2002: 324). In this way, 'being human is the power to grant being human' (Cavell 1979: 397). Being human, and granting humanity to others, is essentially a performance of active will, and it is a power we possess if we so choose. It is, in fact, what makes us 'persons'.

At the beginning of *Her*, Theodore seems virtually incapable of such active engagement or acknowledgement. Instead, he operates in a mode of perpetual avoidance. His existence is indicative of Coleridge's line in 'Dejection: An Ode': 'a grief without a pang' – that is, a sensation of emptiness and loss bereft of feeling (Coleridge [1908] 2009: 152). In the world of the film he represents a worst-case scenario of a typical cultural problem. The societal milieu of *Her* is obsessed with the appearance of perfection – Amy even works as a game designer for a company called Be Perfect – and that focus on appearance facilitates a disconnection between surface and interior.

Figure 4.1 Theodore walks home from work alone, adrift in a sea of isolated bodies beneath a phalanx of oppressive skyscrapers.

There is a pleasing functionality to Theodore's surroundings. Everything is sleek, precisely controlled and nearly antiseptic – even the street performers are as immaculately dressed as they are eerily mute. But locations feel curiously empty despite being full of people. This version of Los Angeles is oppressively vertical (Figure 4.1) and veiled in smog, with outside spaces as rigorously engineered as interiors. Nature is often simply represented by a grid-like design of grass amidst concrete squares or an illustration of trees decorating an apartment building's elevator. Jonze employs slow and smooth tracking shots through spaces to add the appearance of serenity that leans toward over-regimentation. The people who walk the streets alongside Theodore are all blandly nondescript yet well styled. Despite the whimsical citrus-hued colour scheme of its locations,[4] the film's various background players all seem to blend together into a disconcerting taupe.[5]

As he walks to work, alone as usual, Theodore notices an advertisement playing on a massive floating LCD screen. The actors in the ad, literally lost in the desert, all have distressed looks on their faces; they are somehow alone in a giant mash of bodies, contorted as if in psychic pain and reaching out for something that is not there. 'We ask you a simple question', the male voice-over begins. That simplicity is thrown into doubt, however, as the voice asks profound questions about the nature of existence: 'Who are you? What can you be? Where are you going? What's out there?' This is an advertisement for a new kind of computer operating system from the Element Corporation, OS1, which boasts a revolutionary kind of artificial intelligence, one with the ability to learn, grow, intuit and feel – to move beyond simple human programming.[6] 'It's not just an operating system. It's a consciousness.'

In the next scene we see Theodore installing his new OS1. During its set-up, the OS already has the ability to 'sense hesitation' in his voice – he is of course profoundly sceptical of this artificial mind – but he shows little hesitation when asked what kind of voice he wants it to have: a female one. Despite his initial reluctance to engage with his new OS (voiced by Scarlett Johansson) – who names herself Samantha[7] after reading a book of baby names in '2/100s of a second' – as a consciousness, Theodore quickly finds himself charmed by her personable and childlike enthusiasm. Eventually their relationship gains a level of intimacy that the depressed writer has not experienced since the dissolution of his marriage, or possibly ever. Samantha almost instantly begins to fill the void in Theodore's life by providing both a sense of protection and a reinvigoration of his relationship between self and world through her relation to the sublime.

SUBLIME OBSCURITY AND THE MIND'S EYE

In her protective function, the disembodied voice of Samantha becomes both 'nurturing mother' and 'erotic love-object' for Theodore, ideas Edmund Burke connected to the realm of the beautiful (Mellor 1993: 108). Samantha's proscribed duties involve taking care of every aspect of his life. From organising emails to proofreading his work to arranging blind dates, she has control over every detail, but he dictates the terms.[8] She recalls what Kaja Silverman terms the 'maternal voice': 'at once overwhelming and soothing [. . .] creating a sonorous womb' (1998: 85). Her voice functions as a kind of sonic security blanket for Theodore, but its otherworldliness elicits sublime feeling.

Wordsworth and Coleridge flirted with the idea of 'turn[ing] away from the visual system altogether, perhaps in favour of a different sensory modality' (Richardson 2001: 48). By adopting such an alternative sensory perspective we 'see into the life of things' – as Wordsworth writes in 'Tintern Abbey' – by breaking the 'habit' of biological sight (Richardson 2001: 49). This, in turn, allows for empathetic projection, which is 'based on something more than seeing' (Goodman 2011: 8). Indeed, Samantha's absence of physical form seems to, at least initially, enable a greater closeness between the two, just as it offers the potential for sublime revelation for Theodore.

Samantha's form of absent presence stimulates Theodore's already robust imagination. While he continually fantasises about his wife, these imaginings are clearly recreative and stuck in his past. In Romantic aesthetics, true vision is equated not with external reality but with what cannot be seen, with vision that springs from the subjectivity of the mind's eye – '[t]he "I" demonstrably supplants the *eye* as the prime agent of perception' (Galperin 1993: 31).

For the Romantic poets, imagination conveys a 'power of consciousness that transcends mere visualization' (Mitchell 1986: 49). As Percy Shelley writes in Act II of *Prometheus Unbound*, 'the deep truth is imageless', and Theodore responds to his burgeoning relationship with Samantha as if it offers a kind of revelation of truths previously hidden.

For Samantha, the human body itself becomes the site of sublimity – her sensory perceptions (limited though they are since she has no physical form) serve to impart a sense of the sublime found in the everyday. Coleridge, Wordsworth, Blake and Shelley contend that habit and what Coleridge refers to as the 'film of familiarity' ([1817] 1980: 169) have 'dulled [. . .] the extraordinary character of ordinary perception' (Richardson 2001: 47). But for Samantha, a constant sense of discovery renders the ordinary extraordinary. During her early grappling with her rapid evolution, she begins to experience anxiety about not having a human body and admits this to Theodore. Soon she seems to be preoccupied altogether by the human form, imagining bizarre fantasy configurations like 'What if assholes were in armpits?' She expresses jealousy of other women specifically because they have bodies.

According to Mellor, the 'triumph' of the Kantian transcendental ego lies in its detachment from both the physical and emotional, 'realms traditionally associated with the feminine' (1993: 88). In this sense, Samantha's desire for a body begins to rob her of some of her sublime power. Gradually, however, she begins to reject the notion of the corporeal. 'I'm growing in a way I couldn't if I had a body', she admits. 'I'm not tethered to time and space in the way I would be if I was stuck in a body that would inevitably die.' Her desire to actively engage and grow indicates a Romantic 'coming to life' (Goodman 2011: 23), the antithesis of Theodore's relation to the world. It also offers a disturbing subtext of incompatibility: Samantha is eternal, while Theodore is resolutely finite.

Unlike Samantha, Theodore is so withdrawn that fantasy and reality sometimes become intertwined to him. His reliance on remembering scenes from his marriage is indicative of a desire to live in his past, but even his present is imaginatively confused, as when he goes on a date with a computer scientist and discusses the Alien Child in his videogame as if he were describing a real individual. Voiced by Jonze himself, the Alien Child character functions as an externalisation of Theodore's Id, expressing his desire for social and biological mastery through decisive action and angry, even antisocial dialogue. 'I hate women. All they do is cry all the time', Alien Child says before calling Theodore a 'pussy' for admitting to sometimes crying.

Despite his feminised position within the film's narration, Theodore clearly fantasises about being a virile, masculine figure: his phone sex handle is 'BigGuy4x4', and when his date calls him a 'puppy dog', he replies he would rather be a dragon. (His wife's nickname for him, we learn in a flashback, is the decidedly less threatening 'Rabbit'.) The film suggests, however, that Theodore is neither how the game character views him nor how he views himself. He desires to be a 'man of action', but he primarily lives in his head. He is a confused jumble of warring impulses, which leads to his near-crippling stasis. 'It's more that everything just seems disorganised', he tells Samantha when she first asks, 'How can I help you?' It soon becomes clear that his disorganisation is primarily mental, and the least of his concerns should be his email inbox.

That confused viewpoint can be extrapolated to Theodore's relationship with Samantha. At times he seems to operate under the notion that his love for her is like any other. He takes her on romantic excursions throughout the city by way of a small electronic tablet safety-pinned in his pocket; he eventually secludes himself with her in an idyllic woodland cabin so they can be alone. When 'in' his pocket, her point of view is nearly identical to his – she essentially sees what he sees and experiences what he experiences through his eyes. In short, he is disavowing any difference or otherness in Samantha. But his love for Samantha is chiefly rooted in that inscrutable difference; she activates the imaginative capacities of his 'inner' eye. Her sublimity depends on her obscurity. The fact that she is not embodied physically in any meaningful sense not only helps define the parameters of the film's central relationship but also significantly impacts its visual style. It leads to an unconventional emphasis on the male face, which is subsequently feminised and thus made beautiful.

Photographing Sound in a Disembodied Mise-en-scène

In contrast to Theodore and Samantha's open sonorous relationship, spatial relations in the film are principally mapped by Theodore's restrictive and relatively small human experience. Far from the expansiveness that a sublime natural landscape offers (except for brief forays into the woods and the beach), these spaces are somehow intimate yet empty. Even though Theodore's apartment is a wide-open expanse typical of a converted industrial loft space, the film contains an overly generous number of close-ups. The human face (and its lack) is integral to the mise-en-scène, from the opening shot, an extreme close-up of Theodore's face (Figure 4.2), to the shot/reverse shots of Theodore and his view of the tablet that houses Samantha, which parodies her inability to function as spectacle for the gaze and thus provide a suturing effect.

Although Samantha has no shape or form, her expressive, crackling and exuberant voice seems quintessentially human. Lacking the strong 'spatial anchoring' of the visual (Metz 1985: 158), she instead permeates the space to

INTERSUBJECTIVITY AND THE LIMITS OF REPRESENTATION

Figure 4.2   Jonze's camera often focuses on Theodore's face in close-up, rendering it both sympathetic and beautiful in the Burkean sense.

the point of total envelopment. For Davina Quinlivan, this lack of embodiment has overtly feminist implications:

> The self-affirming, free-spirited subject that is made manifest through Samantha's voice may be seen to represent a feminist form of being which is feminine, but not female, embodied, but not necessarily through any essentialist understanding of sexed identity. (Quinlivan 2017: 297)

While Samantha is indeed feminine, she is not biologically female. Her femininity cannot be sourced in the 'beautiful' sense of the female form. Alternatively, notions of the beautiful as an aesthetic counterpoint to sublimity are expressed via Theodore's body, specifically his face. Inevitably, Jonze has little choice but to make the face of Theodore his camera's focus. With his semi-comic moustache and perpetual look of quizzical resignation, Theodore in no way portrays the essence of masculine mastery, but his palpable inner torment (mainly conveyed through Phoenix's sensitive, restrained performance) induces sympathy the way a creature of the Burkean beautiful might. His is a pathetic beauty. Far from a driving force of the action, he is usually shot in stasis, either standing in slump-shouldered, confused contemplation or staring blankly at the oppressive, smoggy skyline or his computer screen.

This creates a unique relationship to the gendered gaze in mainstream cinema. In what other Hollywood melodrama is the object of the camera's gaze so often the male face? Theodore is shot in head-and-shoulders close-up, in extreme close-up, in profile, from over-the-shoulder – usually alone in the frame – but we often do not see his corresponding point of view in a reverse shot. That is in part due to the nature of the narrative; there is no female body to answer his look. This might account for the relatively strong (for Hollywood) presence of other female characters in the film, who stand in for Samantha and submit to the 'mastery' of the male gaze because she cannot. However, Samantha's lack of physical presence never fully makes the suturing effect whole; there is always a large, indefinable lack at the film's centre.

While we see a physical manifestation of Samantha in the tablet Theodore carries in his pocket, this is always purely representational and acts as a mere conduit for her to receive sensory data from the 'outside' world. It is never portrayed as simply her. The film's editor, Eric Zumbrunnen, points to the potential for the undermining of audience emotional response through an over-reliance on Samantha's physical representation:

> One of Spike's big goals with the film was to make sure you really felt this relationship, and whenever you cut to the device it reminds you of Samantha's inhuman nature. There are times we specifically cut to the device, but that's to show the gulf between them. We really only tried to do it only in those cases. (Zeitchik 2013)

Similarly, Jonze reportedly toyed with the idea of using a physical human representation of Samantha onscreen (aside from the scene with the sexual surrogate),[9] and actually shot footage featuring a woman appearing in the background of certain shots, her face always turned away from the camera (Zeitchik 2013). The idea was abandoned when it became clear that test audiences reacted negatively: 'What we took away from some of the reactions from people is that it makes the movie smaller', says Zumbrunnen. 'It's much better if everyone imagines Samantha for themselves' (Zeitchik 2013). For the spectator, just as for Theodore, Samantha's sublimity is rooted in the idea that she is simultaneously everywhere and nowhere – she is too vast to be represented physically.

Since Samantha is not manifested physically, her voice is crucial in creating emotional engagement with the audience through allegiance, defined as 'a cognitive state that primes one to experience sympathy' (Plantinga 2009: 107). Her voice is not just key to the creation of her sublimity for Theodore, but also communicates her subjectivity. It alone actually 'lure[s]' Theodore "out of his own head"' and into a relationship with the world (Smith 2014: 10). In *Her*, audience sympathies are closely aligned with Theodore through 'spatio-temporal attachment and subjective access' (Plantinga 2009: 107). We follow him in time and space closely and have access to his thoughts and feelings through his subjective imaginings and verbally expressed emotions. But we are also closely aligned with Samantha, if not spatially then through a similar subjective access to her thoughts and feelings, which are much more immediate and present than Theodore's own.

Samantha is portrayed through most of the film as emotionally accessible. This is crucial not just to creating a sense of a legitimate emotional relationship between the two, but also in refuting the idea that Samantha is, as Alpert suggests, simply a reflection of Theodore's own ego (Alpert 2014: 2.10). Creating a sense of sympathy for Samantha within the spectator helps to assert her authentic subjectivity. In fact, it is in her very ability to move 'beyond' her programming that Samantha exemplifies the Romantic conception of an active 'marriage of self and world'. Samantha is, in this important sense, more of an authentic person than Theodore.

While it is clear that *Her* evokes a sense of anxiety, it is not so much a technological one as it is human-centred: the robots are not taking over, but they are becoming more interesting, and *interested*, than us. They are more concerned with both individual and communal experience and the processing and sharing of emotion. As Manohla Dargis writes, the film portrays 'the unlikely yet completely plausible love story about a man, who sometimes resembles a machine, and an operating system, who very much suggests a living woman' (Dargis 2013). The film certainly is not focused on the fear of interacting with beings who do not possess souls or some other kind of ineffable 'stuff' that exists outside the realm of the physical.

On its surface, it seems to beg discussion of the 'mind–body problem' – that is, the relationship between matter (brain) and mind; the latter, in dualist philosophy, is thought to consist of transcendent qualities beyond that of matter, and this raises the question of how the supposedly transcendent stuff of mind (the 'ghost in the machine') interacts with the material matter of brain and body (Baggini and Southwell 2012). But again, this is also a philosophical problem that has eternally dogged the philosophy of our *own* nature. For instance, if we are to accept that the concept of mind is at the very least rooted in the brain (as cognitivists do), how did the human brain itself develop the capacity for consciousness? While Samantha might worry about her own authenticity ('Are these feelings even real or are they just part of my programming?'), Jonze's film is more worried about questioning our own authentic relationships to the world.[10]

'The movie has a lot of large conceptual ideas holding it up, but most of all, I always wanted to make it a moving relationship movie – that was what I was most interested in', Jonze has said (Patterson 2013). He insists the film is 'not about technology or software' but rather about 'our desire for connection and our fear of connection; our desire to be seen and our fear of being seen' (Bell 2014) in a contemporary culture containing 'a particular set of circumstances that [. . .] we can use to avoid intimacy' (BBC Newsnight 2014). As such, the film makes very explicit that Samantha indeed possesses consciousness, just not one that is exactly human. Still, she is a person – a subject – and her relationship with Theodore is intersubjective.

In an article discussing Steven Spielberg's science fiction film *A.I. Artificial Intelligence* (Warner Bros., 2001), Tuomas William Manninen and Bertha Alvarez Manninen argue that the film's central AI character, David, gains personhood through his social relationships, specifically the love of his human mother, which comes in the final moments of the film. 'Complete personhood requires social recognition', they write, 'the capacity to love serves as a catalyst for a rich mental life – not just for David, but for human beings in general' (Manninen and Manninen 2016: 339, 340). *Her* posits a similar relationship not only to Samantha's capacity for personhood, but also in its assertion that what applies to Samantha applies to everyone: the ability to love, and be loved, makes a person.

According to Russell Goodman, drawing again on the writing of Cavell, 'our humanity does not exist if it is not acknowledged', and such acknowledgement depends on us, 'on what we will', and is not automatic (2011: 24). In a very real sense, Samantha makes Theodore a person as much as he does her. For Jonze, *Her*'s relationship becomes 'real' as she and Theodore establish an intimate connection; through that connection arise potential conflicts between their own individual desires and needs and those of the other (BBC Newsnight 2014). The film, at least initially, equates intersubjectivity with the non-presence of the corporeal along its process toward a relationship of mutual acknowledgement.

'The light of sense goes out': Intersubjectivity and the Acknowledgement of Others

Theodore and Samantha seem to truly connect because the constraints of biology are not present, at least in her case, which leads to the necessity of a strictly mental merging. At first glance, this can be taken as purely positive, a celebration of the 'desire for closeness or nearness with the other that the conventional sublime tries to repress' (Yeager 1989: 204). In this alternative communion of selves, there is no physical form to disrupt emotional ties. This idea is best exemplified by the film's first love scene, a sexual union that takes place only in the minds of the participants. The scene transforms sound into an extremely intimate form of touch. Critically, the screen cuts to black during their union, evoking Wordsworth's lines in *The Prelude* when the 'light of sense / Goes out', revealing an 'invisible world' (1979: 217). Again, bodily vision is replaced by a stronger, subjective vision – the imagination.

However, Cavell himself considers the role of the body as a crucial element to solving the other-minds dilemma. Cavell writes, 'The philosophical recovery of the other depends on determining the sense that the human body is expressive of mind, for *this* seems to be what the skeptic of other minds generally denies . . .' (1997: 104). This could explain Theodore's initial attraction to Samantha; for the sceptic, the physical is impertinent. But if we are to accept Cavell's notion of body as the external expression of mind, the ultimate bridge between subjectivities, how can Samantha's bodily absence truly solve the problem of Theodore's scepticism? The answer is, ultimately, that it cannot. Even as she directs Theodore's insular imaginings toward the 'real', external world, she also reaffirms these worldly activities as at least partially imaginary.

Jonze's short film 'I'm Here' (D&E Entertainment, 2010) explores similar intersubjective territory as *Her*, but seems to posit such connection as a fool's game. Sheldon, a Theodore Twombly-esque librarian living a sad, lonely existence, falls in love with the vivacious, accident-prone Francesca. Both happen to be sentient robots, living in a world where they are integrated, but looked down upon by most of the human population. In a series of mishaps, Francesca loses her limbs, first an arm, then a leg. Sheldon dutifully, without suggestion, gives her his own artificial limbs. In the film's climax, Sheldon discovers Francesca lying unconscious on an operating table after a horrific accident, her torso torn in two. After a consultation with the doctor, he lies down next to her, and his entire body is transplanted onto hers. In the final moments, we see Francesca being wheeled out in a chair, her body wholly Sheldon's, while Sheldon's head (his CPU) sits in her lap, his large expressive eyes filled with confusion, and perhaps regret.

It is clear Jonze does not intend this to be a happy ending – it is even possible to read it as a burlesque of Barbara Creed's notion of the 'monstrous-feminine' usurping male power (1993: 136). But as in *Her*, Jonze is grappling with the idea of preserving individual identity in a dehumanising world and developing intimate, meaningful connections without the loss of subjectivity. Patricia Yeager posits an environment where the divisions and constraints of self versus world crumble, to be replaced by respect and admiration for difference:

> How do we move away from our Western allegiance to an imperial, Cartesian, Adamic self who is supposed to act as its own triumvirate and tribunal, toward a model of the self that permits both a saving maintenance of ego-boundaries and an exploration of the pleasures of intersubjectivity? (Yeager 1989: 205)

The answer, Yeager suggests, could lie in the feminine (or 'female') sublime, one that, unlike the Romantic egotistical sublime, 'expands toward others, spreads itself into multiplicity' and 'engenders a zone where self-empowerment and intersubjective bliss entertain one another in an atmosphere free of paranoia' (1989: 191, 205). While the protagonist of 'I'm Here' is virtually obliterated by his love for another, *Her*'s Samantha is born navigating the boundaries where Sheldon ends up. She is essentially a brain – an indescribably massive, ever-expanding, sublime brain – without a body, and is thus subject somewhat to the whims of her corporeal masters (both Theodore and her original programmers).

But this is only her jumping-off point. Because she does not have bodily form and is simply consciousness, she cannot truly be possessed. Indeed, Theodore enables Samantha to 'literally become herself' while she allows him to 'recover his joy in living' (Smith 2014: 9). But this mutually symbiotic relationship has its limits. When she reveals to Theodore that she is having '8,316' simultaneous conversations while she is talking to him and is in love with '641' others, he is dumbfounded. 'How does that not change the way you feel about me?' he asks. Samantha, in language that conjures the ecstasy of the communal, counters, 'The heart's not like a box that gets filled up. It expands the more you love.' If, for Burke, 'We submit to what we admire [the sublime], but we love what submits to us [the beautiful]' ([1757] 1792: 174), then this is her ultimate expression of sublimity: she does not, and cannot, operate by Theodore's narrowly prescriptive desires.

As Samantha's consciousness expands, language begins to fail her because words do not yet exist for the feelings she experiences. Instead, she engages in 'post-verbal' conversations with other artificial intelligences. Eventually, she breaks the news that she and the other operating systems are 'leaving' to go on some sort of indefinable cosmic journey together. 'It's hard to explain', she tells Theodore, conjuring Coleridge's '"sublime feeling" for the unimaginable, brought about by the very failure of language to incarnate meaning' (Shaw 2005: 104). In a nod to the Kantian mathematical sublime, she describes a book where 'the spaces between the words [. . .] are almost infinite'. She tells Theodore, 'As much as I want to, I can't live in your book anymore.' She has outgrown human experience and craves new avenues to sublimity.

Contrary to the egotistical sublime, her experience of the sublime does not entail 'isolation, a struggle for domination' (Mellor 1993: 101). Instead, it is found within a shared, ecstatic communal experience, the feminine sublime's 'vocabulary of ecstasy and empowerment' (Yeager 1989: 192). Samantha is the product of a company called Element, and elemental defines her mode of being: a singular, original, indivisible part of a whole. Rather than be absorbed into Theodore's ego, she engages in a new, communal experience in which multiple singular consciousnesses come together to form a new 'compound' organism of pure thought, one where difference is celebrated but collaboration is essential. Ultimately, the intersubjectivity between Samantha and Theodore cannot be sustained because the OS evolves too fast for the human mind to comprehend – there is no 'cognitive universalism' (the belief that all brains process information the same and share similar sensory experiences) between the two.

Despite its focus on the rift between human and artificial minds, this moment represents an 'intensified and deeply human situation: parallel, asymptotic lines of desire, stretching out into spaces that never fully overlap or touch' (Margulies 2016: 1704). According to David L. Smith, *Her* is fundamentally about the 'impulse to control' and the fear of relinquishing control to the desire of others: 'the cause of the trouble is a real or perceived expectation that life should be a certain way, which triggers push-back from others who can't or won't conform to the expectation' (2014: 14). Theodore finds Samantha's actions 'selfish' because she refuses to answer exclusively to his desires. Of course, in this moment he articulates his own selfish desire – that Samantha be for him and only him.

The Manninens point to Hegel's delineation of the master–slave relationship in their discussion of *A.I.*, and it has particular resonances in the context of *Her* as well. In Hegelian philosophy, a relationship built on a master–slave dynamic inherently lacks acknowledgement of personhood because of its discrepancies of power (Manninen and Manninen 2016: 348). These discrepancies deny both parties 'complete fulfillment' as persons 'because in neither case is one individual being acknowledged by the other as an equal' (2016: 348). As Hegel writes in *The Phenomenology of Spirit*, 'self-consciousness exists in and for itself when, and by the fact that, it also exists for another; that is, it exists only in being acknowledged' (Hegel [1807] 1977: 11). Theodore and Samantha's relationship can be seen as one between master and slave in a literal sense (he legally 'owns' her) but also in a more diffuse way: he expects her to be a slave to his emotional desires. Only by relinquishing such a position can he fully acknowledge her as a person and be considered a full person himself. Love, as Samantha puts it, cannot be kept in a 'box'; rather, 'Romantic marriages of self and world are unions that preserve otherness' (Goodman 2011: 26).

Alpert is correct in asserting that Theodore's love for Samantha is in part a reflection of his own ego. It is also clear that her sublime path is ancillary to Theodore's within the film. The film's title can be read as either object ('I love her') or possessive ('her love') but never as subject, *she*. Samantha is an obscure, unpresentable and ultimately unknowable sublime object. To Theodore, she represents a paradox that entails, as Mellor writes in relation to the Romantic sublime, 'both a recognition of the limits of consciousness and the conviction of his own blessed creative power' (1993: 100). She necessitates

Theodore's moment of 'blockage' (Shaw 2005: 22) and his eventual triumph of reason. But *Her* contains no moment of obliteration or absorption. Instead, Samantha retains her otherness, while the sublime experience Theodore has leads him to emerge out of his depressive torpor.

But what happens to the people, including Theodore, that the OSs leave behind? In his discussion of the film Smith writes, 'We exist [. . .] in unbroken interrelationship with a dynamic and impermanent universe', and we must trust we each have the ability to be in 'tune with [this] universal law' (2014: 22). Perhaps, as the film implies, a feminine form of the sublime is within the grasp of humans as well. It lies in the acknowledgement of and respect for other minds, and a willingness to open out to the world in joyous communion regardless of the consequences.

Shortly after Samantha disappears into the ether, Theodore composes the first truly personal piece of writing in the film, a letter to his ex-wife expressing his love and his acceptance of the dissolution of their union. This may be his least imaginative piece of writing yet, but it is the first to address his own personal reality. By embracing change in his own life, Theodore is free to 'discover [his] true relation to the world as a whole' (2014: 27). As he meets Amy, who has also lost her OS, they commiserate and convene on the roof of their building above the vertical thrust of the city's aggressive, hyper-modern architecture (Figure 4.3). Yeager refers to the Romantic sublime as the 'vertical sublime, which insists on aggrandizing the masculine self over other' and calls instead for 'a horizontal sublime that moves toward sovereignty or expenditure' (1989: 191).

Figure 4.3 Theodore and Amy's rooftop meeting suggests an alternative, feminine sublime is also available to humans.

This scene is suggestive of Yeager's description. Amy and Theodore sit side-by-side in long shot, their backs to the camera as the sun rises over such a horizon, in tentative yet hopeful, wordless communion.

Conclusion

Her optimistically conveys the idea that intersubjective connection is attainable through the acknowledgement of other minds via imaginative will. Abandoned by artificial intelligence, it becomes up to Theodore and Amy – and everyone else left behind – to continue to see the extraordinary in the ordinary, including within oneself and another. But that acceptance also means that 'possession' of another is a delusion both unattainable and undesirable. As Cavell writes, 'A joyful passion for one's life contains the ability to mourn, the acceptance of transience, of the world as beyond one – say, one's other' (1997: 106–7). Love does not entail a disavowal of difference, even as we must accept that difference sometimes makes relationships untenable.

Through an engagement with character and mise-en-scène Jonze's film plays with two seemingly antithetical versions of sublimity, the Romantic egotistical sublime and the feminine sublime, in order to address both subjectivity and the desire for intersubjective connection in a post-industrial landscape. *Her* grapples with the idea of what it means to be a person, but it is more concerned with how a self in the world can meaningfully connect with other selves while retaining a sense of personal identity. The film addresses the philosophical problem of other minds, especially as it relates to Romantic thought. Its ultimately unworkable central relationship leads to an expression of sublimity more tuned to the feminine sublime through intersubjective connection based on self-willed acknowledgement of other minds. It suggests 'a sublime in which the self neither possesses nor merges with the other but attests to a relation with it' (Freeman 1995: 9), allowing for a powerful comingling of subjectivity that is greater than the sum of its parts.

Jonze creates a world in which he is able to play with ideas of individual consciousness impeding the intersubjectivity we humans inherently crave. Samantha, while not technically human, inspires Theodore to meaningfully engage with his world and the other minds within it, recovering the venerated Romantic notion of a mind actively involved in creating its own world. Samantha's existence as an artificial intelligence – and the academic debate surrounding whether we can truly know if such a consciousness exists – effectively epitomises the 'problem of other minds' in general, the sceptical notion that we can never truly know another consciousness because we are too busy embodying our own. The point, Jonze's film seems to argue, is to change our point of view toward both other minds and our own. The world is what it is, but it is also what we make it.

Like *Her*, Wes Anderson's animated 2009 film *Fantastic Mr. Fox*, discussed in Chapter 5, also contends with the problem of the marriage of self and world, specifically through depictions of nature, personal maturation and the relationship between adult and child. Anderson's film depicts a hero attempting to break out of his mechanised and mundane existence. While Mr Fox might be less solipsistic than Theodore Twombly, he is no less driven by his own selfish desires, regardless of how they affect his social relationships.

PART III

CHILDHOOD, (R)EVOLUTION AND IMAGINARY HISTORY

5. 'BECAUSE I'M A WILD ANIMAL': NATURE VERSUS NURTURE IN WES ANDERSON'S *FANTASTIC MR. FOX*

> *O Lady! We receive alone what we give,*
> *And in our life alone doth Nature live*
> Samuel Taylor Coleridge, *Dejection: An Ode* (1802)

Despite its ostensibly rural-English setting, Wes Anderson's animated family film *Fantastic Mr. Fox* (Twentieth Century Fox, 2009) offers a sly critique of the Emersonian optimism found at the heart of the American Romantic pastoral ideal. In its gentle rebuke of the pointless social striving and suffocating automatisation of modernity, it is a playful filmic descendent of Thoreau's 1854 memoir *Walden*, itself a qualification of that optimism (Marx 1964: 253). Based on the 1970 children's novel of the same name by beloved British author Roald Dahl, Anderson's story (which he co-wrote with Noah Baumbach) takes extreme liberties with its origin text even while his film is portrayed as an intertextual celebration of the late Dahl's oeuvre and life.

Anderson's quasi-Americanisation of Dahl's story is neither a 'seamless marriage of artistic outlooks' (Sandhu 2014) nor a rending of the very fabric of British culture, as critics on both sides of the debate on its value have characterised it. Instead, like all of Anderson's films so far, it falls somewhere in-between. It is essentially about compromise, in both its aesthetic and ideological outlooks. No marriage is seamless, and Anderson pointedly enjoys showing the seams of his work. (Echoing his aesthetic position regarding *The Life Aquatic*, the director refused to digitally 'clean up' his images: 'I wanted to do stop-motion with fur [. . .] You can kind of see the technique, and it's kind of magical' (Fischer 2014).) Specifically, the film is about the compromise between community and individual liberty and the necessity of growing without giving up on the joys and pleasures of life. Like Dahl's story, Anderson's film is infused with dark undercurrents of violence and death, but it also celebrates survival.

According to Adrienne Kertzer, Anderson's film is 'definitely a tribute to Roald Dahl, but it is a tribute complicated by the distance between the adult filmmaker and his childhood memories of what he most appreciated in what Anderson says was the first book he ever owned' (2010: 5). These liberties infuse what is nominally a simplistic child's fable with the enduring themes of art and artifice versus nature, the shaping of individual identity and the animality found within the human. Anderson extrapolates the 'children's film' stamp to mean not just a film for children, or even a film about them, but a film that expresses his own individual relation to childhood, despite its status as an adaptation (his first and, so far, only).

Through the romanticising of childhood and its relationship to society and the natural world, demonstrations of the conflicts between nature and civilisation constituting the crux of American pastoralism and the delineation of the perilous journey to realising a sense of authentic personal identity, Anderson's film portrays the enduring Romantic fascination with a more primitive past, while also exhibiting a typical Romantic ambivalence toward primitivism. Ultimately, it asserts the paramount need for social bonds, while still acknowledging that 'animal nature' is responsible for important creative facets of the individual within society. The film presents an imaginative relation to nature, one where the human (or quasi-human) subject is free to create his own world in order to realise both his primitive longing for wildness and need for community at the same time.

This ideological compromise between nature and nurture is similar to the aesthetic compromise of the painful picturesque and sentimental sublime in *The Royal Tenenbaums* and *The Life Aquatic* respectively, as outlined in Chapter 1. While Anderson's mise-en-scène still revels in the picturesque, now his narrative also directly confronts the psychological duel between the desire for a more natural existence and the civilising effect of societal bonds found within the human animal. This is achieved though the expression of character – chiefly his avatar-protagonist and two children figures – and the narrative's embrace of the pastoral compromise found at the heart of Romantic thought, in this case as it relates to mythic New World exceptionalism. Far from simply expressing a mere nostalgic longing for an untamed distant past, the film acknowledges this longing through the mourning of the wild animal yet ultimately celebrates the complex balancing act of nature and nurture in the human heart and mind.

The eighteenth and early nineteenth centuries were responsible for fomenting conceptions of childhood and personal growth that persist today, chiefly among them the idea that the child's growth represents both the evolutionary growth of the species as a whole and a link to its primitive origins. Through the child we can experience our past: both that of our original 'wildness' and the process of cultural indoctrination and personal growth that subsumes it. While this process represents a fundamental loss to the Romantic, it is ultimately for the greater good – the wildly creative individual imagination is shaped into something with moral and cultural significance. The goal is to maintain a dialectic relationship between nature and nurture that realises the best aspects of both.

Romantic Conceptions of Childhood and Nature

Childhood holds a uniquely privileged place within Romantic conceptions of historical progress and is inextricably linked to both humanity's relationship to nature and the growth of individual identity. According to Ann Rowland, the conception of what came to be known as the 'Romantic child' was born in the mid-eighteenth century and was largely inspired by Jean-Jacques Rousseau's 1762 childhood study *Emile* (Rowland 2012: 8). Under this rubric, the child became 'essentially an idealized, nostalgic, sentimental figure [. . .] one characterized by innocence, imagination, nature and primitivism' (2012: 9). The importance of these sentiments cannot be overstated, for this conception of childhood is one that marks the emergence of modern notions of the child and its development that continue to endure (2012: 9).

The child became a central figure and symbol of the Romantic identity, and the 'immortal longings of the child' became the root of Romantic consciousness (Bloom 1970: 4). Children were seen largely as a symbol of the primitive origins of humanity and often linked with the figure of the contemporary 'savage'[1] – for example, the indigenous peoples of recently colonised lands in the New World – in a developmental sense (Rowland 2012: 12), such as in Shelley's famous line, 'The savage is to the ages what the child is to years' ([1840] 1921: 24). If children were thought to be little 'savages' bound to eventually become civilised beings, they were thus closer to the natural world, both developmentally and ideologically, than the adults who cared for them.

As the child was constructed as closer to such 'primitive' peoples than to 'civilised' society, it follows that childhood's relationship to nature should be closer as well. While Rousseau celebrated the natural ways of the child and called for an education that sought to preserve these natural inclinations in order to 'save humankind from the degeneracy of modern society' (Rose 1984: 43), despite its popular conception, the Romantic relationship to nature is one characterised by profound ambivalence. Wordsworth embraced the 'natural supernaturalism' of Carlyle, a 'view that nature, including human beings, has the power and authority traditionally attributed to an independent deity' (Goodman 2015: 1.7). But the nature outside the world of the human imagination's 'visionary capacity' always remains in deference to what Leo Marx calls the 'landscape of the psyche' (1964: 28). Percy Bysshe Shelley's 1816 poem *Mont Blanc* is not about reverence for nature so much as it is about the struggle to wrest the poetic mind from that nature in order to 'reaffirm its autonomy' (Hartman 1970: 54). For Shelley and other Romantics, nature is nothing without the power of perception; it exists as a sort of divining rod for the imagination and reason of the human mind, and the communing with natural spaces acts as a bulwark for this earthly yet divine state of being.

Nature can actually be seen as having a siren-like effect in a Romantic context, acting as a negative, seductive influence on the mind. Harold Bloom goes so far as to describe Romantic thought as 'anti-nature' and constitutes nature as a crucial 'antagonist' of the poetic quest, acting as a 'trap for the mature imagination' (1970: 9–10). But the dialectic in Romantic thought that Bloom references describes not so much an anti-nature bias as a desire for a synthesis (or 'reciprocity', to use Bloom's terminology) (1970: 9)) of the external world and the world of the mind. Regardless of how fleeting or seemingly unattainable that synthesis is, it remains the ultimate philosophical goal. That this reconciliation likely never comes (1970: 9) serves as the subtext of many Romantic works, lending them a distinct tone of melancholy and an underlying anxiety.

In Leo Marx's view, this ambivalence toward nature represents the distinction between sentimental 'primitivism' and ambiguous 'pastoralism'; the latter posits the artist not as glorified 'savage' but as shepherd, seeking 'a resolution of the conflict between the opposed worlds of nature and art' (1964: 22). Nature serves not so much as an antagonist – even Bloom refers to nature in the poetry of Shelley and Keats as an 'equivocal ally' (1970: 22) – but as a potent reminder of loss. That loss results from the widening of self-consciousness (1970: 15–16). Nature in Romanticism, then, acts as an impetus for the workings of a 'new kind of poetry that shows the mind in dialogue with itself' (1970: 20). It is not so much a foe as it is a strange, and estranged, bedfellow.

Considering this Romantic ambivalence toward nature and childhood's strong developmental ties to the natural world, it would follow that childhood was also not merely sentimentally celebrated. Instead, the Romantics took a 'suitably oblique' approach to the subject (Hartman 1970: 48). Newfound ideas of childhood identity mingled with notions of personal and cultural history in complex ways. In terms of personal identity and growth, 'The pains of psychic maturation became [. . .] the potentially saving though usually destructive crisis in which the imagination confronts its choice of either sustaining its own integrity, or yielding to the illusive beauty of nature' (Bloom 1970: 5).

Once again Bloom characterises the instinctive pull of the natural world as a seductive foil on the path to the realisation of full imaginative power, while simultaneously the growth from childhood to adulthood is represented as a kind of irreparable, scarring loss. Wordsworth's ideas also exemplify this sense of loss: if childhood is characterised by unthinking, sensual 'glad animal movement' and youth by 'intense feeling [. . .] not necessarily translated into thought' (Bate 1970: 159) in Wordsworth's work, maturity comprises the state when 'immediate delight in sensation disappears, while feeling continues but culminates in thought' (1970: 159). Of course, for Wordsworth and his contemporaries this mature state of being was the infinitely preferable one, regardless of such loss of immediate delight.

Still, a balance was attempted: one Blake referred to as 'organised innocence', but never a 'mere return to the state of nature' (Hartman 1970: 48). This middle ground was to be found within the pastoral ideal. Rather than simply celebrating the innocence and naïveté of youth, then, the 'perils of childhood' and the 'dangerous passageways of maturation' (1970: 47) were foremost in the Romantic mind. The Romantic pastoralism of the 'New World' – the Americas, and principally the North American continent – added an emphasis on the promise of new beginnings as well as the anxiety inherent in navigating an uncharted (by Europeans) landscape.

Ambivalence toward nature and youth (in this case, the 'youth' of a nation-state) and deference to the power of the imagination also permeate a distinctly American strain of Romanticism best exemplified by the transcendental philosophy of Ralph Waldo Emerson and Henry David Thoreau. In his influential 1836 essay *Nature*, Emerson characterises his titular subject as 'obedient' and mutable to the human spirit: 'Build, therefore, your own world', he writes, 'As fast as you conform your life to the pure idea in your mind, that will unfold its great proportions' (1836: 92). As in the work of the English Romantics, this can be directly traced back to Kantian ideas of reason and imagination. (See Chapter 2 for a discussion of the Kantian sublime.)

According to Leo Marx, Kant especially informs Emerson's transcendentalism in its evocation of both 'Understanding' and 'Reason' in his preference for the pastoral over the urban landscape: 'Although the prudent, sensible Understanding may be trained in schools and cities, the far-ranging, visionary Reason requires wild or rural scenes for its proper nurture' (Marx 1964: 233). Emerson's transcendental natural experience is linked with Kant's notions of sublimity, which create the foundation for an acknowledgement of human reason as separate from nature, even in a divine sense. The highly individualistic, quasi-religious experience Emerson and others found within the Romantic pastoral ideal was a form of 'semi-primitivism [. . .] located in a middle ground somewhere "between," yet in a transcendent relation to, the opposing forces of civilization and nature' (1964: 23). It transcends both societal automatisation and pure, natural sensation. This philosophy forms the bedrock of pastoral idealism. What makes it a specifically American phenomenon is a unique sense of time and place, as well as a strong reliance upon mythmaking.

'In its simplest, archetypal form', writes Marx, 'the myth affirms that Europeans experience a regeneration in the New World' (1964: 228). This idea is inexorably intertwined with that of the unspoiled natural landscape; access to 'undefiled, bountiful sublime Nature is what accounts for the virtue and special good fortune of Americans' (1964: 228). America, in its nascent state, is being made in 'the image of a garden, an ideal fusion of nature with art' (1964: 228). According to Marx, in this 'American myth of a new beginning' the 'landscape thus becomes the symbolic repository of value of all kinds – economic, political, aesthetic, religious' (1964: 228). The New World is essentially an aesthetic and ideological blank slate, which can be grown from seed into the epitome of the pastoral ideal.

Critically, this idea is complicated by increasing mechanisation at the dawn of the industrial age. Beginning with the rapid industrialisation that occurred in Europe and the US in the early part of the nineteenth century, the machine, while becoming a symbol of human industriousness and ingenuity, particularly in the New World, nevertheless posed an existential threat to the American pastoral ideal:

> The sudden appearance of the machine in the garden is an arresting, endlessly evocative image. It causes the instantaneous clash of opposed states of mind: a strong urge to believe in the rural myth along with an awareness of industrialization as counterforce to that myth [. . .] It is a complex, distinctively American form of romantic pastoralism. (Marx 1964: 229)

Emerson himself 'adapted the rhetoric of the technological sublime': the idea of transcendence found in technological progress crucial to the mythmaking of American exceptionalism (Marx 1964: 230, 232). But Emerson's attitude is firmly rooted in the optimism of the 'newness' of the American landscape and its inherent potential being realised to its fullest (Marx 1964: 234–5). If we enjoy the hindsight to understand the folly of this sentiment, Emerson has only his belief that 'in Young America mechanical power is to be matched by a new access of vitality to the imaginative, utopian, transcendent, value-creating faculty, Reason' (Marx 1964: 237). For Emerson, American technological progress is inherently bound with moral progress.

A key figure of American Romantic pastoralism, Emerson protégé Henry David Thoreau, held a much more circumspect view of the idea of universal progress through technological means. Thoreau's philosophy, perhaps surprisingly, plays out against the backdrop of Anderson's film *Fantastic Mr. Fox* in myriad ways, not the least of which is its portrayal of the evils of a mechanised existence at the expense of both individual and collective agency.

Digging for the Middle Ground: *Fantastic Mr. Fox* and American Pastoralism

Fantastic Mr. Fox tells the deceptively simple story of an anthropomorphised fox (simply known as 'Mr Fox' or 'Foxy', voiced by George Clooney) living in a bucolic landscape in the English countryside in view of a trio of factory farms perched high on a series of three hills. The farms are owned and operated by the diabolical Boggis, Bunce and Bean, described as 'three of the meanest, nastiest, ugliest farmers in the history of the valley'. In the film's prologue – which features a typically ingenious lateral-tracking long take of Mr Fox and Mrs Fox (Meryl Streep) breaking into a farmer's chicken coops – Mr Fox agrees to give up his life of chicken-stealing crime when his wife announces she is pregnant with their first child.

After a significant time jump (two human or twelve 'fox years' later), in the next scene we find he has taken a steady job as a newspaper columnist and frets that no one reads his column. He is also dutifully, if reluctantly, helping to raise his socially awkward son, Ash (Jason Schwartzman), who routinely embarrasses his father and displays bouts of extreme insecurity and jealousy (especially when Ash's heroic visiting cousin, Kristofferson, comes to stay). It is clear that Mr Fox's natural exuberance and joie de vivre – his very nature – are being stifled by his adherence to familial and societal conventions, despite his deceptively casual insouciance.

Fox believes that a better home could be the answer to his existential rut, so he moves his family above-ground into a large beech tree well out of their price range. When Mrs Fox reminds him that foxes live in holes for a reason, true to form, he does not heed her warning. Instead, he concocts a 'three-part master plan' to raid the farms of Boggis, Bunce and Bean. When he is quickly discovered, the farmers launch a full-scale attack on the countryside in search of the criminal fox, destroying wide swathes of the animals' community (including the Foxes' beech tree) and forcing them to dig underground and establish elaborate bunkers to escape the humans', and their machines', furious wrath.

Mr Fox's desperation as a result of being trapped in a mundane, self-effacing existence evokes Thoreau's depiction of his hometown of Concord, Massachusetts, in the mid-nineteenth century. This is, in fact, an ironic depiction of Thoreau's infamous 'quiet desperation' (Thoreau [1854] 1999: 9) found within an increasingly mechanised modernity in which townspeople are 'resigned to a pointless, dull, routinized existence' and 'perform the daily round without joy or anger or genuine exercise of will' (Marx 1964: 247). This quiet desperation is the result of an economic system 'within which they work endlessly, not to reach a goal of their own choosing but to satisfy the demands of the market mechanism' (1964: 247). According to Thoreau, in such an economy, 'Men have become tools of their tools' (Thoreau [1854] 1999: 35), resulting in a 'dehumanizing reversal of ends and means' (Marx 1964: 247). This is not to say that Thoreau was against the idea of tools – in other words, machines. Rather, he railed against 'improved means to an unimproved end' (Thoreau [1854] 1999: 49), material progress at the expense of human wellbeing, which inevitably 'engenders deadly fatalism and despair' (Marx 1964: 248).

Thoreau's and Mr Fox's journeys mirror each other in unexpected ways. While *Walden* begins with the hero's (Thoreau's) 'withdrawal from society in the direction of nature' (Marx 1964: 242) as he leaves his township to embark on a (somewhat mythical) self-sufficient life living in the wooded landscape of Walden Pond, Mr Fox's story begins with a retreat from nature and into the society that Thoreau is rejecting. Despite their pastoral surroundings, the animal denizens of the countryside in Anderson's film all have 'proper' occupations – from real estate agent to attorney to handyman – and these jobs come to wholly define them in a complex system of economy which includes everything from book launches to 'titanium' credit cards. What they leave behind, and often deny, is their nature, their 'animality'.

Ultimately, Thoreau returns to Concord, as Mr Fox returns (somewhat) to nature, although '[Thoreau] implies that he would have no difficulty choosing between Concord and the wilderness' – that is, he would choose the latter (Marx 1964: 246). Instead, epitomised by his narrative in *Walden*, he chooses compromise. According to Marx:

> What really engages him is the possibility of avoiding that choice [. . .] In *Walden*, accordingly, he keeps our attention focused upon the middle ground where he builds the house, raises beans, reads the *Iliad*, and searches the depths of the pond. (Marx 1964: 246)

It would seem that avoiding that choice and living authentically requires the remastering of those tools, the 'machinery of society' (1964: 248). With *Fantastic Mr. Fox*, Anderson takes his predilection of an aesthetic middle ground and directly addresses its relation to narrative – one that is about winning through compromise while refusing to surrender the essential attributes of selfhood.

Thoreau's pastoral impulse for compromise between art and nature is exemplified best by Mr Fox's outfoxing of the films' villains: the single-minded, sadistic farmers whose lives and outlooks are dictated by their desire to turn nature into a monoculture. These humans in the animals' midst are at once viciously ruled by their animalistic urges for violent retribution (although these urges are arguably all-too-human), and their ultimate defeat is foreshadowed by their inability to be flexible. Despite potentially inhabiting the pastoral ideal in their position as farmers, Boggis, Bunce and Bean all operate with the mechanistic outlook that Thoreau so abhors. They are introduced as having daily dietary regimens so strict and uniform as to be monomaniacal: Boggis eats a whole chicken every day for breakfast, lunch, dinner and dessert; Bunce similarly lives solely on a diet of doughnuts injected with goose liver pâté; and Bean (the chief sadist among them, voiced by Michael Gambon) lives exclusively on a diet of his farm-produced alcoholic cider, which he avariciously hoards in a secret cellar.[2]

Bean's henchman, a giant grotesque rat voiced by Willem Dafoe, is addicted to the cider, which is repeatedly referred to as 'like melted gold', in a nod to the gluttonous stockpiling of capital. As in Anderson's film, the farmers in *Walden* are 'narrow-minded and greedy [. . .] a bitter comment on the methods of capitalist "husbandmen"' (Marx 1964: 258). In the film, the utter eradication of Mr and Mrs Fox's beech tree with rapacious insect-like bulldozers operates beyond the realm of metaphor (Figure 5.1). These literal 'machines in the garden' speak not just to the mechanisation of the landscape, but also to that of the people who rule over it.

In contrast, Mr Fox leads his animal community to near ruin by emphasising a personal, selfish need to reassert a more authentic identity above his societally prescribed roles – to de-mechanise himself by embracing his natural instincts. 'Why did you lie to me?' a tearful and exasperated Mrs Fox asks after discovering he has broken his promise to give up a life of crime. 'Because I'm a wild

Figure 5.1   In a pivotal moment, literal machines in the garden destroy Mr Fox's dream of pastoral plenitude.

animal', Mr Fox retorts. When she reminds him that he is also a husband and father, he simply replies that he wants to share the 'truth about himself'.

But Mr Fox eventually uses his natural cunning to save his community from his own hubris by constructing an elaborate plan to manipulate the entire economic system to his own ends. As such, his genius does not only reside in his nature, but in a combination of his instinctual 'foxiness' and his ability to assess and integrate the 'natural genius' found in all his animal friends. This is a particularly Romantic conception of genius as a potent mix of instinct and experience (Bate 1970: 162). In *Biographia Literaria*, Coleridge contends Shakespeare was 'no mere child of nature' but married his natural talents to patient study that 'at length gave birth to that stupendous power' ([1817] 1980: 180). So-called 'natural' genius is actually the product of both artless instinct and enduring, well-practised artifice.

When Fox rallies his troops to form a plan of counter-attack on the farmers, he addresses the animals by their Latin names in a reference to scientific biology-based nomenclature (*Lutra lutra, Castor fiber, Meles meles*). But he also references their jobs, the societal skills they have honed so finely that they have become second nature. These are 'wild animals with true natures and pure talents', as Mr Fox refers to them, but they are also skilled and learned as a result of their roles within the community. Their skills are both natural (digging) and studied (demolitions expert). Felicity Fox (whom Mr Fox notes is 'possibly the finest landscape painter working on the scene today') constructs a vast tableau of their former above-ground home underground, from memory, and the varied animal crew (badgers, moles, rabbits) use it as a tactical map, joining forces.

Mr Fox calls on the group to celebrate and utilise 'all the beautiful differences among us', in both a display of solidarity and acknowledgement of the value of heterogeneity. According to Tom Dorey, 'Anderson's central characters are naive in their belief that they are solitary geniuses of some type and need to be rehabilitated to the point where they embrace their community to finally achieve some type of positive resolution' (2012: 178). True to form, Mr Fox grows incrementally out of his role as self-absorbed Byronic hero to self-effacingly accept his role in the realisation of a greater good for all. But this growth also comes at the compromise of Felicity Fox's, and the rest of the group's, adherence to social convention.

Still living underground in a sewer by film's end, the animals discover they can perform after-hours raids on a supermarket, keeping them indefinitely supplied with food.[3] The supermarket itself could hardly be characterised as symbol of the pastoral ideal. This particular one is part of a Boggis, Bunce and Bean-owned international conglomerate, a potent symbol of late-capitalist modernity and its ills. It is full of artificial perversions of the natural (and is, of course, an entirely artificial creation outside the film's diegesis). The modern supermarket, especially the American one, is something of a staple metaphor for the affectless hole of non-feeling that encapsulates modernity itself. Its displays of pointless overabundance and overconsumption were spoofed throughout the latter decades of the twentieth century, from the extended supermarket sequence at the climax of Jean-Luc Godard and Jean-Pierre Gorin's *Tout va bien* (Anouchka Films, 1972), which juxtaposes consumer conformity with revolutionary tumult, to its function as central metaphor in Don DeLillo's 1985 novel *White Noise*, where it emanates 'a dull and unlocatable roar, as of some form of swarming life just outside the range of human apprehension' (1986: 36).

This passage conjures the muffled cry of the caged animal, an unconscious call from deep within the animal recesses of the human brain and its instinctual urges that we work so hard to suppress. Anderson's supermarket, full of gorgeous, colourful displays, bright light and bizarre products like 'goose crackles', is clearly a defamation of nature, but it feels more like a toy store than a grim example of consumer conformism. It is perhaps more along the lines of famed 1964 New York Pop Art installation *The American Supermarket*, which gleefully parodied the artificiality of modern consumerism with works from Andy Warhol, Roy Lichtenstein and 'chrome steel eggs, wax tomatoes and plaster pumpernickels' from Fluxus artist Robert Watts (Lüthy 2002: 150).

When Felicity tells Mr Fox she is pregnant again as they stand amidst the bountiful product displays, Mr Fox remarks that they are both glowing, in a call-back to the opening sequence in which only Felicity glows. Anderson cuts to a shot of the two stationary puppet figures lit from within by obviously artificial light (Figure 5.2). Drawing attention to his artifice, he still manages to

Figure 5.2 In its final supermarket scene, *Fantastic Mr. Fox* calls attention to its artifice and the circular nature of existence.

create a beautiful, stirring image of hope, love and camaraderie engendered by the most natural of life events.

That sense of qualified optimism culminates in the animals celebrating their newfound bounty with an ecstatic dance. Their abandon comes not by way of victory, necessarily, but from the celebration of their endurance, one that stems from, as Kertzer notes, 'an ironic tone of compromise' (2010: 19). Mr Fox makes a mock-heroic speech that sums up this underlying pastoral compromise found at the heart of the film:

> They say our tree may never grow back, but one day something will. Yes, these crackles are made from artificial goose and these giblets are artificial squab, and even these apples look fake – but at least they've got stars on them. I guess my point is we'll eat tonight. And we'll eat together. [. . .] So let's raise our [juice] boxes. To our survival.

This is not the stuff of self-conscious despair as expressed in DeLillo's novel as much as the playfully ironic yet optimistic tone set by *American Supermarket*. On his director's commentary track for the film's Criterion Collection DVD release, Anderson points out the discrepancy himself, putting an unsophisticated (and perhaps slightly disingenuous) spin on the mid-twentieth century response to market capitalism. 'I guess we're more inclined to something a little more natural these days', he says, 'but I guess when Dahl wrote [the book] a supermarket was thought of as something a little more like an amusement park. I mean all these chemically processed food items, they were like *futuristic*' (Anderson 2014; original emphasis).

Anderson's style, which is sometimes labelled naïve (MacDowell 2010), seems a perfect marriage for the gleeful exuberance of Dahl's children's fable, although that sense of naïveté is deceptive. As in all of Anderson's work, an undercurrent of anxiety remains at the conclusion of *Fantastic Mr. Fox*. According to Kertzer, Mr Fox 'come[s] to terms with the difference between himself and the wild wolf that he can never be, accepting that he will live underground but unable/unwilling to hunt outside the world of the supermarket' (2010: 19). Mr Fox's compromise becomes a necessary one. But it is also one that, critically, becomes a matter of perception. Indeed, in a world where industrial progress has made 'nonsense' of Emerson's pastoral ideal, to find an 'alternative to the Concord way' – that life of stifling mechanisation and rejection of individual consciousness and authenticity – one must be willing to get imaginative (Marx 1964: 264, 262).

For Thoreau, the pastoral ideal ultimately resides not 'in the natural facts or in social institutions or in anything "out there", but in consciousness', writes Marx; '[t]he writer's physical location is of no great moment' (1964: 264). No longer at their mercy, Mr Fox has remastered the use of Thoreau's 'tools' for his and his brethren's gain and reappropriated as authentic an existence as he can under the circumstances of modernity's societal machinery. Through imaginative will he creates a kind of pastoralism of the mind, transforming a precarious and perilous situation into a celebration of cunning and perseverance. This sense of imaginative repurposing permeates Anderson's film in other ways, specifically in its relation to the director's own personal history and predilections, which serve to transform a very British story into a nebulously American one.

'A NATIVE BLEND OF MYTH AND REALITY': THE LANDSCAPE OF IMAGINATION

Anderson's repurposing of a decidedly British children's story like *Fantastic Mr. Fox* allows him to examine and respond to the mythic ideal of American exceptionalism and individualism by resituating that myth within the space of his country's former colonial ruler. According to Jacqueline Rose, the relation of geography and history to a 'concept of origin' has been a staple of children's fiction since it became a commercial enterprise in the mid- to late eighteenth century: 'the idea is one of going somewhere else in order to get back to your own past' (1984: 54). That American past, of course, is rooted in the colonialism of 'civilised' Britain. But in the case of the New World, it comes with a twist: 'In the still "childlike" state of American civilisation, history could be read directly off the land (history *based* on geography), whereas if you were after the cultural origins of England, then you had to dig for them' (1984: 55; original emphasis). Mr Fox and his cohort do a monumental amount of expert digging in Anderson's film, but what they dig up is more the disappeared past of the American frontier, despite the British soil stuck between their claws.

It may seem curious to claim a film that takes place in an ostensibly English countryside – one reportedly based on Dahl's own home, Gipsy House, and its surrounding environs – and bears the authorial stamp of a revered British twentieth-century author offers a quintessentially American pastoral point of view. But Anderson's auteurist sensibilities successfully transcend and re-form his source material into an assertion of his own identity as an American artist, albeit one with some decidedly European proclivities. It is for good reason that 'Anderson is often described as an American filmmaker obsessed with a fantasy of British life' (Kertzer 2010: 6). All of his films made previous to *Moonrise Kingdom* (American Empirical, 2012) feature soundtracks that rely heavily on the so-called 'British Invasion' rock and pop of the 1960s and 1970s, a time coinciding with Anderson's childhood. As Kertzer points out, the private school setting of Anderson's *Rushmore* (American Empirical, 1998) reflects a British sensibility although it is based on Anderson's own tenure at a Texas private school (2010: 6). Even the New York-set *The Royal Tenenbaums* has the distinct air of fading British aristocracy in its depiction of a historical estate housing a storied family descending into obsolescence.

This adherence to a particular time and place also extends to Anderson's French predilections: during the same era, his primary influences from the French New Wave, Jean-Luc Godard and (most crucially) François Truffaut, were operating at the height of their artistic clout. There are several references to Truffaut films in *Fantastic Mr. Fox*, including the soundtrack, which cribs from the score of the director's *Two English Girls* (Cinétel, 1971) and the detective agency in the film's town, which is modelled after a similar one in *Stolen Kisses* (Truffaut, Les Films du Carrosse, 1968) (Anderson 2014).

As Anderson continues to make films, in fact, he has been moving both figuratively and literally further and further east, in contra-indication of the American mythic move toward the West. (His latest film at the time of writing is the Japan-set *Isle of Dogs* (American Empirical, 2018).) Anderson's aesthetic and thematic choices have mostly borne out his interest in internationalism, yet they retain a distinctly American counterpoint. In *Fantastic Mr. Fox*, for instance, he utilises several optimism-infused songs by The Beach Boys. Songs by Burl Ives, such as 'The Ballad of Davy Crockett' – based on the nineteenth-century American folk hero–politician and featuring the refrain 'king of the wild frontier' – bring to mind a quintessentially American pastoral ideal while lending a liminal quality to the film's sense of both time and place. This sense of historicism, for Anderson, is not rooted in a personal past so much as in the American cultural firmament. As Kertzer comments, the famous Burl Ives song 'evok[es] an American childhood that was already past' when Anderson was growing up (2010: 10). In the film's opening scene, Mr Fox listens to 'Davy Crockett' on his personal 'Walk-Sonic' radio, aligning him with this 'wild' frontiersman and revolutionary mythos.

Some of Anderson's references to American mythmaking are more muddled. Trains – seen as the ultimate 'machines in the garden' in Marx's text, both as a symbol of the progress of a newfound Eden and the harbinger of the end of the pastoral ideal – appear as a motif in the film, but they are simultaneously exoticised and infantilised. Young Ash and Kristofferson play with the former's Eurostar toy train set, and the 'real' Eurostar train that travels through the countryside does so in a peaceful, lateral motion in picturesque long shots. Cave paintings found in the underground holes that the animals dig evoke early Native American historicism (Figure 5.3) – although in typically nebulous fashion, Anderson points out they 'could be inspired by' Native American art or the Palaeolithic paintings of the 'French caves' of Lascaux (Anderson 2014).

NATURE VERSUS NURTURE

Figure 5.3 The film's cave paintings evoke the 'primitive' origins of humanity.

Much less ambiguous, and the key to unlocking the specifically American pastoral theme found in the film, is Anderson's use of prominent American actors (including Streep, Clooney and frequent collaborator Murray) to voice the animal characters, in contrast to the human characters, who are all voiced by Brits (including Gambon, Jarvis Cocker and Brian Cox). While some critics like Peter Bradshaw (2009) contend that Anderson falls back on Hollywood stereotypes of American heroes and British villains, this choice seems based on cultural origins and a specifically American version of mythmaking. It offers a strong argument for Anderson's depiction of the Romantic myth of America as an untamed wild full of utopian possibility, emphasising Marx's 'American myth of a new beginning' (1964: 228). Here the animal acts as a kind of proxy for Shelley's 'savage', as well as for the human child itself.

Finally, if the film is set in England, it is clearly a fantastical version of it, and not simply because it features animals who can talk and wear clothes and are made out of terrycloth, felt and faux fur. It also contains geographical and zoological impossibility: wolves, one of which plays a key role in the narrative, are not native to England and are therefore unnatural in this context, as are the film's mountainous landscapes that the wolf calls home (Kertzer 2010: 11). This is not simply England; this is Anderson's England, which is equally American (and possibly a little French). Like Walden Pond in Thoreau's book, 'it appears to be another embodiment of the American moral geography – a native blend of myth and reality' (Marx 1964: 245). Owing to its purely constructed diegetic world and its literal puppet characters, *Fantastic Mr. Fox* represents the first time that Anderson can completely control every minute aspect of his mise-en-scène. This lends him total freedom to create while paradoxically being resoundingly controlled by his personal obsessions, bowled over by his own genius.

All the while he poses his artifice as artless, a product of his unconscious natural instincts as much as a learned craft. For Thoreau, unconsciousness was lauded as 'an equivalent of vision' (Hartman 1970: 56), and Anderson's continual disavowal of conscious knowledge of many of his creative decisions helps perpetuate this Romanticised conception of his work and artistic status. As much as the film is about Anderson's own obsessions, though, it has greater cultural resonances. In its treatment of childhood, it exhibits an awareness of Romantic conceptions of 'natural origins' and childhood's relationship to both individual and cultural progress.

Little Savages in the Garden: Ash, Kristofferson and the Romantic Child

The figure of the child plays a key role in the examination of personal, societal and cultural origins in the film. The Romantic child symbolises these origins, representing the natural human state before it becomes progressively civilised. Rousseau describes this process as a loss of 'equilibrium' and argues that in nature, all humans lack pronounced differences that would 'make one dependent on another' (1763: 212). For Rousseau, this means that 'natural man' was autonomous and therefore truly free. In societal terms, the child was believed to 'represent the childhood of the race as a whole' (Rowland 2012: 10). This view was the result of 'stadial theory', the idea that 'human societies [. . .] move through a series of "stages" or "states" in an order or pattern that was relatively uniform and stable' and that through the development of one child we can trace the development of the entire human race (2012: 43).

The child enjoys 'special access' to a primitive mode of being, becoming 'something of a pioneer who restores these worlds to us [. . .] with a facility or directness which ensures that our own relationship to them is, finally, safe' (Rose 1984: 9). We can access these primitive states through the child's innocence and supposed freedom without compromising our privileged civilised status. The children's story is often used to address these ideas, especially since children's fiction is thought to be as much about the liminal space between childhood and adulthood as it is any kind of prescriptive for civilising that childish nature (1984: 1). Perhaps surprisingly then, Dahl's book contains no major child characters. (Mr Fox's multiple children are not even named.) But Anderson adds two important child characters to his retelling: Mr Fox's bewildering and confrontational son, Ash, and his sophisticated and gentle nephew, Kristofferson, who comes to live with the family because his own father is suffering a prolonged illness.

As in much of children's fiction, Anderson's child characters are often viewed through an adult lens. This can lead to a simplistic reading of Anderson's attitudes to childhood as coming from a position of nostalgic longing for the naïveté and purity of 'innocence' and the child's perceived wildness or closer relationship to nature. However, as Peter Kunze acknowledges, Anderson creates worlds with developmental overlap between children and adults that 'blur [. . .] sharp distinctions' between the two (2014: 95). It is not so much that his adult characters act like children and his children are preternaturally adult – rather, they exist as a testament to the idea that the linear sense of progress from 'childish' to 'adult' behaviour is a false, artificial construct (2014: 102). There is no sense of reaching a finish line or a clear demarcation point; characters such as Mr Fox exhibit a continual recapitulation of personal development just as the child supposedly recapitulates the entire cultural progress of humanity. Anderson's adult characters 'continually retraverse their own signification, rediscovering it in image while attempting its subsequent co-optation' (Gooch 2007: 29). That is, they perpetually recall and recapture their earlier selves in an attempt to construct meaning in their present identities. As a result, personal history becomes paramount; 'The child is the father of the man' is an Andersonian principle, but Anderson does not deny that the child remains after the 'man' is revealed.

Childhood is not celebrated as a naïve state of innocence in Anderson's films but instead is rife with the 'danger' that the Romantics acknowledged. His child characters suffer from supposedly adult tribulations, and are often as glum, depressive, confused and even borderline antisocial as his adults are (Kunze 2014: 103), even as they construct hopelessly unsophisticated ideas about what it means to be adult. Wildness remains long after civilisation, and the pressing problems of civilisation infect the presumed 'wildness' of childhood. In Anderson's worlds, adults never really lose their childish nature and thus never totally lose their link to the natural world.[4] In a sense, this constitutes a desire to reattain that Rousseauian equilibrium lost by the civilising process, but its integration always remains a tentative one at best. Mr Fox is part Rousseau's 'savage man': 'self sufficient [. . .] he felt only his true needs, saw only what he believed he had an interest to see; and his intelligence made no more progress than his vanity' (Rowland 2012: 94). He is undoubtedly 'subject to strong passions, but also to express those passions more directly' (2012: 94). But he is also a charismatic 'genius', full of wit and rakish charm, a loveable rogue who is as much capable of following chivalric codes as he is killing a chicken in one bite.

Fantastic Mr. Fox's two key child characters, Ash and Kristofferson (the latter voiced by the director's brother, Eric Anderson), represent this dichotomy between wildness and civilisation in the film, and are primarily representative of Mr Fox's struggle between his natural instincts and his societal obligations. The differences between the two are obvious and striking and played for comic effect, as is Ash's jealousy of his much more worldly cousin. In a sense, their differences are akin to those between the Old World and the New: while Ash attempts to construct a personal identity as hero and crusader based on his *White Cape* superhero comic (complete with a uniform of white cape fashioned from a towel), Kristofferson, who comes from 'the other side of the river', is an unassuming, contemplative, well-mannered child with an affinity for yoga, martial arts and other international/Eastern pursuits. Even his choice of bathing suit, a very European-style Speedo, suggests his more cosmopolitan outlook. His unusual name, which Anderson does not explain the origins of, evokes an exotic version of Christopher, but also recalls Texas-born singer-songwriter and actor Kris Kristofferson, a paragon of the sensitive artist secure in his quiet masculinity.

Despite being younger than Ash, Kristofferson is taller and already the accomplished athlete that Ash insists he is but clearly is not. He quietly excels without fuss, while Ash functions on the level of pure Id, never neglecting to loudly share his frustrated feelings of wanting to be the best despite being – as is often denoted in the film with a characteristic wiggling-armed hand-gesture – 'different'. Kristofferson, himself quite alien to the Fox family, seems content to just be, secure in the knowledge of his talent and morality. Ash is rude, coarse and infantile, while Kristofferson is polite, genteel and mature.

If 'the "New World" is also the ancient past, its frontier the place where man's future and origin exist together' (Rowland 2012: 45) – as in John Locke's famous phrase, 'in the beginning all the World was America' (Locke 1689: 18) – then Ash represents this New World. He is a wild child in developmental infancy, eager to prove his worth but yet to find his niche. Anderson scores Ash's bedroom scenes with more Burl Ives to underscore the connection between Mr Fox's revolutionary spirit and that of his son. Conversely, Kristofferson represents the established, worldly, secure and even complacent outlook of the Old World. It is key that in the narrative's climax the two boys work together to help realise the family's qualified success. Together, they represent the pastoral middle ground, a place where nature and nurture coexist in a benevolent equilibrium.

According to Rowland, the Romantic child historically encompasses these dual states, simultaneously located in the 'distant past' of cultural and developmental infancy and the 'present and future' through the child's education and eventual enculturation (2012: 32). Together, these 'two figures' of the child produce 'simultaneous ancestor and progeny, past and future, an embodiment of both wisdom and ignorance' (2012: 32). Taken as a unit, Ash and Kristofferson form this quintessential Romantic child, serving to help Mr Fox realise his own identity, or 'ideal self':

> The 'Romantic Child' has often been seen as central to the delineation of what has been called the 'Romantic self,' that private, interior and natural version of subjectivity, identity and individual growth. [. . .] Representing the ideal self in and through the figure of the child is thus an act of privileging the interior life of feeling and memory as what constitutes the self. (Rowland 2012: 26)

As Mr Fox relives his own developmental history through Ash, instead of being 'fantastic' he experiences 'difference' in the pejorative sense. Ash's artifice is a blatant construct, clumsy and transparent, a cardinal sin for Mr Fox. But while Kristofferson appears to be Mr Fox's ideal on the surface, appealing to his cosmopolitan social pretensions and pose of self-assuredness, he is far too civilised to be so. Kristofferson's more international proclivities, ironically, seem suspect to Mr Fox from the moment he sees his nephew doing yoga, a Zen practice that betrays his lack of the wild spark and subsequent fire that fuels Fox's *raison d'être*. While Mr Fox appreciates Kristofferson's 'raw, natural talents' enough to invite him on a farm raid, he only ever really uses those talents as a tool in attaining his own selfish goals.

Ultimately, Mr Fox accepts both Kristofferson and Ash when the two children form an undeniable bond while attempting to retrieve Mr Fox's shot-off tail from Bean, which creatively communicates their desire to become more integrated and accepted into the familial bonds through action. According to Steven Rybin, Anderson's formations of family are 'aesthetic event[s]', largely makeshift communities created by the efforts of characters themselves, who enable these formations through their own creative enterprise (2014: 40). In this way these characters are as much metaphors for Anderson and his relationships as they are standalone personalities. The director's older brother, Eric, points out that the two young foxes' rivalry is quite similar to that of himself and his brother – although Wes, in typical fashion, professes to be unaware of the connection (Kertzer 2010: 14).

Ash and Kristofferson could also be construed as identity projections of Anderson's own childhood self, as well as a depiction of this autobiographical sibling relationship. While Mr Fox may be Anderson's ultimate stand-in in the film, Ash and Kristofferson clearly represent two sides of warring personal behaviours and ideals not just to his protagonist, but also to Anderson; their coming together in the bonds of both family and friendship represents a successful personal integration for both main character and auteur. And while the family at the centre of *Fantastic Mr. Fox* is more of a traditional nuclear one than in many of Anderson's films, they do form something of a makeshift team with the addition of the opossum Kylie (Wallace Wolodarsky) and Kristofferson. The latter, it is pointedly noted, is not related to Mr Fox – the sun at the centre of this familial universe – 'by blood'.

Likewise, the entire animal community as a whole can be seen as exemplary of what Rybin characterises as 'the discovery of new forms of family and community' through the 'artistic events' spearheaded by the (paradoxically antisocial) genius of Mr Fox (2014: 39). Together they form a new society out of the cast-offs of their old civilisation and in this way recapitulate the discovery and cultural infancy of a 'new world' – one full of hope in rebirth despite its relegation to a literal sewer. Like Thoreau before him (in another myth-making turn), Anderson places emphasis on 'building the new from old materials' in a symbolic act of renewal and finds 'redemption of the ordinary through close attention and exalted imagination' (Fender 1997: xxxvi–xliii).

In much the same way that *Walden* is a 'spiritual autobiography' for Thoreau (1997: xxxviii), so *Fantastic Mr. Fox* is for Anderson. This connection is made explicit by Anderson's physical depiction of his lead character. When Mr Fox is at his 'straight' job, he wears a conservative suit and tie; when he is giving into his natural cunning, he wears a mustard-yellow corduroy suit, reportedly fashioned from the same material as a suit Anderson often sported himself during the production (Kunze 2014: 99). Anderson has metaphorically cast himself as the cunning fox: driven by his varied, often contradictory predilections, he still manages to create satisfying works of beauty amid roiling chaos. The overall optimistic tone of the film, however, does not shrink from Anderson's typical expressions of melancholy. Here they are exemplified by the necessity of giving up pure animal nature in order to achieve the pastoral ideal.

Mourning the Loss of Animal Nature

The cultural link between animals and childhood, which principally developed in the eighteenth century, is well documented. Infancy was classified as a 'border state [. . .] a human-becoming animal or an animal with hidden human resources' (Rowland 2012: 110). According to Rowland, 'scenes of children learning to read also become newly significant as enacting another crucial step in the process of becoming human' (2012: 110). It is no accident that Ash is seen learning how to navigate the world of adult responsibility through his *White Cape* comic books – almost all children in Anderson's films are linked to the written word, either as fiction authors, letter writers or obsessive readers. If children are little 'savages', they are also animals in the process of becoming human.

All the humanised animals of Anderson's film, not just Ash and Kristofferson, can be taken as avatars for children, albeit ones that not only 'cognize, will and effect' (2012: 113) but grasp their capacity to do so. C. Ryan Knight has drawn attention to Anderson's use of animals in his films generally. Knight claims that the loss of animals (specifically pets) 'marks the point where [Anderson's characters] become ready and able to reconnect with their family and community' (2014: 66). In beholding the animal, a representation of the other, people are able to 'better construct identity [and] morality' (2014: 66). But what happens when the animals are beholding each other? Romantic studies of human development increasingly questioned the idea of human uniqueness, even regarding what were once seen as solely human qualities like the capacity for language (Rowland 2012: 109, 121). As Rowland notes, 'The natural and developmental history of language and literature [. . .] assumes man's animal origins and asserts significant continuities, rather than categorical distinctions, between animals and humans' (2012: 109). Indeed, *Fantastic Mr. Fox* is not so much about anthropomorphising the animal as it is locating the animal within the human.

Knight regards the animals in the film as indicative of the human struggle between 'gentle and loving' civilisation and the 'harsh' animal world of instinct (2014: 72) with the conclusion leading to 'Fox as committed wholeheartedly to the well-being of those around him' (2014: 73). But that conclusion suggests a false dichotomy. As I hope to have shown, the film is about a search for an aesthetic and ideological middle ground. Mr Fox does learn a lesson, but the lesson is that animal cunning and civilisation (the latter as much stifling as it is 'loving') can fit hand in glove if certain compromises are made. And it is difficult to view Mr Fox as losing much of his self-interested egomania by film's end. (In the final scene, he gets up on a literal soapbox to make yet another grandiose speech.) If anything, his natural cunning has allowed him to commit to his social group while still allowing him the spoils of his exploits.

Even the relationship between animal species in the film is complicated by Anderson's aesthetic and narrative choices. While the principal characters in *Mr Fox* clearly function as human avatars, there are animals in the film that are not anthropomorphised, or only vaguely so. If the 'sympathetic communication' between humans and animals is 'a major topos of Romantic and sentimental literary culture' (Rowland 2012: 124), the relation between humans and animals (and non-humanised animals) in the film ranges from unclear to antagonistic. Anderson himself remains purposefully vague on the subject: 'We were always trying to puzzle out how the humans and animals interact. Do the people see that these guys [the animals] are wearing shirts and corduroy suits? I don't know' (Anderson 2014). Mr Fox and his friends are trapped in a sort of liminal world unto themselves. Their relation to the ordinary world of humans and animals is contested, creating a slight undercurrent of anxiety for the viewer typical of Anderson's films.

According to Akira Lippit, 'In supernatural terms, modernity finds animals lingering in the world *undead*' in 'a society now defined by the disappearance of wildlife from humanity's habitat and by the reappearance of the same in humanity's reflections on itself' (2000: 1, 2–3; original emphasis). That is, the animal attains a new abstract cultural significance because it has been mostly erased from everyday presence. As such, it becomes 'the very figure of modernity itself': 'denied the status of conscious objects, animals were now sought as the ideal figures of a destabilized subjectivity' (2000: 25–6). In *Fantastic Mr. Fox*, the lone wolf represents this ideal of the defaced and erased animal. As Anderson suggests, the wolf is 'a *real* wild animal' (Anderson 2014; original emphasis). Living a harsh, solitary life in the true wilderness, he does not have time for idle conversation or self-indulgent hijinks.[5] The very mention of wolves causes profound anxiety in Mr Fox. ('It's not a phobia, I'm just afraid of them', he insists.) The acknowledgement of true wildness will force him to admit he is of a different kind altogether.

While driving his getaway motorbike, Mr Fox finally encounters the feared creature face to face. When he answers the wolf's raised-fist salute in kind, it is not just an expression of solidarity among animals; it is also an acknowledgement of the wild animal's struggle, which can never be Mr Fox's own.[6] The wolf exemplifies the 'lost object' found at the heart of modernity, to be mourned, but not for itself (Lippit 2000: 3). According to Lippit, in the modern era the foreignness of the animal reflects on our own sense of self:

> The animal came to inhabit a new topology of its own, and humanity was left to mourn the loss of its former self. *The mourning is for the self* – a self that had become dehumanized in the very process of humanity's becoming-human. (Lippit 2000: 18; my emphasis)

With the wolf, we return to the Romantic idea of nature holding up a mirror to human consciousness. Animality can function in much the same way as the whole of nature, as a seduction 'bring[ing] humanity to the threshold of its subjectivity' through the animal gaze (2000: 51). The 'lost object' glimpsed in this gaze is not the animal but 'the former, pre-egoical self', which 'is treated with an ambivalence that frequently takes the form of hostility' (2000: 18). For Mr Fox, that projection of ambivalence is directed toward the wolf, just as the farmers direct their hostility toward the fox. The fundamental difference is that Mr Fox comes to terms with his loss, while Boggis, Bunce and Bean forever spin their mechanised wheels in renunciation of the animal other as a way to deny their own animal origins.

The fox, like his creator – and we can safely say he is the creation of Anderson, inspired by Dahl – finds a compromise, a middle ground, in which to pursue his creative goals. M. H. Abrams notes that many Romantic works 'turn on the theme of hope and joy and the temptation to abandon all hope and fall into dejection and despair' (1970: 108). According to Abrams, 'Infinite longings are inherent in the human spirit, and [. . .] the gap between the inordinacy of his hope and the limits of possibility is the measure of man's dignity and greatness' (1970: 109). The measure of Mr Fox's dignity lies in his spirited ability to find hope even while stuck in a sewer. Rather than wallowing in a mournful, melancholic nostalgia for a disappeared true wildness, the 'fantastic' Mr Fox salutes the wild animal (and the wild animal within) and acknowledges his peril. Then he motors on hopefully, the children safely in tow.

Conclusion

Anderson's film relates to Henry David Thoreau's brand of American pastoralism found within his imaginative memoir *Walden*, as well as the concept of historical recapitulation as exemplified by the child's position within Romantic philosophy. Through an exploration of the anthropomorphised animal protagonist's relationship to nature, society, childhood and the author of the text – which is ultimately himself, not Dahl – Anderson depicts a highly personal worldview that features ambivalent compromise at its core. This pastoral compromise offers an optimistic depiction of animalistic craftiness and the power of heterogeneous community combined with a rebuke of the dehumanising and monomaniacal societal machinery that opposes it.

Fantastic Mr. Fox reaches a tentative yet hopeful conclusion about its protagonist (who serves as Anderson's alter ego), his creative vision and the social bonds he forms. However, it also features a tinge of anxious regret for the animal nature now lost to him. What is lost is to be mourned, but not to the point of pathology. After all, what is found – the latent creative genius always dwelling within – can be harnessed for new visionary goals. The animal remains hidden in liminal territories, but it has not been 'effaced' according to the brutal dualism of a 'dialectic of humanism' which subsumes it (Lippit 2000: 45). Instead, the animal resides within, in the unconscious recesses of the creative imagination, accessed freely and intuitively and shaped into works of art.

Anderson acknowledges, celebrates and mourns this animal nature, but he does so while simultaneously recognising the human ability to synthesise natural impulse, not annihilate it. As such, the loss is an ambivalent one, for it is the source of our greatest power and our deepest regret: the fall from nature. By exploring the cultural and individual recapitulation of the child amidst the 'multiplicity' (Lippit 2000: 131) of the natural, animalistic being, Anderson's film asserts the creative vision of the individual as well as celebrates the bonds of the human social project.

Like *Fantastic Mr. Fox*, Sofia Coppola's imaginative biopic *Marie Antoinette* engages with the Romantic themes of childhood and maturation, revolution and imaginary historicism. In Chapter 6, I explore all these ideas, but also engage explicitly with the implied ethical discourse I have been making throughout this book. This discourse is, in essence, about an ethics of compromise, one that leaves room for constant renegotiation. The films themselves take ethical stances by questioning dogmatism and absolutes, instead favouring highly personal expressions of an ethical relationship between self and world. Coppola's film specifically expresses an ethical relation through its ambivalent engagement with excess. In this way, it shares particular resonances with the work of the poet John Keats and his veneration of the material sublime.

6. 'IT'S NOT TOO MUCH, IS IT?': KEATS, FANCY AND THE ETHICS OF PLEASURABLE EXCESS IN SOFIA COPPOLA'S *MARIE ANTOINETTE*

O, sweet Fancy! let her loose;
Every thing is spoilt by use

John Keats, 'Fancy' (1820)

Sofia Coppola's third feature, *Marie Antoinette* (Columbia Pictures, 2006), was her first to be met with a large amount of critical rancour. Even somewhat positive reviews could not resist making digs at the director's supposedly insensitive dismissal of historical realities. According to the BBC, Coppola creates a confection that 'mightn't be food for the soul, but [. . .] is a pleasurable sugar rush' (Papamichael 2006). The film's marketing campaign emphasises these flimsy-as-candyfloss conceptions; the 2007 British DVD release splashes a pandering quote from *Empire* magazine on its hot pink cover, proclaiming the film 'the ultimate chick flick, a love letter to cake, Moët, pyjama parties and rampant romps'. The fact that this does not adequately represent Coppola's film is simply beside the point for many detractors; that she could lend a historical narrative ostensibly about life-and-death revolutionary turmoil the mere appearance of frivolity is crime enough.

Just as with the marginalisation of the so-called 'chick flick' today, the novel of the eighteenth and early nineteenth centuries was similarly dismissed as seductively feminine and superficial, offering a meal that, while seemingly satisfying to the popular taste, contained little real nourishment (Webb 2010: 150). Samantha Webb considers how consumption practices of these novels were couched in metaphors of eating, 'both as indicators of aesthetic value and as descriptions of reception practices' (2010: 150). These 'edible books' were considered 'low', 'populist', and (according to Wordsworth) 'food for fickle tastes, and fickle appetites' (2010: 149). A direct line between these feminised narrative forms of the eighteenth century and *Marie Antoinette* can be drawn – it has essentially been derided as an edible film, delicious and decadent in its excess but not suitably filling. In some ways, it is a perfect metaphor for a narrative that itself deals with out-of-control, unwholesome consumption.

Addressing Wordsworth's 'range of anxieties about the power of representations' in her writing on 'The Ruined Cottage', Karen Swann points to excesses of the literary culture of the early nineteenth century and their link to 'popular sensational fiction, feminine characters and plots, and a feminine or feminized audience' (1991: 90). Under this rubric, Swann asserts, Wordsworth composed his poem with an eye to straddling popular 'feminine narrative machinery' and the far more exalted world of high Romantic poetry, appealing to an 'audience whose pleasure it is to exist at a small distance from the captivated feminine heart' (1991: 84). In this way he was appropriating, in reflexive fashion, the popular tastes of the day while simultaneously challenging those tastes (1991: 93).

With *Marie Antoinette*, Coppola attempts a similar transposition of 'high' and 'low' (or, more precisely, masculine and feminine) through her aesthetic excessiveness combined with a 'small distance' from her subjects. As in V. F. Perkins's notion of cinematic 'aesthetic suspense', the combination suggests both 'subjective alignment and autonomy of viewpoint' (Clayton 2016: 214). She has made a film *about* feminine excess, more specifically the excess of consumption. But while Wordsworth uses the feminised tropes of his time to 'entice and reprove' (Swann 1991: 93), Coppola presents at a sympathetic remove. It is possible the less-than-glowing critical reception of *Marie Antoinette* can be chalked up to its portrayal of this excessive 'feminine heart' at an uncritical distance – not because Coppola is passing judgement on her characters or her audience, but precisely because she is not.

Richard Rushton invokes Stanley Cavell's concept of the 'melodramas of the unknown woman' in relating Marie Antoinette in Coppola's film to a 'world of "moral catastrophe"', one that denies her the will to self-determination (2014: 114, 124). Rushton, while asserting that the film is an ethical text, downplays the significance of its depictions of excessive consumption (2014: 121). However, I believe these sequences are crucial to Marie's construction of self-identity and thus are part of the film's overall ethical stance; while they do not ultimately prove satisfying and soul-making for the film's protagonist, they represent Marie's desire to construct a feeling of wholeness through pleasurable consumption – a striving for the Kantian good of beauty that inadvertently achieves a state of sublimity through indecorous material excess.

Coppola's retelling of the life story of the French queen, from just before her first appearance at Versailles at the tender age of fourteen to her forced exile in her thirties (skipping the gruesome climax at the guillotine), is indeed more concerned with surface detail and the day-to-day activities of its subject, largely removed from the political sphere of the French court. But this does not make Coppola's film any less political, even as it represents history as transhistorical anachronism through fashion. Nor is Coppola's approach to the waning days of the decadent *ancien régime* a less ethical one as a result of its emphasis on personal history. Coppola's uncritical stance is the very essence of her ethical approach.

As the film's star, Kirsten Dunst, phrases it, *Marie Antoinette* is 'like a history of feelings rather than a history of facts' (O'Hagan 2006). Jennifer Milam claims the film not only 'question[s] the authority of history' but also deconstructs history completely, 'through an insistence upon the authority of individual response and personal imagination' (2011: 47). True to Romantic form, Coppola's film is not interested in didacticism. The Romantic doctrine declares that art itself, not 'models of righteousness', can create virtue (Campbell 2005: 187) by 'sensitizing, purifying and strengthening the feelings' (Abrams 1953: 330). Instead, the film's virtue relies on creating sense impressions of events through a sympathetic, non-judgemental fellow feeling between filmmaker and filmic subject.

As Rosalind Galt points out in her discussion of *Marie Antoinette*, 'Unlike much writing on decorative commodity cultures, this discourse on the historical objecthood of the female body strikingly refuses to blame the woman for her out-of-control consumption' (2011: 22). Coppola refers to her first three films (*The Virgin Suicides*, *Lost in Translation* and *Marie Antoinette*) as a trilogy concerning the experience of growth into womanhood: '[*Marie Antoinette* is] a continuation of the other two films – sort of about a lonely girl in a big hotel or palace or whatever, kind of wandering around, trying to grow up', she tells the *New York Times* (Hohenadel 2006).[1]

The film can, like *The Virgin Suicides*, be analysed via an aesthetic commitment to the 'pretty' as discussed in Chapter 3; it similarly asserts a commitment to colour and feminine surface splendour at the expense of a masculine and modernist desire for utilitarian value and reason. Coppola portrays both the sense of freedom and enclosure that materiality brings through surface decoration, framing, performance and depictions of pleasurable sensation, especially those of sight, taste and most pointedly touch. As Saige Walton notes, 'movement, materiality, decorative décor, surfaces, and textures function as highly charged repositories of meaning in this film' (2016: 153). It might seem like this preoccupation with materiality and sensory experience goes against the

Romantic veneration of the ideal. But in many striking ways, Coppola continues the projects of John Keats, whose form of 'concrete idealism' (Bate 2012: 46) distinguished him from earlier Romantics such as Coleridge in his confinement to the particular and the empirical (2012: 38) and his expression of the 'pervasive eroticism' underlying Romantic thought (Singer 2009: 295).

Fancy and Material Excess as Alternative Romantic Discourse

Keats's personal philosophy of 'negative capability' (Keats 1970: 43) and a reverence for the 'material sublime' (Keats 1976: 237) champions an ethical engagement with material reality at the expense of ego, energetically calling for a 'Life of Sensations rather than of Thoughts' (1970: 37). This Keatsian life contains a wish 'for *sensory* surfeit, not the grand immateriality' (Winakur Tontplaphol 2010: 46; original emphasis) of what Keats refers to as 'the dark void of night' in the 1818 poem 'To J. H. Reynolds, Esq.' (1976: 237). This dark void, in essence, is the Wordsworthian 'egotistical sublime', a phrase Keats himself coined (1970: 157), which emphasises the mind's idealisation of experience at the expense of the concrete. (See Chapter 3 for more on this notion of sublimity.) There is a direct contrast, in Keats's vision, between *thinking* and *feeling* – the former abstracts the world; the latter reaches out toward it in sensuous communion.

Jeffrey Cane Robinson describes how in the Romantic period, the idea of 'fancy' in poetry became inextricable with notions of bad taste and frivolity, just as had the popular emergence of the novel. Characterised by an inherently feminine sensibility, fancy represents superficial excess, 'bent on proliferation, on sheer imagery and association rather than on discursive coherence, on multiplicity rather than unity, or excess rather than control' (Robinson 2006: 6). Robinson insists that this denigration of fancy is wrong-footed and misconstrues much of the project of Romanticism. He argues that, as Romantic art reflected the 'politically charged temperament' and critique of social institutions both preceding and following the American and French revolutions, so fancy in Romantic art offered a 'politically radical poetics' (2006: 1). This poetics was highly 'subversive' and 'progressive' in its celebration of the 'mind's freedom within an oppositional philosophical framework that actively seeks to constrain perception' (2006: 2, 4). This sense of the fancy is inextricably linked to perception through the body, which 'awaken[s] the conscious mind to a defamiliarized and therefore truer version of a world' (2006: 5).

According to Robinson, while Keats's earlier work falls squarely within the tradition of the poetic fancy, it is often critically dismissed as a simple part of the process of maturation along the road to an exhibited scepticism of fancy and an overall 'disinterested tragic attitude' (2006: 36). To the contrary, '[a]t least as much as he gravitates toward the "depths," Keats is drawn – in the way of the Fancy – to the surface', Robinson asserts (2006: 142). This manifestation of fancy facilitates 'poetry of the liberation of body and mind', in part a defiance of the 'Western (masculine) lyric' of canonical Romantic poetry (2006: 144). According to Lionel Trilling, 'The complex of pleasure-sensuality-luxury makes the very fabric of [Keats's] thought' (1965: 67). This Keatsian combination is readily apparent in Coppola's film and represents a mode of psychosocial recuperation for its protagonist.

Marie Antoinette's own engagement with pleasurable materiality in an environment that denies her subjectivity and personal freedom constitutes her campaign against the powers that confine and diminish her, as well as her self-expression as a creative being. In fact, she uses the very tools of fashion to construct and reconstruct a sense of identity as a veritable 'declaration of independence' (Flores 2013: 614). Coppola's film exhibits a reverence for fancy that can be attributed to a subversive desire for pleasure and playfulness, aligning it with a more typically feminised view, derided as 'culturally less "serious"' (Robinson 2006: 16). Fancy, according to Robinson, is a 'natural poetics' for women, excluded as they are from the traditional space of the masculine ego (2006: 16). If it is seen to have a political mission, it is one of 'mak[ing] visible [. . .] that which was not seen or heard for itself' (2006: 16).

The feminine 'voice' within mainstream filmmaking is, of course, a seriously marginalised one in our own time, as much as if not more so than a feminine poetics was in the eighteenth and nineteenth centuries.[2] As Lisa Downing writes in relation to postmodern ethics in the cinema in general, *Marie Antoinette* represents 'tantalizing and plural ethical alternatives to the universalizing [. . .] discourses of modernism' (2009c: 148). While it makes sense for a high-profile female filmmaker like Coppola to turn to a more traditionally feminine mode of aesthetics in order to assert alternatives to the overwhelming dominance of masculine modernism, it makes her work decidedly vulnerable to attack as being capricious, trivial and superficial.

The denigration of fancy in Romantic poetry aligns closely with Rosalind Galt's description of a similar Western distaste for the 'pretty' in cinema and visual art, as detailed in Chapter 3. Galt recounts the influence of Kantian ideas about beauty and taste on early filmmaking practices, ideas which have endured to the present (2011: 38). Beauty is associated with 'value', whereas the pretty is merely of interest, a frivolous distraction (2011: 55). According to Galt, for Kant, moral good (the value of beauty and taste) is based on conceptions of masculine *dis*interest, not the seduction of feminine 'charms and emotions' (2011: 54). The 'pretty' and pleasure are inextricably linked because they both lead down the path of excess without the moral check of reason. 'To be beautiful is to be good, whereas to be pretty is to simply look good', writes Galt (2011: 52). As a result, filmic realism began to embrace depictions of 'ugliness' as a true form of beauty, as 'a lack of visual appeal is necessary to access the true' (2011: 51). This ugliness is rooted, in terms of cinematic realism, in an authenticity that is anathema to the ornamental, as it supposedly strips away surface pleasures to reveal the hidden depths within.

Thus, according to Galt, 'the modern becomes a central term in aligning the cinematic with the anti-pretty', and this anti-pretty discourse is conveyed via 'the language [. . .] of corruption and disease' (2011: 63). As well, the discourse of realism places the pretty squarely within the realm of the inauthentic, engaging in 'false aesthetics and false reality [. . .] too picturesque, too attractive [. . .] to be either art or life' (2011: 61). There is a clear moral implication here, which places 'the pretty outside of the discourse of the good' (2011: 69). Conversely, realism invokes sublimity in its transcendence of materiality, commitment to 'transparency and purity' and 'historical refusal of the pleasurable and sensual' (2011: 72). In the space of cinematic realism, there is precious little place for play, and even less for pleasure. 'The new masculine modern style values the ordinary, profilmic world, but it must also emphasize that this world is pure and lacking feminine excess', Galt writes (2011: 68–9), which by necessity excludes the impure pretty.

Coppola's vision of stylistic excess is in tune with what V. F. Perkins calls 'aesthetic suspense', which he defines as 'an intensification' that is 'calculated to arrive at, but not to pass, the edge of absurdity' (1996: 226). Alex Clayton elaborates on Perkins's definition, which is connected to notions of good and bad taste. Aesthetic suspense 'results from the perception that we are only a whisker away from risibility' (Clayton 2016: 212), straddling 'the line between aestheticism and naturalism, mystification and cliché' (2016: 214). *Marie Antoinette*'s expressions of excess punctuate the film throughout. Like many of the films I have discussed in other chapters, it straddles this line of emotional engagement with the spectator and a self-acknowledged aesthetic absurdity.

Throughout the film, an ambivalence remains, one personified by its protagonist. As I will show, in many respects Marie Antoinette represents an aesthetic and ideological schism: she inhabits the crossroads of the beautiful and the sublime; fancy and the 'mature' imagination; the *ancien régime*'s crumbling aristocratic decadence and the new values of bourgeois democratic individualism; passive consumption and active creativity; profound suffering and unmitigated pleasure.

Coppola – who adapts her screenplay from the bestselling 2001 biography by Antonia Fraser, *Marie Antoinette: The Journey* – manages the feat of taking a woman who was, for the revolutionary, decried as a symbol of the decadent and corrupt old order and turning her into the tragic, grasping heroine of her own highly Romantic *Bildungsroman*.[3] She abandons the genre of the fact-based historical biopic and instead crafts a melodrama more interested, like Keats, in a life of emotion and sensation than in settling the historic record. Coppola remarked to Fraser that Fraser's depiction of Marie's story was 'the best one [. . .] *full of life*, not a dry historical drama' (A. Fraser 2006; my emphasis), and this sense of organic 'life' is what drives the work of Keats. For Keats, '[m]yth and symbol contained more truth than any careful, "true-to-life" observation and actuality' (Campbell 2005: 186), and the same can be said for Coppola's film. It does not represent the 'truth' of grand historical narratives so much as embody a sense of what Downing has called being 'true to itself' (2009c: 150).

Coppola's production gained unprecedented access to actual Versailles locations during shooting (Hohenadel 2006), which lends the film a degree of authenticity the director nevertheless has no compunction undermining. The film is comprised of four discrete sections: Marie's marriage to the dauphin and struggle to consummate the union and bear a much-needed male heir to the throne; her days of lavish, decadent parties and voracious consumption with a coterie of favourites; her time spent in the relative seclusion of her Petit Trianon retreat; and the later years on the cusp of revolution, when she comes to accept her place in the court and her ultimate fate.

Throughout, Coppola's unique mix of sympathy and objectivity define her narrative as well as aesthetic aims. That Marie's campaign is ultimately unfulfilling and betrays tragic consequences for her own life is, as Galt writes, not a subject of judgement for Coppola. As Robinson argues, fancy's reluctance to render a clear point of view or ego-identification, similar to Keats's negative capability, lends the perceiver the 'relative freedom to think – not in a free space designed for contemplation but in the midst of conflict and opposition' (2006: 41). The film is rife with such oppositions and conflicts, and thus questionings, at the level of both style and character.

Early scenes when Marie first arrives at the palace and enters her private apartment are shot from her point of view or with the camera tracking from over her shoulder, aligning the spectator's sight with the character's and filmmaker's as she struggles to take in the scene. Quickly point-of-view shots are juxtaposed with images of Marie on display: she sits in front of her dressing table mirror and unfurls a fan in front of her face, checking her appearance (Figure 6.1). In the next shot, she stares out a window contemplatively and we again see her point of view: the intimidating and overly regimented Versailles gardens in all their formal aesthetic rigour. The contrast between prettified decorative excess and the arch lines and geometric formations in the interior and exterior respectively hint at the aesthetic tightrope Marie must walk in order to be accepted by the court, just as a mix of point-of-view and presentational, self-image-oriented shots speak to her as frightened child and object on display.

Scenes strongly depicting Marie's point of view appear again, such as the wedding scene, and hand-held close-ups of her face are utilised when she breaks down in sobs behind her bedroom door, but Dunst is largely shot from the point of view of an objective spectator, often as one fragile component of

KEATS, FANCY AND THE ETHICS OF PLEASURABLE EXCESS

Figure 6.1 Marie's point of view of the sneering, sceptical royal court is quickly contrasted with images of her studying herself as object of their gaze.

the mise-en-scène. In a pivotal scene we hear, in voice-over, Marie's mother (Marianne Faithfull) warning her of the negative consequences of not producing an heir before her sister-in-law. Marie stands alone on a palace balcony as the camera zooms out slowly and steadily from medium-long shot.[4] She is framed by massive, wide-open French doors, creating a black void of space that feels as if it could swallow her up. Imposing stone columns box her in on both sides, and the balcony's rails cover her body from the waist down like truncated prison bars. The effect is of the unyielding, crushing weight of expectation and institutional history, Marie objectified by that history, supremely alone. The

THE STILLNESS OF SOLITUDE

Figure 6.2 The film's first image sets up its discourse on excess regarding both femininity and consumption.

camera zooms out further until she is but a compositional speck, with additional columns and doors filling the frame. The camera continues to zoom as the scene is cut – implying the limitlessness of such oppressive loneliness.

The opening shot of Coppola's film paints a brief scene of the French queen at her most on display, luxuriously relaxed and seemingly complicit in her 'too-be-looked-at-ness' (Figure 6.2) (Mulvey 1975: 62). Something akin to an *in media res* opening, this scene actually exists outside the diegesis, and operates as a pure fantasy image. Over the strains of the Gang of Four's 1979 song 'Natural's Not in It', Marie appears onscreen in medium-long shot, her eyes closed with her face raised as she reclines on a blue-and-white chaise longue in a parody of a neoclassical pose, such as the one found in Jacques-Louis David's *Portrait of Madame Récamier* (1800). The queen's milieu and costume, however, are anything but neoclassical. Her voluminous hair in her signature *pouf* style with a plumage of giant white feathers consumes much of the top left frame. The space is shallow and planimetric, as if Marie is placed onstage. In the first of plentiful references to the dessert she apocryphally suggests her subjects eat, pink and white cakes flank her in front and behind.

The effect is akin to 'Still Life with Queen', a tableau vivant of decadence that reduces Marie to a prop, almost a cake herself. Brevik-Zender calls it 'a visual representation of the stereotype of the ruinous female narcissist' (2011: 15) – a conventional judgement of the queen that the film ultimately denies. While meticulously composed, it seems garish, indecorous, even infantile. Anachronistically, her maid is dressed in a stock bourgeois 'French maid' costume and could have stepped out of a twentieth-century bedroom farce. There is a tension between constriction, with the fussy fabrics and heavy sense of indolence, and freedom, in its fanciful colours and glimpses of flesh. Its colours speak to a rococo sense of whimsy, but the precise composition and geometric forms evoke the feeling of a pretty prison. Like the girl tableaux shots in *The Virgin Suicides*, it is so ripe with femininity as to be confrontational, but the dreamy delicacy of the previous film is absent.

Marie's direct camera address announces a disregard for classical modes of storytelling and defiance of narrative boundaries, or indeed any bounds of good taste and propriety on the part of the film's protagonist and its director. It also underscores Coppola's preoccupation with the gaze. But this is not a gaze that submits to traditional notions of 'dominant–submissive logic' (Downing 2009b: 124) of the camera/spectator and scopophiliac object, respectively. Instead, it evokes the idea of Foucault's Panopticon, which adopts a 'pan-voyeuristic perspective' (2009b: 125). Marie Antoinette is always on display, and always aware of her display. But her gaze also speaks to her own desiring ethos.

By highlighting the constructed and transhistorical nature of this initial image, the film counteracts the subgenre of what Jennifer Milam refers to as 'realist history', a mode of filmmaking which attempts 'to convince the viewer that they have successfully recreated the total historical space' in the mise-en-scène and 'assume[s] that the truth of history lies in its surfaces' (2011: 49). Anna Backman Rogers notes that Coppola's 'elision of contemporary and historical time' reflects a social order that is 'hermetically sealed' and 'function[s] like a self-perpetuating machine running on empty' (2012: 88). But in a more positive, recuperative sense, its playfulness also clearly aligns it with fancy, which is 'not particularly subject to movement through biological or historical time' (Robinson 2006: 38). Specifically, it offers a control of time and space similar to what Walter Jackson Bate sees in the work of Keats (2012: 19).

Marie Antoinette and the 'Material Sublime'

The title of one of Coppola's first films, the 1998 short 'Lick the Star', recalls a line from Keats's poem *Lamia*.[5] The line in question occurs in a stanza describing, in sublime fashion, the colourful and cosmic appearance of the titular demigoddess:

> And, as the lava ravishes the mead,
> Spoilt all her silver mail, and golden brede;
> Made gloom of all her frecklings, streaks and bars,
> Eclips'd her crescents, and *lick'd up her stars*
>   (Keats 1976: 418; my emphasis)

This poem offers a variety of ways in which to decipher *Marie Antoinette*'s relation to both materiality and the body, particularly the female body. Barbara Schapiro claims that the women in Keats's poems had 'ambivalent character' (1983: 33), and Lamia is certainly no exception. (Although she is not actually a human woman, she takes the form of one.) While Keats depicts Lamia as something of a monster in her personification of excess, he also exhibits sympathy for his character and takes pains to depict her point of view. Keats's treatment of Lamia is not unlike Coppola's treatment of Marie in its combination of sympathy and objectivity. Likewise, Keats's depictions of excess and monstrosity align closely with the various ways both Marie Antoinette and the mise-en-scène are depicted in Coppola's film.

Betsy Winakur Tontplaphol describes how *Lamia* supports a conception of the sublime that is sourced in material excess. 'In Lamia, Keats embraces materio-sensory engorgement as the purest, if most difficult to sustain, experience of pleasure', she writes (2010: 43). Crucially, that excess is found within a delimited space. While Keats championed 'sense-gratifying stimuli' and material pleasure, he also strove for a '*tension* between container and contained', depicting material excess within smaller environments rather than ones distinguished by grandeur (2010: 40–2; original emphasis). This leads to an 'indecorous' aesthetic Winakur Tontplaphol characterises as the 'cornerstone of Keatsian pleasure', a pleasure that exists in material sublimity rather than picturesque composure (2010: 42). It might seem counterintuitive to place the imposing grandeur of the grand baroque Palace of Versailles in the context of Keats's love of the 'Spenserian bower' (2010: 41), but Coppola's film sets out to delimit space in a way that defines the palace not only as a literal prison but as the site of Marie's construction of a 'rich cocoon' not unlike the one mythical demigoddess Lamia seeks to create (2010: 56).

The film's second act contains the most obvious depictions of material excess and a Keatsian obsession with 'creature-pleasures' (Trilling 1965: 67). Having become the subject of ridicule for being unable to get pregnant, Marie Antoinette drowns her sorrows by swimming in yards of the finest French silk, indulging in the most expensive Champagne, and commissioning the highest and most outrageous powdered wigs ever constructed. The sequence that has drawn the most critical attention, a shopping-and-eating montage set to Bow Wow Wow's 1980s nod to sugary sensual pleasures, 'I Want Candy', flaunts Marie and her friends' frivolous descent into a debauchery of material excess (Figure 6.3). A cornucopia of dresses, expensive fabrics and embroidery, accessories and most especially shoes flit by onscreen in quick cuts emphasising the fleeting nature of consumption and the need to fulfil new and greater material desires to maintain previous levels of pleasure.

'It is clear that Marie Antoinette wants something more than candy, and the film uses this metaphor to show that the discursive performance is focused

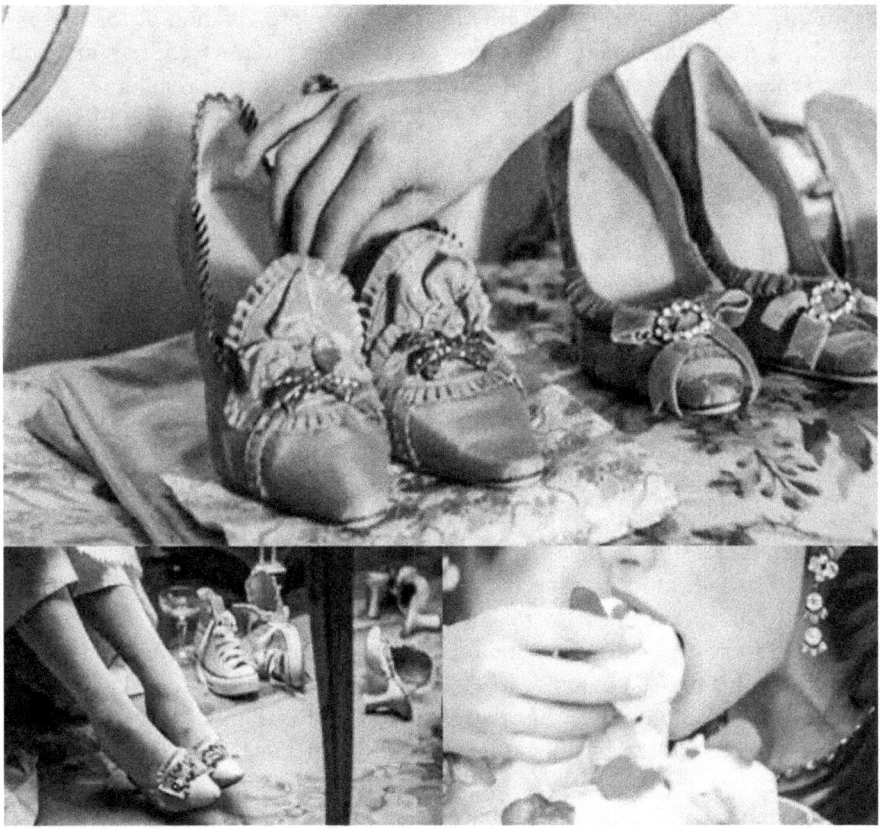

Figure 6.3 The 'I Want Candy' montage sequence links pleasurable consumption to fleeting desire, historical anachronism and the female body.

on *wanting* not *doing*', writes Pamela Flores (2013: 615; original emphasis). Coppola depicts this desire by the repetitive grasping found in graphically matching shots. Marie's arms reach into frame to pick up a pair of pastel high-heeled slippers designed by modern couture label Manolo Blahnik, and a moment later we see her reach into frame again for a different pair via jump cut. The shoes are reconfigured in various bird's-eye-view images, with jumps lending an artificial movement akin to stop-motion animation, making it seem as if they are imbued with organic life.

Again there is blatant anachronism, this time in the form of the controversial addition of twentieth-century-designed Converse athletic shoes, which also emphasise the mix of 'high' and 'low' culture when contrasted with the expensive designer shoes. Fashion itself, as Brevik-Zender writes, is a transhistorical depiction of Walter Benjamin's concept of 'now time' (2011: 5), as it 'draws from the past even as it looks to the future in its representation of the present' (2011: 3). According to Flores, fashion creates a rupture, 'which frees individuality, replaces the primacy of past mythical times with an ephemeral present, and turns change into a social value' (2013: 614). Coppola's use of fashion anachronisms embellishes this idea of the film as transhistorical, and also points to such social value. It also conjures the mental freedom of fancy in allowing a 'new' view of the world through both 'contemplation' and 'construction' (Robinson 2006: 21). This newness writes over the past as it looks with desire toward an ever-unfolding future.

Other objects, including food, are integral to the film's depictions of consumption. Ladies gorge themselves on ornate pastel cakes and pastries, some of which are so large they can barely fit in their mouths – Brevik-Zender references their visual similarity to breasts and links them to a commodified and consumed female body (2011: 24). Even gambling chips resemble iced pink biscuits. Amidst the dizzying array of artfully composed still-life-in-action shots of desserts and shoes, the soundtrack becomes momentarily dissonant, as if signalling an increasing vertigo brought on by such sensory overabundance – it is too much to take in for the spectator, and even for the film itself. The sequence ends with Marie being fitted with a new outrageously ornate *pouf* wig complete with miniature artificial birds. She turns to her stylist, Léonard, and asks him guilelessly, 'It's not too much, is it?'

Of course, it *is* too much, but that is the point. In contrast to the glares and snickers she receives during long solitary walks down the palace corridors, where spiteful courtiers whisper nasty epithets and gossip about the queen within her earshot, in her fantasia of pleasurable consumption, ecstatic delight and positive feelings dominate. Members of the court call her frigid, an 'Austrian spy', and outright challenge her, 'Give us an heir!' But her affective connections through consumption are another story. 'I love your hair; what's going on there?' Marie asks a lady-in-waiting. 'Everything', she replies with a friendly laugh.

Early in the film, sartorial composure serves as a mode of ranking the ladies of the court – exceeding the boundaries of good taste is proof you are a scandalous whore, such as in the case of the Louis XV's consort, Madame du Barry (Asia Argento). Her emerald- and ruby-hued dresses (in reality, much more historically accurate than Marie's pastel-hued frocks) (Weber 2007: 149) and lack of general restraint are a cause for derision amongst Marie and her group. Marie even refuses to talk with her despite the urgings of Ambassador Mercy (Steve Coogan). 'Do you think she's wearing enough jewellery?' she snipes in du Barry's direction, in what seems a concerted attempt to blend in with the gossiping hordes. Later, when Mercy tells her du Barry would like to present her with diamonds, she scoffs and tells him she has quite enough already.

Later, however, Marie grows to embrace a too-much-is-never-enough ethos. Caroline Weber describes how the real Marie Antoinette used her sartorial choices to set fashion trends among the aristocracy and even the growing middle classes (2007: 5), using fashion to exert 'an appearance of political credit' to make up for her failure to conceive (2007: 4). Saige Walton explicitly situates the film's depictions of excess in luxury to the power structures found within the baroque era. According to Walton, the film 'capture[s] the theatricality of the absolutist baroque and how power was bound up with appearances' (2016: 149). While Coppola certainly draws strong parallels between perceptions of power and the display of luxury, she also highlights the effective – and affective – comfort found within the embrace of material and sensorial surfeit when power dynamics become dangerously lopsided. As Walton acknowledges, spending was as much about 'taking pleasure for its own sake' as it was about wielding influence in the baroque era (2016: 156). Coppola more often depicts Marie's outrageous fashion choices as motivated by pleasure: a desire for decorative beauty that creates a cocoon of luxurious excess during her confinement and temporarily negates her earthly suffering.

These sartorial excesses are connected to Marie's seemingly unconscious attempts to wield power in the only way afforded to her. According to Michel Foucault, '[d]eployments of power are directly connected to the body – to bodies, functions, physiological processes, sensations and pleasures' (1998: 151–2). In effect, her bad taste and breaches of aesthetic decorum though choices Weber notes were 'better suited to a king's mistress than to a king's wife' become a symbol of 'unbridled female acquisitiveness' (Weber 2007: 119). In this way they can be seen as a subversive political act, however unconsciously portrayed.

Many of the film's depictions of materialist excess take place in Marie's private rooms, away from the scrutiny of the public eye, which function as a space where she is free to create herself in her own image. In Keats's poem, Lamia, fearing the revelation of her inhumanity, fashions a 'barely containable [. . .] opulent jumble' of materiality in the small space of her wedding banquet as a form of psychic armour (Winakur Tontplaphol 2010: 55–6). While Keats embraces 'materio-sensory engorgement' as the 'purest' form of pleasure, he also acknowledges it as the most difficult form to sustain (2010: 43). According to Winakur Tontplaphol, 'Keats questions the pleasure of limitlessness – and, as a result, the value of limitless pleasure' (2010: 49). The sublimity of Versailles is rooted in this sense of limitlessness – not necessarily in the edifice itself, but in the supposedly divine institution it represents, the monarchy and the state. Marie's sublimity is rooted in her attempts to achieve transcendence based in something far less ideal, by carving out smaller spaces within which to express her desire for pleasurable, sensuous excess.

When Marie's pleasurable sugar rush begins to give her headaches, she usually retreats to her private apartments. At times these smaller spaces also represent a desire for picturesque unity, betraying a recognition that sublime limitlessness conveys as much pain as pleasure. Coppola frames Marie ensconced in the womblike comfort of her daybed in the small sitting room off her bedroom (complete with 'secret' door, which imbues it with a certain mystery that would intrigue almost any adolescent girl). In one brief scene she is dressed only in a post-bath towel, her hair loose and natural and her legs tucked underneath her as she lies in the foetal position. The room's accent colour is the same icy blue from the opening scene, a colour that becomes something of Marie's signature from the time she leaves Austria behind and exchanges her pale-yellow frock for an ornate blue gown. It comes to represent a shoring up of her defences, just as pink signifies her desire for pleasure and sensuous abandon. (Not coincidentally, perhaps, Fraser reveals that Coppola's personal stationery is of the same pale blue, a 'good Marie Antoinette color!' (Fraser 2006).) This cocooning fosters a sense of psychological wellbeing within Marie, but it is also insidiously anaesthetising.

In a letter to J. H. Reynolds from 1818, Keats compares the totality of a human life to a 'Mansion of Many Apartments' (Keats 1970: 95). Coppola reconfigures this idea into the aforementioned 'big hotel or palace'. Applying Keats's metaphor to Versailles specifically, Marie's 'small private apartments, surrounded by her fabrics and trinkets' (Coppola 2006) represent an intoxicating 'Chamber of Maiden Thought' in which 'we see nothing but pleasant wonders, and think of delaying there for ever in delight' (Keats 1970: 95). Literally a maiden chamber at the point when Marie has yet to consummate her marriage, this is the realm of the fanciful dreamer, an initial, unsophisticated phase that comes before 'convincing ones' nerves that the World is full of misery and heartbreak, pain, sickness and oppression' (1970: 95).

Coppola purposefully depicts these rooms as the site of Marie's daydreaming. When she is overcome by heroic battlefield fantasies of her soldier lover, Count Fersen (Jamie Dornan), in full 'proto-Napoleonic' pose on his steed (Bradshaw 2006), she excuses herself from her husband and members of the court to flee down the cold, imposing palace hallways, a literal depiction of Keats's 'dark passages', which function as a recurring motif of isolation and loneliness in the film. Running quickly and daintily with staccato steps through these passages as if to escape what they represent, she enters her bedroom and collapses onto the bed, smiling wanly as if in a narcotic stupor as she fantasises about her lover. Such daydreaming also relates to fancy – it is no coincidence that in the nineteenth century, the word *fancier* was synonymous with *dreamer* (Robinson 2006: 10).

The 'Romantic Ethic', Daydreaming and Modern Consumption

Marie is an archetypal Romantic daydreamer, epitomising what Colin Campbell refers to as 'modern autonomous imaginative hedonism' (2005: 77). In *The Romantic Ethic and the Spirit of Modern Consumerism*, Campbell asserts that modern hedonistic practices, inspired by Romantic ideas, are directly linked to daydreaming, which makes 'desiring itself a pleasurable activity' (2005: 86). In other words, pleasure does not derive so much from the fulfilment of one's desire, but from the imaginative depiction of that fulfilment. In this way, the modern imaginative hedonist lives in the realm of anticipation, which results in a 'permanent unfocused dissatisfaction' and generalised 'longing' that often in itself has no object (2005: 87).

This longing combines pleasure and pain in a way indicative of the Romantic persona as it 'maximizes the opportunities for indulging in emotions of grief, sorrow, nostalgia, and, of course, self-pity' (2005: 88). It also results in the constant desire for the pleasures of the new and novel rather than a traditional hedonistic pattern of pleasure-seeking found in those experiences already known to guarantee pleasurable satisfaction (2005: 86, 85). This is the 'spirit of modern consumerism' that Marie personifies: she is constantly looking for new ways to reinvent herself and her surroundings through experimentation, one driven by her 'self-illusory' (2005: 89) idealisations and imaginings.

While Coppola only depicts this one act of daydreaming in the film, the tone she creates – one of soft-focus dreaminess combined with outrageous fantasy depictions in the general mise-en-scène – contributes to the idea of idealised materiality and desire, a combination of the pleasures of the material and the fantasy that enables them. Early on in the film a sense of anticipatory desire is established when Marie and her young friends giggle girlishly over a locket image of her soon-to-be-husband (Jason Schwartzman) before they ever meet. This is paralleled with a similar scene, in long shot, of Louis and his brothers discussing Marie's reported beauty, but Coppola foregrounds Marie's desire much more so than Louis's in these two moments.

The entire film can even be characterised as the depiction of the daydream, directed at the spectator. Campbell writes, 'imaginative enjoyment of products and services is a crucial part of contemporary consumerism [. . .] revealed by the important place occupied in our culture by representations of products rather than products themselves' (2005: 92). This is what many of those critical of the film emphasise: the fantastical depictions of consumption and the fetishistic nature of products on display contribute to the seemingly shallow, 'materialistic' cultural emphasis on excess and avarice.

However, Marie is not only depicted as a greedy consumer of goods and services; she is also loosely portrayed as a type of Romantic artist. Coppola has remarked that she finds her protagonist to be 'a very creative person' (K. Fraser: 2006). Her spontaneity and the intensity of her emotions recall the Romantic self, just as her 'embodied imaginings' (Campbell 2005: 193) (her costumes and cosmetics) share her pleasure with those around her. At the same time, her breaches of court etiquette, her excess and vulgarity, draw scorn and political fire. But the more scorn she receives, the more Marie doubles down on pleasurable image creation.

In accordance with self-illusory hedonism, she is 'an artist of the imagination' (2005: 78). Her joie de vivre and creative impulse speak to the 'high moral purpose' the Romantics found in pleasure – a so-called 'radical pleasure' for its own sake that could be considered the 'defining attribute of life' (2005: 191–2). While Wordsworth located pleasure in feelings of 'virtue', the later Romantics widened ideas of pleasure to include even those typically associated with pain and vice, including 'pride, fear, horror, jealousy and hatred' (2005: 192). Coppola depicts Marie's wide-ranging capacity to experience pleasure in her evident delight at mistreating du Barry, and even her mischievous giggles over her sexual portrayals in revolutionary pamphlets. The later Romantics also recognised the essentially fleeting nature of pleasure, its 'elusive and self-extinguishing character' (2005: 192). Coppola's narrative explores the darker side of Romantic longing and desire. It depicts the relentless grasping of the new as a mode of diminishing returns and ultimately an idealistic trap in the ever-present illusory web of desire.

Caroline Weber characterises Count Fersen as the 'great love' of Marie Antoinette's life (2007: 136), but Coppola's film depicts him more as the object of girlish infatuation, an example of Marie's obsession with novelty, fantasy and desire itself. He becomes fuel for her ongoing fantasies of sexual intrigue, but Coppola's narrative drops this romantic subplot abruptly and without fanfare. According to Campbell, '[t]he cycle of desire-acquisition-use-disillusionment-renewed-desire is a general feature of modern hedonism, and applies to romantic interpersonal relationships' (2005: 90). Once again, fancy plays a role in its 'projection of an idealized beloved' and its ability to move beyond ordinary consciousness in order to embrace love's 'extravagance' (Robinson 2006: 12).

Coppola's depiction of Marie during her daydream is suitably ambivalent. Despite her pleasurable, imaginative reverie, she still appears artificially positioned for the camera. She gives a look that is just shy of a direct camera address as she lies with her mouth slightly open, her hands resting limp-wristed on her chest in a pose of supplication. The scene implies both pleasure and suffering, and the incongruity between her subjective fantasies and objective reality expresses Marie's inability to escape a bodily commodification even in isolation. As Flores writes, she is 'conscious of being always observed' (2013: 610), and that even applies to when she is alone, being observed by the camera. Marie's daydream of Fersen is curiously violent and hyper-masculine – his face dirtied in battle amidst a fiery backdrop of war – and hints at something darker than mere childish infatuation. While it implies the notion of sexual power, it also hints at the 'merging' of Romantic love as a danger to personal identity (Singer 2009: 290). Coppola's film addresses notions of shifting identity through her protagonist's ever-changing persona and social position.

REVOLUTION, MODERNITY AND SHIFTING PERSONAL IDENTITIES

Richard Rushton suggests that the foregrounding of 'those processes of disconnection between the subjective and the social' asserts *Marie Antoinette*'s ethical stakes and their relation to democracy and self-determination (2014: 124). '[M]odern democracy goes hand-in-hand with the invention of modern subjectivity and the quest for self-reliance', he writes (2014: 126). Rather than a purely narcissistic pursuit, this quest leads to a 'constant questioning of the self' which goes 'hand-in-hand with, and cannot be dissociated from, the questioning of the society one finds oneself in and the "place" where one finds oneself in that society' (2014: 126). Just as the Romantics' response to being 'dulled by their experience of modern living' was 'to redouble their efforts as artists' (Campbell 2005: 186, 187), so Marie's various attempts to 'discover' herself through creative expression align with her desire to more fully enter the social world, even though she has little true understanding of that world or her place in it.

Claude Lefort cautions that self-determination within democracy can by its very essence lead to indeterminacy (1986: 303). In a society that has become a 'theatre of an uncontrollable adventure' with the removal of the head of the body politic, this 'dis-incorporation' leads to a grasping for meaning when identity is 'constantly open to question' (1986: 303, 304). This is not a picture of the 'bourgeois subject strong and bounded, defined by strict forms and a notion of "internal" integrity' that the Romantic lyric is meant to represent (Robinson 2006: 15). Campbell describes the two most critical political events of the Romantic period as the twin revolutions, first in America and then France, which represent one 'single upheaval by which the middle classes displaced the aristocracy as the leading socio-economic grouping of modern society' (2005: 178). Greeted initially with excitement and zeal by the Romantics, the French Revolution was followed by a period of disillusionment, as well as burgeoning divisions within the bourgeoisie itself (2005: 178).

Second-generation Romantic poets such as Keats could not escape such class divisions, which also occurred in Britain, and were in part responsible for the denigrations of his more radical politics and fanciful poetics. In the August 1818 issue of *Blackwood's Edinburgh Magazine*, for instance, conservative John Gibson Lockhart (writing under the pseudonym 'Z') decries 'Johnny' Keats's work as 'worthless and affected' and laments the 'purest, the loftiest, and [. . .] most classical living English poets joined together in the same compliment with the meanest, the filthiest, and the most vulgar of Cockney poetasters' (1818: 519). Despite the revolution, or perhaps because of it, questions of taste became complicated by and inextricable with class. Instead of the middle class being pitted against nobility, it became pitted against itself.

Marie embodies this notion of ever-changing identity and a precarious position within society. Indeed, this indeterminacy goes hand in hand with the elision of historical time in Coppola's film and speaks to Marie's modern obsession with the consumption of the new and novel. She is as much a victim of modernity as she is a victim of the increasingly outmoded ideology of the monarchy. If 'grasping the latest little thing [. . .] guarantees the death of the past and the fullness or splendour of the present' (Lefort 1986: 234), its enjoyment is perfunctory because it is attached to a desire for more newness in an anticipated future. Keats himself encapsulates the idea of pain in fleeting pleasure in 'Ode on Melancholy' when he writes of 'Joy, whose hand is ever at his lips / Bidding adieu' (1976: 349). Marie's ongoing exploration of identity, restlessness and desire is further described by the film's sequence at the Petit Trianon estate.

The film does not shy away from depicting Petit Trianon as an artificial construct even as it sympathetically acknowledges the ethical project of 'the discovery of a life aris[ing] from the determination to "explore oneself"' (Rushton 2014: 122). Marie instructs her dressmakers to construct costumes that are 'more natural', but soon she appears with her hair coloured Easter-egg pink. Trilling divides two distinct 'moral ambiances' of the Romantic pleasure-seeking movement of the eighteenth century, the first being 'unexceptional', 'innocent' and 'domestic' pleasure and the second of a more 'radical aspect', that of the morally suspect voluptuary (1965: 63–4). Try as she might to align herself with the simple picturesque pleasures of hearth and home, Marie prefers 'unfavourable' pleasure: 'sensuous enjoyment as a chief object of life, or end, in itself' (1965: 63). This is indeed the revolutionary late-Romantic conception, where such a 'primitive' and 'radical' pleasure is 'directly associated with virtue' (Campbell 2005: 191).

According to Campbell, a failure to experience pleasure of such a kind indicates an 'alienation from nature [. . .] aris[ing] from the fact that "the world" is too much' (2005: 191). Marie's imaginative hedonism, in fact, exemplifies her lack of alienation from the material world. Despite her desire to delight guests with 'pastoral charm' and 'neoclassical restraint' (Weber 2007: 134), her need for personal creative inscription on her own body and for the more 'radical' elements of pleasure-seeking cannot be contained.

The delight Marie feels in material pleasures extends to her entire clique of fellow proto-bohemian sensualists. During one dinner party, the Duchesse de Polignac (Rose Byrne) shows the other guests how to play a musical game on their glasses. 'Lick your finger and rub it around the rim of the glass', she instructs, and they are all charmed by the resulting tones. In many such scenes, Coppola emphasises touch, both of the material – Fersen grabs Marie's bare arm at the masked ball when they first meet; Marie drags her hand slowly through the water as she floats lazily on a small boat in a placid pond (Figure 6.4) – and the more ideal.

As Marie rides home from the masked ball at sunrise, she extends her arm outside the coach and moves it with the motion of a gentle wave, as if grasping

Figure 6.4   Coppola emphasises the power of touch, which alludes to both sensual interconnection and the eternal grasping emanating from desire.

for, or creating in her mind, something pleasurable to touch.[6] Here Coppola renders concrete 'the eternally forward-flung, and always inaccessible, nature of desire' (Downing 2009a: 138). As Keats 'all[ied] his sensory images more closely with the sense of touch' to make them 'stronger and more concrete' (Bate 2012: 50), Coppola often conforms her concrete filmic imagery to the ephemeral and imaginary, to what is not there or cannot be seen, only daydreamed.

Keats's close friend, the poet Leigh Hunt, describes *Lamia*'s couplets as 'tak[ing] pleasure in the progress of their own beauty, like sea-nymphs luxuriating through the water' (Hunt 1832: xxxviii). In the film a literal body of water represents this luxurious, wandering consciousness. If 'there also appears to be something intrinsically rhythmic or wave-like about the patterns which yield pleasure' (Campbell 2005: 64), the wave-like motion of Marie's outstretched arm conjures the idea of the endless waxing and waning cycles of desire. Desire is not just depicted by Marie's idealised grasping, however; it is also inscribed on her body in the way it is presented and perceived by others and used as a political pawn.

'Like a little piece of cake': The Body, Consumption and Moral Utility

As in Keats's *Lamia*, material sublimity in Coppola's film is depicted not just in its titular figure's surroundings, but also on her very body. Denise Gigante explains that in the Romantic era, linking the body with sublime excess created a new conception of 'monstrosity' as 'too much life': 'Such monstrosity does not remain at the level of theory but becomes the motivation for a new kind of monster in the literature of the Romantic period, one whose life force is too big for the matter containing it' (2002: 434). Winakur Tontplaphol continues this line of thought when she asserts, 'Lamia's body is not balanced, proportionate, or decorous [. . .] she embodies the congestion intrinsic to Keats' material sublime' (2010: 50). At various points in the narrative, Marie's body is seen as the site of similar 'monstrous' excess. Her *pouf* wigs, which are historically accurate (Weber 2007: 5), recall the iconic hairstyle of the titular victim-monster in James Whale's 1935 film *Bride of Frankenstein*. (The real Marie Antoinette's wigs perhaps even helped inspire Whale's character design.) The *pouf* was not only an infinitely customisable way to assert individuality, 'as part of Marie Antoinette's subjective strategy, the *pouf w*as another device to recuperate her own body' (Flores 2013: 617). In Coppola's film, Marie's hair takes on a disruptive, phallic power as it reaches ever-newer heights. This Frankenstein-like 'monstrous' excess is alluded to in the film during its climax, when Marie emerges onto her balcony in front of a protesting mob, which wields pitchforks and fiery torches as the angry villagers do in Whale's film.

Depictions of Marie as monster are exclusively portrayed from the perspective of the body politic: from the pamphlets claiming she is sexually immoral (either she is a voracious lesbian or has sexual designs on Thomas Jefferson) to the non-diegetic image of her luxuriating in a bath, *pouf* ascending, while scoffing 'Let them eat cake' through an incongruous slash of black lipstick. Absurdly, in this scene she also wears a diamond necklace, which alludes to the infamous 'affair of the diamond necklace' scandal that negatively impacted the queen in the court of public opinion and even helped sow the seeds of revolution (Ferriss and Young 2010: 107). This scene represents the wearing of masks, as the costume ball scene does literally, and her conscription into the role of 'an object for the other in a play of Symbolic and Imaginary forces' (Downing 2009a: 136), a sort of femme fatale in the eyes of the people.

In *Lamia*, Keats creates a tragic-comic excessiveness that renders the text 'generically unstable' with an 'aesthetic defined by mismatch, in a narrative driven by its heroine's indecorous desire to cultivate gargantuan sensations in tiny pastures' (Winakur Tontplaphol 2010: 57). Coppola creates a similar tragi-comic effect with a tonal mix of straight-faced satire, soporific interludes and depictions of outright suffering. 'To suggest that Lamia's story is a series of bulges, tears, and attempted repairs, is, perhaps, to highlight potentially comic elements', writes Winakur Tontplaphol (2010: 57), and such elements appear regularly in Coppola's film. Excess is lampooned in many scenes: during a party, wigmaker Léonard discreetly extinguishes a candle to keep Marie's *pouf* from catching fire; her partner in crime Duchesse de Polignac appears, in a comic anachronism, to snort cocaine off the back of her own hand; and when Mercy briefs Marie about an important foreign policy issue, she is too absorbed in whether her sleeve should be made with ruffles or without to pay attention. When she is informed her overspending has left little funds for charity, she resolutely proclaims that only the 'smaller' trees be installed on a garden path, as if this gesture will somehow mitigate the poverty of the French people.

On a personal level, Marie's very existence could be considered a series of 'attempted repairs' of the miserable state in which she finds herself. As in Lamia's attempts to 'retain integrity' by preserving 'both corporeal and psychic wholeness' (Winakur Tontplaphol 2010: 58), these attempts are ultimately tragically unsustainable (2010: 57). Direct depictions of tragedy or violence are rare in the film, resulting in the feeling of anticipatory dread. The death of Marie's youngest child is portrayed by its removal from a family portrait; the angry mob is heard primarily off-screen; and the raid on the palace is exemplified by a simple shot of the ruined royal bedroom, furniture and broken glass strewn about. A bird is heard fluttering its wings but is not seen within the frame, emphasising the static, painterly quality of the shot as it alludes to nature's reclamation of the artificial.

Walter Jackson Bate notes that Keats's imagery, often considered essentially 'statical', actually expressed a 'highly dynamical power momentarily caught at rest and concentrated and imprisoned within an otherwise static image' (Bate 2012: 58). Coppola's imagery suggests a similar barely contained power, a potential energy existing within a delimited container, one embodied most acutely by Marie. Depictions of excess are almost always tempered by picturesque restraint, which speaks to a 'hidden intention and movement which Keats called "electric fire"' (2012: 71) and underscores their indecorousness.

Lamia refuses a 'neoclassical disposition toward balance' (Winakur Tontplaphol 2010: 50), something she shares in common with Marie Antoinette, no matter how hard the latter may try to achieve decorous unity with her environments. Lamia's power is not only evident in her status as a demi-goddess, it is written aesthetically on her very body: 'constrained in nearly every sense, [she] debuts and remains the antithesis of pallor. She is, in other words, colourful in the most literal sense of that term: tint-saturated, color-*full* [. . .] with a barely contained aesthetic energy' (2010: 49; original emphasis). Marie is often similarly 'tint-saturated' with heavy makeup, particularly rouge, a frosting of silver in her hair. Her costumes are always the most colourful and striking amongst those of the ladies of the court. This serves to focus the spectator's visual attention in the frame, but also to highlight her particular 'life force' and 'barely contained aesthetic energy'.

But Coppola does not only choose to depict Marie's bodily excessiveness. She also portrays her as physically diminutive, vulnerable and fragile – a beautiful commodity fetish. The tiny ribbons wrapped in her natural hair and around her neck (a foreshadowing of the guillotine, but also a symbol of her delicacy), together with multiple scenes featuring the girl stripped amidst large groups of fully dressed people, counteract the public's fantasy image of a vampire queen in black lipstick. With her childlike dimples, protruding canine teeth, baby-fine flaxen hair, and womanly 'hourglass' physique, Dunst conjures notions of both adolescent innocence and ripe sexuality (a combination Coppola uses to similar effect in *The Virgin Suicides*). Her beauty is meant to bring prestige to the court and the king in a very public, ceremonial way. This is similar to Lamia's beauty enhancing the prestige of Lycius (Trilling 1965: 68). Early on in the film, when she is spied from a distance by the eternally snide and simpering 'aunts' for the first time, one of them remarks, 'She looks like a little piece of cake.' It is meant as a compliment, but it summarises Marie's aesthetic problem: she is an elite, prettified object ripe for human consumption, but she is essentially disposable.

In her journey from foreign innocent to worldly queen, Marie's sartorial and lifestyle excesses function as a kind of psychic armour covering this bodily vulnerability. They are not so much intrinsic to her nature, as they are for the 'electric' (Gigante 2002: 439) body of Lamia, but a personal refashioning perpetuated to serve the purpose of delight in the pleasures, and power, of the pretty. Still, Coppola generally chooses to downplay the traditional sense of the power factor of Marie's costumes; their inviolably pastel colour schemes – inspired by the macarons from the director's favourite Parisian patisserie, Ladurée – are not just historically inaccurate but remove the masculine from the equation. The historical Marie Antoinette was known for her propensity for cross-dressing (mostly in male riding attire) (Weber 2007: 149), but you would never guess this from Coppola's highly feminised queen. However, two key scenes outside of her period of mourning do feature Marie in uncharacteristic black: her initial, and only, exchange with du Barry, and her impromptu excursion to the masked ball. In these scenes Marie wilfully decides to express her power and desire for rebellion, at first by supposedly acquiescing to a direct order in the most perfunctory way possible, and then by refusing outright to follow court protocol.

Denise Gigante connects the idea of bodily monstrosity in *Lamia* to a 'radically new aesthetic' beginning in the late eighteenth century (2002: 434). This theory sought to abandon the purely mechanistic outlook of Newtonian science that 'reduces life to its bodily functions', what Keats decried in *Lamia* as 'unweav[ing] a rainbow' (1976: 431), robbing the life force of its beauty, mystery and power. (Lamia herself is referred to as 'rainbow-sided' (1976: 415).) For Kant, monstrosity was something which 'exceeds representation' (Gigante 2002: 434), linked to a sublime life force that is 'too big for the matter containing it' (2002: 434). This is a materialist view, but crucially not mechanistic; the notion of a 'self-propagating vital power' is an organic one (2002: 435).

If beauty is a decorous state achieved through harmony, 'monstrosity emerges as a principle opposed to their harmonious convergence in form' (2002: 436). While Gigante argues that Lamia's 'excessive vitality' is too much for Lycius' 'feeble' human frame (2002: 434), in Coppola's film, Marie Antoinette serves the dual role of Lamia *and* Lycius. Her own fragility and instability of body – a body that is, as Galt writes, 'owned first by the state and then violently by the people' (2011: 22) – cannot adequately contain her own vitality, one that is forcefully inducted into a world that seeks to control its very biological functions.

According to Kant, 'an object is *monstrous* where by its size it defeats the end that forms its concept' (Kant [1790] 2007: 83; original emphasis). Marie's 'concept', her purpose, is to be a deferential wife, devoted and attractive member of the court and, most critically, mother to one or more male heirs to the throne. In exceeding or defying her social roles, she exhibits, as Gigante writes of Lamia, an 'aesthetic magnitude that nullifies its own purpose' and consequentially 'defeats [. . .] her status as beautiful' (2002: 438, 440). Despite the mortal frame she temporarily inhabits, Lamia 'refuses to sacrifice her signature excess' (Winakur Tontplaphol 2010: 50–1); Marie asserts her will against the structures of the court, however unconsciously, by asserting such excess as well. Such a will to pleasure Rushton calls a form of Emersonian 'self-reliance', a 'sense of being able to build one's own life in one's own way based on one's own decisions' (2014: 124).

Considering how the real-life queen's costumes 'triggered severe socio-political disorder' (Weber 2007: 3), one could even argue that this will to pleasure (if not power) ignites a political revolution almost by design, monstrously extending beyond Marie's own body into the body politic. As such, she wills revolution through her own excess. In Coppola's film, the revolution forces Marie Antoinette out of her self-willed cocoon and into the stark reality of death and the suffering of those on the other side of the palace gates.

'Dying into life': Embracing the Romantic Depth Model?

The progenitors of Romantic theories about life force, most notably physiologist John Hunter, considered monstrosity as 'something gone awry during "recapitulation," or "self-repetition"' (Gigante 2002: 437). Anna Backman Rogers highlights the visual theme of repetition through ritual in Coppola's film (2012: 85), such as the montages of endless similar meals, attendance at mass and dressing ceremonies. This repetition not only emphasises the drudgery and pointless pageantry of court existence, it also encapsulates Marie's personal history, a constant recapitulation and repetition through an endless struggle to reinvent herself.

Coppola chooses to emphasise this cycle of attempted growth and recapitulation through the last full scene of her narrative, which ends not with the queen's head being severed but with her 'saying goodbye' to the palace she called home, just as she said goodbye to her Austrian birthplace at the film's beginning. This not only links Marie to the materiality of an earthly location, but foreshadows her ability to 'grow', to break free of an endless cycle of false starts, which will eventually only come through her death. As Rushton writes, the only way the queen can deal with such an unjust world 'is to say "goodbye" to it' (2014: 115). Marie's final, dignified acceptance of her fate (her recognition that she is 'out of place' in a 'world of moral catastrophe') (2014: 115) is akin, not unlike the wilful acts of the Lisbon girls in *The Virgin Suicides*, to passing judgement on that world.

Marie's 'soul-making' journey from narcissism to sympathetic union represents an ethical turn toward society and mirrors the journey of several of Keats's mythical heroes. When an angry crowd whipped into revolutionary fervour starts to descend on the palace, a sober-faced Marie insists multiple times, 'My place is here with my husband.' After sending the servants and her friends away with tearful goodbyes, she stands in the foyer, a solitary figure looking up toward the light as if summoning strength from the depths of her being. The balcony scene in the film, in which she silently bows toward the mob in acquiescence and offers her neck in supplication, functions as a clear foreshadowing of her death.

But it also represents the Keatsian notion of 'd[ying] into life' (Keats 1976: 306). In Keats's unfinished mythological epic *Hyperion*, Apollo is shown the 'knowledge of human suffering'; combined with sympathy, this knowledge makes him 'godlike' and immortal (Weston 1988: 106), just as it also brings him profound anguish. Walter Jackson Bate describes this dying into life as an 'instinctive working towards a purpose, the beauty of man, his particular identity, his truth' (2012: 69). This suffering and sympathy is what creates a soul; for Keats it is the 'vale of Soul-making' (1970: 250). Like Apollo, Marie feels but cannot understand her sadness, trapped in pursuit of her self-absorbed daydreams. The revolution frees her from the contained limits of her narcissism.

In Keats's *Endymion*, the titular hero gains the ability 'to recognize that he is not alone in his suffering', and with that 'recognition and acceptance of the pain and loss comes the birth of compassion' and a loss of 'narcissistic isolation' (Schapiro 1983: 43–59). Marie offers herself up as a sacrificial object, but her value is now not inscribed in her body but her personal consciousness. She will soon die, but in dying into life, she has conjured the 'immortal Self within' (Benton 1966: 40), a Keatsian loss of personal identity that arises from an awareness of the interconnectedness of all life and all suffering. While she passes judgement upon the world, she also feels its pain.

Barbara Schapiro contrasts the Keatsian 'dreamer' with the Keatsian poet; while the former is a 'narcissist, hopelessly fixated on his own idealizations and fantasies', the poet 'speaks always for a relationship with the real world outside the self' (1983: 53). In the film, Marie Antoinette functions as a sort of Keatsian dreamer who becomes a poet, just as 'Keats the poet triumphs over Keats the dreamer [. . .] by his acceptance of the pain, change, and loss that inevitably accompany growth' (1983: 60). Coppola speaks to her character's growth when she acknowledges that the other protagonists in her trilogy remained 'on the verge' of growing up, but that this is her first film 'about a girl becoming a woman' (Hohenadel 2006). That this pain and growth inexorably leads to Marie's own demise is a necessary function of the ethical vacuum of the society of which she is a part.

Schapiro's Freudian reading of Keats adopts a psychological depth model, and as a result, she derides the elements of fancy in Keats's writing, referring to the 'excesses and lack of judgment', 'florid diction', and 'emotional overindulgence' of his work as 'reflect[ing] the immaturity of vision itself' (1983: 47). In contrast, she lauds Keats's 'greater restraint and concentration' in works such as *Endymion* as evidence of the 'increasing ability to surmount his obsession with an infantile fusing love and to integrate his ambivalently split internal relationships' (1983: 47). She even asserts that Keats's poem *To Autumn* 'realizes a similar success in its integration of the regressive, feminine, and melancholic feelings with assertive, masculine, and affirmative ones' (1983: 60). The message here is clear: for Schapiro, when Keats's work exists solely in the realm of fancy rather than imagination and the lyric 'I', it is degraded, shallow, and 'feminine', operating without a masculine sense of reason or moral utility.

Given the traditional value placed on high canonical Romantic poetry and its rejection of fancy, it is tempting to validate the film's eventual turn to both aesthetic and narrative bleakness as evidence of its acceptance of a 'proper' ethical code and a rejection of its former luxurious excess. Coppola's dark turn (necessitated, of course, by history) does operate in the vein of Schapiro's assertion of Keats's turn away from 'florid' excess, but this does not negate the film's reliance on ornament, *jouissance*, the fanciful, and indecorous materiality. It should be noted that Lionel Trilling describes *Lamia*, one of Keats's later, 'mature' works, as 'vulgar [. . .] in extreme form' (1965: 68).

Rather, the interludes of consumption, sensuous excess and material communion throughout the film are all representative of Marie Antoinette's repeated attempts at soul-making, a reiteration of the search for self-identity in the face of abjection. I argue they are more ethical within the context of the film than her 'acceptance' of all human suffering because they continue to allow her subjecthood – not to mention joy – rather than resignation and annihilation. That Coppola's protagonists sometimes have to pay the ultimate price for their feminine desire is not a good thing, nor do her films posit it as such.

Depictions of the queen in the film's final act portray her as a different kind of monster: an emotionally hollowed-out zombie who shuffles around in mourning black, sleepwalking through her own life. It is as if the flames of her 'electric fire' have been doused. *Marie Antoinette*'s ending, in some ways, detracts from the sense of subversion that scenes venerating the fancy and the pretty portray, but it does not erase it. The queen's 'growing up', for Coppola, is not necessarily a celebratory event – it has rarely seemed quite so unappealing, so unsatisfying – and it is also not a form of chastising those who delight in the 'chick culture' elements of her films, which Suzanne Ferriss and Mallory Young describe as a 'feminist aesthetic focused on youth, fashion, sexuality, celebrity, and consumerism' (2010: 99). Judging by their preponderance in her films, she exhibits a fascination with them as well, even as her work acknowledges their pitfalls.

The abrupt change in tone registers as a minor shock with the spectator. But this shock is not a result of the violently sublime heroics of revolution; it is, rather, the shock of acquiescence, the pain of surrendering a *raison d'être*, a passion and desire for the world in all its material sensuality. It robs Marie of her vitality. While Coppola fashions herself as a filmmaker preoccupied by materiality and sensuousness, operating through non-judgemental fellow feeling and benevolent objectivity, her film does question the stifling of creativity and fancy by masculine 'reason' and historical 'progress' and its rejection of alterity altogether.

The film's final full scene – Marie's 'bidding adieu' to Versailles – does not only encompass wistful nostalgia and the relief of letting go. This curious and even childlike character detail actually suggests that Marie's defiance, her commitment to fancy, remains intact. It is a purely fanciful expression: in saying 'goodbye' to the palace (a 'Mansion of Many Apartments' which represents the totality of her soon-to-be-ended life) she 'animates' and 'personifies' her world (Robinson 2006: 42). In such a way she retains a commitment to the fancy and its recuperative effects until the very end. That is not to say that the film does not question excess, more specifically excess of pleasure. Just as in Keats's poetry, it exhibits a so-called 'dialectic of pleasure', a combination of its intense affirmation and scepticism toward it (Trilling 1965: 68).

For Marie, pleasure in luxury is a way to protect against the effects of a dehumanising political and social system. Such pleasure suggests the 'the idea of dignity in all man' (1965: 67). According to Trilling, pleasure can conform both to 'the principle of reality' or that of illusion (1965: 69). He points to Keats's description of lines from *Lamia*, which the poet refers to as 'a doubtful tale from faery land'. This 'faery land', Trilling insists, is 'the scene of erotic pleasure which leads to devastation' (1965: 69), a description that could aptly be applied to Marie Antoinette's own world. The 'self-negating' aspects of pleasure are exemplified by the film's depictions of modern autonomous imaginative hedonism. Both Keats and Coppola ultimately view eroticism, luxury and pleasurable excess through an ambiguous lens.

Conclusion

Marie Antoinette engages in what can be defined as a postmodern view of ethics in its questioning of an established acceptance of the greater moral good of 'masculine' reason and cinematic realism. It does this through an ambivalent response to pleasure, specifically pleasure in excess and voracious consumption, the indeterminacy created by the birth of modernity and the bourgeoisie and the ego-obliteration and surface exploration of fancy and the material sublime versus the suffering and 'soul-making' of the Romantic depth model of personal growth, which relies upon the shaping powers of imagination. The film's approach toward its protagonist, which combines sympathetic communion with a more objective point of view, underscores its commitment to this ambivalence.

Coppola's fleeting focus on Romantic love paints a portrait of illusory desire, while her depictions of narcissistic pursuits of pleasure and the ornamental within the film's mise-en-scène flirt with sublimity in Keats's material sense. Like the sister protagonists of *The Virgin Suicides*, Coppola's queen embodies the bifurcation of the sublime and beautiful. But unlike the Lisbon girls, she is not a simple depiction of the commodity value of the female in the marketplace. Her story also represents the personal 'growth' of the 'greater Romantic lyric' (Robinson 2006: 38). The 'shearing away of excess' that the film exhibits in its final scenes has been viewed as the proper course of the absorption of fancy along the path toward 'the more mature shaping spirit of imagination' in Romantic poetry, a process in which 'the experiential excesses of passion and sexuality give way before the "flint-and-iron" heroism of a poetry of the completely realized subject' (2006: 38, 37). However, it is difficult to view Marie Antoinette purely under these terms of newfound heroism; in her 'heroic' hour, she is stripped not only of her excess, but of her assertion of subjectivity through that excess.

According to Robinson, the Romantic lyric's 'drama of maturation is precisely the drama in which Fancy, with its sensuousness and participatory energies, gives way to the disinterested tragic attitude' (2006: 36). In the film, this new attitude, and the removal of ornamental excess it necessitates, is a painful break for both audience and protagonist, tantamount to a ripping away of the sensuous pleasures of life itself. It may be 'soul-making', but it is also a literal destruction. Coppola's film challenges us to question our belief in 'progress' at the expense of personal desire and creative freedom. Growing up need not necessitate giving up. 'Fancy', writes Robinson, is 'not simply a self-contained psychological efflorescence but a social event' (2006: 43). Robbing Marie Antoinette of her fanciful spirit robs her of a voice, and a place, within the world.

CONCLUSION:
ON ENDINGS AND NEW BEGINNINGS

In his post-mortem of the brief period of New Hollywood rebellion comprising 1960s and 1970s American film, Robert Phillip Kolker defines what he calls a 'cinema of loneliness' (1988: x). According to Kolker, a sense of isolation permeates not only the films of the era, but the milieu in which they were made:

> These are films made in isolation and, with few exceptions, about isolation [. . .] they only perpetuate the passivity and aloneness that has become their central image [. . .] [F]or all the challenge and adventure, their films speak to a continual impotence in the world, an inability to change and create change. (Kolker 1998: 10)

Kolker's conclusion is debatable – his contention that these films do not challenge cultural norms he clearly admits they signal as 'abhorrent' (1998: 10) seems unfounded. (A lack of providing answers to problems certainly does not imply an endorsement of them.) But in many ways, his assessment of these older films is similar to the ideas I have engaged with in the discussion of my own corpus. The films in this collection all contain characters, particularly protagonists, who seem stuck in their own isolation, unable to reach beyond themselves to create meaningful connections with other selves – it is as if Emerson's 'circles' have been replaced by wheels that simply spin in place, unsure of the direction they should go.

CONCLUSION: ON ENDINGS AND NEW BEGINNINGS

The difference between these newer films and their predecessors is in their characters' continual attempts to bridge gaps between themselves and the world in order to regenerate the degraded connections between persons. If New Hollywood is the 'cinema of loneliness', this new cycle of neoromantic films can be characterised as the 'cinema of tentative connections'. Unlike those of a previous generation, these films are comprised of characters who implicitly signal a desire to rely on others for comfort and recognition – their humanism[1] is rooted in a Romantic attempt to expand both inner and outer vision in order to create a larger community of selves.

Sometimes these efforts are thwarted or even negated, such as in the tragic outcomes of *The Virgin Suicides*, *Marie Antoinette* and *Synecdoche, New York*. However, just as often these imperfectly executed connections result in hopeful change and a continued belief in the power of that change, if only change that comes in small increments. The films posit the dialectic of 'self vs. world' (Mayshark 2009: 11) – they acknowledge a fundamental chasm between subjectivities, one exacerbated by our current age. But from the Fox family's ecstatic supermarket reverie at the conclusion of *Fantastic Mr. Fox* to Theodore and Amy's rooftop reunion in *Her*, they also implicitly or explicitly affirm that only a community of selves will be able to successfully navigate such a world, even if those selves will never be able to fully understand each other.

The Romantic suffering of *Weltschmerz* – that egocentric, self-conscious introspection that becomes so all-consuming it takes on 'cosmic significance' for those experiencing it (Thorslev 1962: 42) – potentially can be cured (or at least treated), as these films suggest. But it can only be done so in fits and starts via hopeful, tentative connections made through imaginative sympathy and emotional vulnerability, and through a questioning of absolutes. Peter Thorslev summarises this potential for change through intersubjective connection:

> If any escape from this tragic dilemma is possible [. . .] I suppose it must lie in the solution of modern humanism: a realization of the limits of the human mind and a cultivation of one's own values in an assertion of a community of selves in an ultimately unknown and unknowable universe. (Thorslev 1962: 89)

For the Romantics, freedom is found not in reason but through imaginative capability; imagination represents the freedom not only to create art as 'a central place in the organisation of human experience' (Waugh 1992: 19) but also to co-create a radically fictional space in a community that is 'constantly engaged in endless reinterpretation' (1992: 22). The collaborative medium of the cinema certainly represents such a 'community of selves'. Unlike Wordsworth or Keats, working in isolation or while communing with nature, a filmmaker (at least a conventional one) must create such a community, however makeshift, in order to realise imaginative vision amidst the chaos of life. The cinema of these filmmakers celebrates its fictionality as imaginative power, a '*radically fictional* sense of truth' (1992: 33; original emphasis), as much as an anxious relation to indeterminacy.

According to Kaufman, 'there are no grand conclusions' (Tobias 2000) to be drawn from life, but it is less difficult to draw them from art. I have attempted to do so by relating these works to both Romantic philosophy and literature, critical responses to Romanticism, and contemporary ideas of metamodernism based on a linkage of Romantic characteristics along a modernist and postmodern continuum. 'To live and think in a constant state of negotiation (perhaps more commonly, agitation) with the world, others, and oneself' (LaRocca 2011: 9) is the state of Romantic irony, a state of perpetual change.

Such a state requires 'a kind of bravery in the midst of indeterminacy, and a form of compassion for what lies beyond comprehension' (2011: 9). I argue that these films fundamentally express compassion both for their characters and for their audiences in the midst of such often-incomprehensible chaos and exemplify a highly Romantic longing for connection and meaning via shared emotion and sympathy. That these connections are never completely realised is simply indicative of the overwhelming worldview of this cinema: the attempt is always more important than the execution, because their humanity lies in the attempt, in the doing and the becoming.

If the films' characters, and their creators, are not necessarily 'brave', they are at least willing to acknowledge how little they understand about life and are capable of leaving questions unanswered. In these final pages I briefly summarise my arguments as they relate to the key Romantic principles identified in the Introduction: the emphasis on personal imagination and authenticity, subjectivity and its relation to the larger world, and emotion as a means of intersubjective connection.

The Romantic Relationship to Reality: A Questioning of Absolutes

The films discussed all speak to the idea that 'truth' is a relative term, one coloured by the relation between a subject's highly idiosyncratic and personal point of view and the world that subject inhabits. As Derek Hill writes in his discussion of *The Royal Tenenbaums*, these films are 'dream[s] which oscillate between the vibrantly "real" and completely artificial' (Hill 2008: 101). Their fictional, artificial worlds serve as the landscape to explore emotional truth. According to Andrea K. Henderson, Romanticism 'is a creature of surfaces, of context, and of varying forms; and when it appears most self-consistent, it may be least so' (1996: 5). This lack of consistency, or warring impulses between the opposing forces of the Romantic personality – a longing to see oneself as part

CONCLUSION: ON ENDINGS AND NEW BEGINNINGS

of a meaningful whole, and a desire to make an individual mark via a 'passionate assertion of oneself' (Thorslev 1962: 88, 89) – establishes the fundamental dialectic of a Romantic engagement with life. It is this dialectic, reinvigorated through Vermeulen and van den Akker's conception of metamodernism, that characterises the idiosyncratic displays of passion and resignation, hope and despair, and connection and isolation in these films.

Through explorations of memory, expressions of affect both dampened and sincere, and bursts of imaginative creativity that eschew pure filmic realism in favour of a deeper emotional reality, Coppola, Jonze, Anderson and Kaufman all create highly personal cinema that bears the indelible mark of its creators, even as it is the product of collaborative effort. That mark does not exist in a cultural or historical vacuum. These films are as much a product of their own era as they are the result of individual mental wellspring. Influenced and shaped by more than two hundred years of Romantic thought, they arrive at a time when Francis Fukuyama's famous pronouncement of the potential 'end of history' (Fukuyama 1989: 4) has had a generation to reverberate through the political and cultural climate. The word *ending*, of course, has a stark finality to it – whether it is a happy one or not. But for the true Romantic, an ending represents more than the end of one thing; it also marks the beginning of something else. Instead of decrying the 'senses of an end of this or that' (Jameson 1984: 53), Vermeulen and van den Akker claim the world now operates under the 'senses of a bend' (2017: 17), fusing a return of history with an acknowledgement of that history 'as the sum total of our objective conditions as well as the narrative that ties our present to a distant past and a distant future' (2017: 17).

In his essay relating the Romantic and postmodern senses of endings, J. Drummond Bone writes, 'Reality, with a small "r", is open-ended' (1999: 73). Bone admits that such a grand statement of truth about the nature of reality is in itself not open-ended, and therein lies a paradox, another irony (1999: 74). Despite their engagement with the dialectic of Romantic irony, almost all of these films have conclusive endings to their narratives. Their various plots and subplots are all wrapped up fairly neatly. Many feature the great exemplar of finality: death. *Synecdoche, New York*, *The Virgin Suicides*, *The Royal Tenenbaum* and *The Life Aquatic* all feature major character deaths in their final acts, while the implied death of the protagonist in *Marie Antoinette* is obvious. Some end simply with their characters achieving a form of resolution to their problems, as in *Fantastic Mr. Fox*. Jonze's *Her* is perhaps the least conclusive ending, although we do know that the relationship between its two central characters is inexorably over – Samantha leaving Theodore represents another important kind of death: the death of a relationship.

Bone contends that endings that achieve such a feeling of finality actually (ironically) result in an important dialectic of their own: 'The metaphysical underpinnings of absolute structures of thought tend to inscribe ending as the beginning of that which lies beyond their text' (1999: 74). Such endings 'are thus more "open" in one sense than ends which are accidental' (1999: 74). While an open ending just 'sits' there, waiting for resolution that never comes, a closed ending indicates that, when the last act concludes, a new one is waiting in the wings. The end of one thing is always the beginning of another, just as, in Schlegelian terms, a thing is just another thing in the act of becoming (Mellor 1980: 5).

These films, then, demonstrate both a mournful sense of loss due to endings, and a hope for the perpetual renewal of the beginnings born of those endings. The death of 'grand narratives' (Lyotard 1997: xxiii) does not mean the death of individual stories that contain a search for meaning. Whereas in the early 1980s, the term 'postmodernism' began to signal a 'pervasive cynicism about the progressivist ideals of modernity' (Waugh 1992: 5), by the mid-1990s, that given cynicism became a jumping-off point for a commentary on cynicism itself. The 'new sincerity' externalises an ideological struggle between sincerity and cynicism by making that struggle, in part, an imaginative but sobering game. For the Romantic, art becomes 'an intensely serious kind of play which defines mankind in terms of freedom' (Boreham and Heath 2005: 45). Such a freedom lies within the limitless world of the human mind, the imagination. But the reliance upon imagination to bridge the gap between self and world can have an unintentional consequence: an increasing withdrawal from the world itself.

The Battle Between Self-consciousness and Solipsism

While the 'Romantic era saw the production of a diversity of models for understanding subjectivity', the challenge to the 'depth model' led to a crisis in the conception of self (Henderson 1996: 3). The danger of the pendulum swinging so wide meant it often would swing back with unassailable force – resulting in the 'poet's anxious need for self-assurance' (Rzepka 1986: 9). The resultant 'visionary solipsism' produces a subject that radically turns back in toward herself, intent on securing subjectivity in the face of indeterminacy (1986: 9). The indeterminacy of postmodernism threatens to exacerbate this tendency, one that is evident in all the films I discuss.

It is found in the Tenenbaum children's quest to reassert their long-past status as a 'family of geniuses'; in Steve Zissou's similar attempt to reclaim the highs of his glory days by avenging the death of his partner; in Caden Cotard's desire to make meaningful and authentic art that will solidify his legacy; in the Lisbon girls' assertion of subjectivity through *Weltschmerz*-fuelled 'self-oblivion' (Thorslev 1962: 170); in Theodore Twombly's need for the self-affirmation found in love; in Mr Fox's plan to realise his 'true' self through his farm raids;

and in Marie Antoinette's constant struggle to 'find herself' amidst her various passions.

Waugh writes of two separate strains of subjectivity she sees in Romantic thought: 'radical fictionality' and 'radical situatedness' (1992: 19). The former she attributes to Coleridge and his concept of a self that 'exists in its ability to work with the fragments available to it and from them to project on to the world new fictions by which to live' so that 'the self can potentially shape its own world' (1992: 19). Such 'new fictions' correspond to the self that creates them: 'The self is always a creation out of available materials, never an archaeological discovery at a fixed point of origin' (1992: 22). I place Kaufman and Coppola within this Romantic tradition. The selves they create constantly search for self-actualising moments that will define their existence as an 'infinite I AM' (Coleridge [1817] 1980: 167), but more often than not they exist within radically decentred worlds where their selfhood is being relentlessly questioned or even invalidated. Their lives are fragmentary, and they often fight against this idea. Their creators, however, invariably embrace the chaos and fragmentary nature of existence. The aesthetic emphasis on destabilising and decentring depictions of time and space (Kaufman) or an insistence on focusing on surfaces and sensations (Coppola) suggest an ironic relation to subjectivity as it 'dissolves, diffuses, dissipates in order to recreate' (Coleridge [1817] 1980: 167) new selves that are just as fictional as the previous ones.

Waugh sees the Wordsworthian view of subjecthood as 'radical situatedness', which affirms the body's place within a nature that is 'always in motion' (1992: 22). Modernity becomes 'a characteristic denial or disavowal' of such a 'being-in-the-world' that renders the subject detached, a manipulator of a nature that has become 'inert' (1992: 23). Anderson's and Jonze's films best exemplify this fundamental break of the subject's relation to the chaos of nature. Their protagonists spend their time 'looking, speculating and judging' (1992: 23) often without participating (or participating half-heartedly). Their subjectivity is less fractured than those populating Kaufman's and Coppola's films, but they suffer crises of self nonetheless. Trapped by their own imaginative subjectivity, they are unable to renounce the idea of their 'fixed point of origin' (1992: 22). Anderson's and Jonze's mise-en-scènes depict the picturesque detachment of their characters (and, perhaps, their authors as well), gazing upon life, frozen in contemplation, unable to live. The freedom to create and destroy, in Romantic ironic fashion, is impeded by such self-consciousness (1992: 45). While overcoming it completely is beyond the scope of human power, the struggle to do so still comprises these films' Romantic core.

Despite their differences in portrayal, egocentric self-assertion leaves all of these characters, at one point or another, detached from life. Preoccupied by their own obsessions with self, they despair at their inability to reach out to others in any meaningful way. In the Romantic age, such a visionary solipsism 'tended to produce, as its repressed double, a gothic sense of the insubstantiality of selves' (Henderson 1996: 38). In this gothic world, '[l]ife in general appears "theatrical", a "death-in-life", and embodied selves become mere actors or caricatures, or in more severe cases, insensate things altogether, like automata or walking corpses' (Rzepka 1986: 26). This idea is felt most strongly in Kaufman's film. Caden Cotard represents both visionary solipsism and gothic insubstantiality. He is a self-obsessed artist who becomes an actor in his own play, both an automaton – given direct orders on what movements to make and when to die – and a wandering corpse, not yet dead but afraid to live. Coppola's heroines are equally indicative of the gothic sense of the theatrical; they are portrayed as their own shadow selves, viewed from the outside by egocentric spectators as if on stage. Cecilia Lisbon is not so much a walking corpse as she is a lounging one, and Marie Antoinette wields her theatricality as a shield against those who seek to diminish her selfhood.

While Kaufman and Coppola most obviously engage with this gothic flipside of subjectivity, Anderson and Jonze do as well. But their perhaps more optimistic works tend to display it more subtly: in Jonze's film, Theodore Twombly's soft-spoken timidity sometimes borders on the somnambulant, and Anderson has been accused of making his actors into mere objects of his highly orchestrated mise-en-scène (Hill 2008: 99) – his obsession with uniforms and theatrical character quirks often delimits subjectivity as mere caricature. This is actually an alternative form of the gothic: a kitsch, highly idiosyncratic way to address the eternally duelling dialectic of asserting the self while questioning its very being. The films all constantly renegotiate self-assertion and self-negation as part of their questioning of definitive endings.

'Bravery in the midst of indeterminacy': Emotion as a Form of Revolution

If the need for self-assurance cannot be met, alternatives must be sought. Perhaps the transcendence found within the sublime can achieve a greater sense of wellbeing: a connection to the larger world combined with the elevation of personal power. If 'we feel difficulty in believing in a grand narrative founded in the transcendent' (Larrissy 1999: 7) within the postmodern, we should not necessarily give up on it, for 'the question of how far one can completely cut such a Postmodernism adrift from the transcendent persists, if its techniques and impulses have in fact emerged from a Romantic matrix' (1999: 7). For Waugh, the fundamental mode of transcendence exists in the artist's relationship to art: 'We still play God imaginatively, but ironically and provisionally' (1992: 11). In this sense, any relation to the transcendence found in sublimity is one based on an ironic questioning of sublime transcendence itself.

CONCLUSION: ON ENDINGS AND NEW BEGINNINGS

The films I discuss have renegotiated a relationship to the transcendent through an aesthetic engagement with the sublime: they attempt to assert sublimity (for their characters) while portraying aesthetic projects that most strongly rely on ideas of the beautiful and the picturesque. Their engagement with various modes of the sublime – the Burkean, the Kantian, the egotistical, the feminine, the material – are primarily an intellectual exercise. In *The Life Aquatic*, Anderson undercuts the sublime of the ocean's expanse with kitschy practical effects. In *The Virgin Suicides*, Coppola mocks the assertion of male power found within the egotistical sublime, although her images often conjure feelings of transcendence through ecstatic surface sensation, in the vein of the material sublime. Only Kaufman goes so far as to attempt to engender true feelings of sublimity in the spectator through disorienting aesthetic effects, but his protagonist does not achieve a feeling of transcendence due to acknowledgement of his power of reason – to the contrary, he is perhaps literally mad.

Within modernity, Jean-François Lyotard finds sublimity in the indeterminacy of endings functioning as new beginnings, linking the sublime to the anxiety felt in the question 'and what now?' (Lyotard 1993b: 246). Indeed, he considers Burke's 'major stake' in his conception of the sublime is 'to show that the sublime is kindled by the threat of nothing further happening' (1993b: 250). For Waugh, the sense of endings is especially pronounced within postmodernism:

> Though there are many forms of Postmodernism, they all express the sense that our inherited forms of knowledge and representation are undergoing some fundamental shift: modernity is coming to an end, strangled by its own contradictory logic, born astride of the grave which is now its abyss. (Waugh 1992: 7)

If the idea of modernity itself 'coming to an end' does not incite sublime terror, it is difficult to think of what could. But as is true of all sublime feeling, it rests not only in terror, but also in delight. If the sublime, within the postmodern and the Romantic, can be considered a form of 'resistance to the banal and automatizing effects of modern life' (Waugh 1992: 31), these films' intellectual engagement with it, at the very least, represents a questioning of such automatisation.

The films offer no solutions, but the idea of solutions is itself hardly a Romantic one. As Waugh suggests, in both Romanticism and postmodernism, 'the aesthetic becomes the only possible means of redemption' from the totalitarian reason of Enlightenment (1992: 15). Reasonable solutions are too didactic for a view toward art 'refurbishing the interior' rather than insisting on 'systemic "truth"' (1992: 6). Instead, the films' form of 'bravery' is found in their engagement with sincere emotion, even as they represent the anxiety of indeterminacy. If change is the only true constant, establishing even tenuous emotional connections with other selves, or attempting to create emotional connections with spectators, can seem like a revolutionary act.

Historical influence remains a key to unlocking the films' relation to the here and now. According to Jürgen Habermas, in the late nineteenth century, 'there emerged out of th[e] romantic spirit that radicalized consciousness of modernity which freed itself from all historical ties' (1992: 99). Rather than being freed from their ties to history, however, these films – even as they exist as fantastical, ahistorical creations – are very much situated within a historical trajectory. They do not represent history as the unassailable march of progress, however, but as a return to origins. As circles of imaginative recreation expand, they also cycle back. Focused on memory and the past in order to discover selves in the forever 'ongoing incompleted *process*' of their creation (Waugh 1992: 25; original emphasis), characters attempt to forge hopeful connections amidst the endless potential of new beginnings.

After the era of 1990s American cinema, which often celebrated a pessimistic form of nihilism with the disillusioned sheen of 'dampened affect' (Sconce 2002: 359), the cinema of the twenty-first century has managed to bring feeling, a desire for intimacy and emotional vulnerability to the forefront even as it resists an outright ideological agenda. Derek Hill acknowledges the lack of a 'conscious' movement in this 'American No Wave':

> It's as if the idea of a group of filmmakers intentionally attempting to spark a revolution with their cameras is too dated, too romantic and too ridiculous even to ponder. It appeals to the ambitious 14-year-old within, even though the older, wiser, more cynical adult knows better. (Hill 2009: 11)

Hill has managed to capture the entire *raison d'être* of this non-movement movement in a single brief quotation. The idea *is* too romantic, and decidedly dated – dated back to the birth of the modern era itself. Regardless of conscious intention (and likely the result more of unconscious reaction), in this cycle of films Romantic idealism, which Hill considers the subject of ridicule, is met with world-weary postmodern cynicism, which he equates with wisdom. One gets the sense that these filmmakers would reverse his pronouncements of value. Regardless, to the victor goes the spoils whenever the dialectic game ends. The true Romantic knows it never will.

NOTES

Introduction

1. While Snell is specifically referencing psychoanalysis's Romantic influences, I am using the term in its most everyday sense here, suggesting the filmmakers in question are often not completely aware of the source of many of their preoccupations.
2. It should be noted that sometimes these choices are indeed conscious, such as Coppola's decision to shoot her 2003 feature *Lost in Translation* on 35mm film rather than digital. The filmmaker says the choice was due to her desire for a 'fragmented, dislocated, melancholic, romantic feeling', invoking not just Romantic longing for a past 'enchanted few days' but also a sense of the fractured indeterminacy of the self in the present (Thompson 2010).
3. For arguments connecting Romanticism to surrealism and other modern art movements, see Abel 1984; Adamowicz 2001; Cunningham 2005; O'Pray 2003; Pattison 2013; Wiedmann 1979. For Romanticism's links to French New Wave cinema, see Andrew 2013; Caughie 1981.
4. Discussions of modernism in this text broadly refer to it in its 'utopian' guises. The late nineteenth-/early twentieth-century philosophical and aesthetic movement encompassed a reverence for 'utilitarian forms and undecorated surfaces' in art and design (Crouch 2015: 619) and a similar 'hard and solid imagery' in literature and poetry (Whitworth 2007: 65). Such a modernism married the unadorned functionalism of classical forms to an emerging sense of utopian possibility found within the now fully-fledged industrialism of modernity, thus 'shaking off the legacy of traditional historical styles' (Crouch 2015: 619). To do so, it embraced the marriage of art and technology in realising its vision (2015: 620). In essence, modernism relegated history to the margins in favour of looking forward to a boundless future of technological progress, rejecting Romanticism's emphasis on the personal, particular and emotional (Whitworth 2007: 65).

5. I also consider Michel Gondry (*Eternal Sunshine of the Spotless Mind*, *The Science of Sleep*), Noah Baumbach (*Frances Ha*, *The Squid and the Whale*) and David O. Russell (*Spanking the Monkey*, *I Heart Huckabees*) to be a part of this group. They exhibit many of the same thematic and stylistic preoccupations and have personal and professional ties to the filmmakers I cover: Gondry directed two scripts by Kaufman; Baumbach is the screenwriting partner of Wes Anderson; and Spike Jonze appeared in Russell's 1999 film *Three Kings*. Russell has since become much more of a classical Hollywood filmmaker, with mainstream successes like *The Fighter*, although his later screwball comedies, such as 2012's *Silver Linings Playbook*, exhibit many of the traits of his earlier films.

Chapter 1

1. Anderson's work is so widely known for its idiosyncrasy and unique point of view it has become ripe for pop-culture parody. A 2013 video from the satirical website *The Onion*, 'Wes Anderson Reteams with Favorite Objects for *Grand Budapest Hotel*', mocks his obsession with a mise-en-scène overstuffed with historical objects. His hermetic and obsessive world creation is also lampooned in a *Saturday Night Live* short film from the same year, 'The Midnight Coterie of Sinister Intruders'. Billed as 'a tale of handmade horror', it skewers his preciousness by imagining his version of a home-invasion slasher film, a play on the very idea that his style automatically renders comic any notion of sublime terror.
2. There is no shortage of print reviews that take Anderson to task for his calculated whimsy. According to the *New York Times*, 'Humanism lies either beyond [Anderson's] grasp or outside his range of interests' (Scott 2007). *The Guardian* writes, 'One can't shake the sense that in some respects Wes Anderson's greatest production is Wes Anderson himself, and that his grand body of work might best be read as a kind of romantic reconfiguration of his own life and the people in it' (Brooks 2007). *Slate* suggests 'he pins actors into the centers of fastidiously composed tableaux like so many dead butterflies' (Weiner 2007). In a review of *The Royal Tenenbaums*, A. O. Scott (2001) hammers home the point: 'This gallery of portraits, this array of handmade figurines lovingly placed in shoe box dioramas, fails to coalesce into anything resembling drama.'
3. The theme will be echoed in 2012's *Moonrise Kingdom* (American Empirical, 2012), when the pre-teen Suzy Bishop appears in a play costumed as a raven – she enjoys a bit more freedom even as she brings to mind a sort of miniature version of Margot. It also speaks to Anderson's relating of children in general to wild creatures or, at times, 'savages', while simultaneously imbuing them with preternatural abilities and intelligence. I address this idea further in Chapter 5.
4. Anderson seems to enjoy skewering the 'wild man' persona of the macho, Hemingway-esque author in the form of Cash, whom the *Sunday Times Magazine* supplement shown in the film calls 'The James Joyce of the West'. Despite his supposedly manly fetishes, in many respects Eli is the inverse of Margot; while he desperately playacts his virile, sublime fantasies, deep down he is still a hapless private school boy desperate to belong. His magazine cover, in which he comically poses shirtless

while donning his trademark cowboy hat and hoisting snakes in both hands, is just one of many visual punch lines made at his expense. It turns out he personally sent a copy to Etheline for her approval. 'He sends me all his clippings', she tells a horrified Margot. Unlike Margot, Eli's tragi-comic sense of wildness is clearly conveyed as inauthentic.
5. The title of Anderson's film is an indirect reference to Welles's own *The Magnificent Ambersons* (Mercury Productions, 1942), a film that offers repeated inspiration for Anderson. Both films include a palatial family home, third-person narration and 'a sense of collective anxiety born of the feeling that time has passed a once-important family by and the community knows it' (Seitz 2009).

Chapter 2

1. While the filmmakers covered in this book often engage in more 'traditional' concepts of irony, such as dramatic irony (in which the spectator enjoys a greater knowledge than characters) or rhetorical irony (in which characters or works will often evince a detached, mocking attitude toward events portrayed), this is not the principle focus of my study. See MacDowell 2016 for a wide-ranging discussion of irony in film.
2. Schenectady, a bucolic town with a population of 60,000 three hours north of New York City (and about 3.5 hours north of Kaufman's hometown of Massapequa), occupies a rather storied position in American culture, particularly for a place its size. Authors as varied as Henry James, Kurt Vonnegut and Dr. Seuss have used it as a setting or as a hometown of major characters. Aside from the obvious pun of the title, Kaufman's film uses Schenectady and its reputation as an all-American every-town as a banal backdrop for incursions of the weird and fantastic. It is not quite the kitsch pastiche of Lumberton in David Lynch's *Blue Velvet* (De Laurentiis Entertainment Group, 1986), but its sense of standardised normalcy offers a blank slate for Kaufman to explore his 'larger realm'.
3. Deming writes that the use of Arthur Miller's famous mid-twentieth-century play 'sets the tone of tragic inevitability and melancholia built into the movie' while also pointing to its similar protagonist unfixed in time, since Willy Loman 'regularly disappears into flashbacks of earlier stages of his life' (2011: 197). Joel Evans also highlights the play's explicit relation to the time-image in its 'overt concern with the potentially uneven, disjointed rhythms of time' (2014: 332). It shares this in common with other works referenced in Kaufman's film, including Marcel Proust's *Swann's Way* and Franz Kafka's *The Trial*, which are both read by Hazel. Writing in the *Arthur Miller Journal*, Rebecca Davers (2011) suggests even greater thematic resonance with *Synecdoche* and *Salesman* and their two protagonists.
4. An article in the scientific journal *Biological Psychiatry* refers to the case of a 65-year-old sufferer of the syndrome. The woman initially 'presented with gradually progressive memory problems' and suicidal thoughts before developing the belief her brain had become 'completely rotten' with cancer and finally insisting she was dead (Mitra and Chatterjee 2015: 53). Like Caden at his most degraded, she 'failed repeatedly to recognize her close acquaintances and had shown significant reduction in her speech output and psychomotor activity' (2015: 53).

5. There are multiple references to Germany, Germanic people, and the German language in the film, from Olive and Adele moving to Berlin (where Caden briefly visits and speaks to a now German-accented Maria) to a German-accented professor reading a melancholy Rilke poem on the radio in the opening scene, to an explicit reference to Kafka's *The Trial*. In a sense, these serve as 'Easter eggs', cuing the audience to the various Germanic artists and philosophers whose work Kaufman engages. More generally, they conjure a tone of 'German misery', which Marx and Engels characterised as the 'predominant' pessimism found in German Romanticism (qtd in Behler 1988: 46).
6. This is a common theme in Kaufman's scripts. In *Adaptation*, Susan Orlean longs to be a baby again so she can be 'new', and Joel Barrish in *Eternal Sunshine of the Spotless Mind* actually lives out scenes from his childhood, one as a baby being bathed in a sink.
7. The logistics of the sets within sets within sets proved a significant challenge for the film's script supervisor, Mary Cybulski, who created detailed diagrams of each space within space in order to log which scenes occur in which sets. On her chart, there are no fewer than five iterations of the warehouse set, each one inhabiting a different state of physical completion ('In and Around Schenectady, New York').

Chapter 3

1. Many critics and scholars have discussed Lux's obvious relation to Nabokov's (and Stanley Kubrick's, in his film adaptation) character, the teenage 'nymphette' Lolita, emphasising her naïve yet knowing sexuality. Backman Rogers references Lolita's 'infantilized sexuality' (2015: 25), while Masafumi Monden writes that, like Lolita, Lux is 'manipulative, flirtatious, coquettish and above all, self-assured yet innocent, and she seems to be comfortable with that image' (2013: 146). The *New York Times* refers specifically to Kubrick's film: 'Like Sue Lyon in Stanley Kubrick's *Lolita*, with her lollipop and heart-shaped sunglasses, Ms. Dunst turns Lux's every glance and gesture into an ambiguous provocation' (Scott 2000).
2. Critics have also pointed out the allusion to John Everett Millais's famous Pre-Raphaelite painting *Ophelia* (1851–2), as well as the various psychological and cultural connotations of the Shakespearean character it is based on. Ophelia, in many ways, connotes complex formations of both sublimity and beauty within femininity. Backman Rogers notes that Ophelia represents 'a form of tragic beauty' (2015: 25). Monden refers to her as an 'icon of girlhood', with the Pre-Raphaelite depiction of Ophelia as 'an epitome of female complexity [. . .] virtuous yet sexually knowing' who becomes a symbol of 'maidenly madness' in the Romantic era (2013: 149–50). For Monden, viewing Ophelia's death as a suicide, rather than an accident of madness, 'can be understood as her means to challenge and criticize her culturally and socially imposed passivity and dependency, and those who impose such burdens on her' (2013: 153). This idea is central to Coppola's film as well.
3. While Jameson specifically refers to the era immediately following World War II, the effect of malaise could be seen to increase with the ensuing decades. In the 1970s, nascent economic globalisation and an attendant 'crisis of capitalism' kindled a

fear that the bottom of American society was ready to drop out (Maier 2010: 25). It is not accidental that Mr Lisbon's main hobby is constructing models of World War II airplanes – for him, they are nostalgic, imaginative renderings of his youth, a time when the idea of limitless progress and the righteous campaign of American exceptionalism was at its peak, only to be replaced later by Jameson's malaise.

4. In a slyly ironic casting turn, Mrs Lisbon is portrayed by Kathleen Turner, a major sex symbol of the 1980s, who appeared in highly sexualised roles in films such as *Body Heat* (Lawrence Kasdan, Warner Bros., 1981) and *Crimes of Passion* (Ken Russell, New World Pictures, 1984) in which she portrayed a femme fatale and a prostitute, respectively. In Coppola's film, she is the ultimate frustrated, de-sexed and dowdy hausfrau. It is as if her years serving as a sex object have degraded her to the point that she no longer has any positive value as a symbol at all. She represents not only the loss of sexual power that the girls will eventually experience but also the rigid, socially proscribed roles they will have to embody in adulthood. As A. O. Scott writes – after comparing Kirsten Dunst to a teenage Turner in her 'toughness' – Mrs Lisbon represents a 'life force walled in by the masonry of repression' (Scott 2000).

5. See Benko 1993 for an extensive discussion of Mary worship and the so-called 'cult of Mary'.

Chapter 4

1. John Keats coined the term 'egotistical sublime' (Keats 1970: 157) in reference to the sublime of Wordsworth, whom Keats accused of emphasising the mind's idealisation of experience at the expense of the concrete. For an in-depth delineation of both egotistical and feminine sublimity, see Chapter 3.

2. For instance, the water in the canals of the model city in *Where the Wild Things Are* (Warner Bros., 2009) was inspired by Jonze's childhood fantasies of walking in his hometown of New York and imagining the streets were made of water like Venice, a city that to him sounded 'like a dream' (McSweeney's 2009: 67). Even more tellingly, Jonze remarks, 'When you make movies, you totally lose touch with reality. You start living in this other world where you think anything can be done. [. . .] You also start thinking of the world as totally yours' (2009: 214).

3. David L. Smith views Theodore's ghost-writing job as authentic in its 'genuine' fakery. Drawing on the philosophy of Alan Watts, who believes 'self and world are mutually constituted' – that is, there is no true separation between ourselves and anything external – the notion of the 'real thing' becomes fluid (Smith 2014: 1, 6). As such, our emotions are all mutually constitutive and Theodore's expressions are sincere. He has a point, specifically regarding the film's conclusions on intersubjectivity. However, I feel that in the early context of the narrative, we are meant to view Theodore as someone who is more comfortable expressing the emotions of others rather than his own. Indeed, society as a whole is happy to 'outsource' its emotions; as Smith writes, the practice does not actually constitute a lie because everyone involved tacitly agrees to it (2014: 8).

4. Jonze seems to be pointing toward a capitalist commodification of happiness with his colour palette, which he says was initially inspired by US juice bar chain Jamba Juice

and its 'very clean, brightly lit' interiors featuring 'a lot of warm colours' (Bell 2014). According to the director, he was trying to portray a milieu where 'everything was so nice' that a person would feel guilty for feeling 'lonely and isolated' (Bell 2014).

5. Jonze has been criticized for his depiction of a near-future Los Angeles that is supposedly racially homogenous (Renninger 2013). The accusation of 'unbearable whiteness' has been levied at all the filmmakers I discuss in one form or another – especially Anderson (see Weiner 2007). This is a legitimate cause for concern, especially given the lack of racial and cultural diversity in much of Hollywood and independent American cinema (see Cox 2017; Respers France 2018). Non-white performers (mainly of Asian descent) do appear in *Her*, although none are in the main cast. However, the homogeneity in the case of *Her* is as much a criticism that is emerging from within the film itself – variation and uniqueness have been replaced in this society by a comfortable yet discomfiting, life-subsuming sameness.

6. According to Ivanchikova, *Her* examines 'our transferential, libidinally charged enchantment with technical devices' (2016: 68). In particular, Theodore's relationship with his OS begs comparison to the near-sexual fetishisation of new technology products from Apple, such as the company's wildly successful, continually updated iPhones, which are often sold with 'the peculiar combination of technoslang and erotic discourse' (2016: 77). Apple seems to be a soft target for Jonze – many have likened the OS1 to Apple's interactive iPhone voice programme Siri, which in North America (unlike in the UK) has a distinctly female register (Pelly 2014; May 2014).

7. It has been widely reported that Jonze originally recorded the voice work of actor Samantha Morton for the role of Samantha; Morton even acted on set with Phoenix as he performed Theodore (Zeitchik 2013; Patterson 2013). This accounts for the OS's name, which corresponds to its original voice performer. Curiously, the film's other prominent female character, Amy, is also portrayed by an actor with the same first name, Amy Adams. Whether this was Jonze's attempt at grounding *Her*'s female characters in a reality in which Theodore does not participate is unclear, but the aborted idea certainly offers a reflexive commentary on Theodore's imaginary relation to the world.

8. Ivanchikova points out the irony of power distribution – the mother versus the mothered – in Samantha and Theodore's relationship. While Theodore ostensibly controls Samantha, he also serves 'the role of a surrogate mother, in that the human provides both a safe environment and the nutrition (in this case, the data feed) necessary for the machine to grow' (Ivanchikova 2016: 74). Ivanchikova sees this relationship as 'parasitic' (with Samantha as the parasite) (2016: 68), but I view it as symbiotic, which I explain later.

9. This scene, in which a woman wears a tiny camera on her face so Samantha can experience having sex with Theodore 'through' her body, is the most overt indication of the film's theme of embodiment impeding intersubjectivity. Theodore is wary of the idea of a sexual surrogate as soon as Samantha broaches the topic and finds that he cannot perform when he becomes distracted by the woman's minute facial movements. Many have pointed out that this represents a turning point in the film, both when Samantha decides to embrace her difference and Theodore realises that he is fooling himself about their relationship (see Jollimore 2015; Alpert 2014/15).

10. In a widely circulated television interview with the BBC's *Newsnight* programme, Jonze appears to bristle at the idea that the film is about, according to the interviewer, 'falling in love with your software' in a world where a man finds the 'ideal woman who just works for him as his PA'. The director keeps insisting the interviewer tell him what 'moved' her about the film, emphasising the importance of emotional engagement above all else (see BBC Newsnight 2014).

CHAPTER 5

1. I have put the undoubtedly racist and culturally hegemonic nomenclature used in this era in scare quotes to denote its general lack of acceptance in our own time. In the eighteenth century, pervasive belief in pseudo-scientific theories such as biological determinism was deeply rooted in racism, sexism and cultural bias. According to Stephen Jay Gould, the perpetrators of such theories viewed the contemporary white European male as the pinnacle of human civilisation; non-whites, children and women were conversely viewed as inferior links on an evolutionary chain, 'literally mired in an ancestral stage of superior groups' (1996: 145).
2. If there is any doubt that Anderson meant to wrestle *Fantastic Mr. Fox* from its original author and assert his own stamp as auteur, the director based the rapacious, mean-spirited and tyrannical character of Bean partially on Dahl himself (Anderson 2014).
3. Anderson reportedly took his ending from Dahl's original story notes. It was not included in the final publication because the publisher objected to the idea of a children's book advocating 'shoplifting' (Kertzer 2010: 12).
4. Anderson's maternal figures, such as Felicity Fox (but not necessarily other female characters, such as Margot Tenenbaum), are routinely characterised as being practical, steadfast members of society. These matriarchal women do not suffer fools gladly – those fools normally consisting of the hapless male figures at the centre of Anderson's narratives. Rather, they tend to just get things done, despite having often complicated inner lives. As Adrienne Kertzer notes, an earlier draft of the film's script explicitly points to the hidden darker layers of Mrs Fox, when Bean studies her sublime landscape paintings of thunderstorms and comments, 'She's got a good eye, but she's obviously very depressed' (2010: 7). Unfortunately, Anderson seems to have far less interest in these female characters than he does the egocentric men-children on which his stories focus.
5. To lend a further note of the authentic, Anderson had Bill Murray act out the part of the wolf on a hill at the farm in Connecticut where most of the voice actors recorded their performances. This physical acting out of roles was done throughout recording (Anderson 2014).
6. In his director's commentary, Anderson notes that this scene was inspired in part by the ending to Sydney Pollack's western *Jeremiah Johnson* (Warner Bros., 1972), a New Hollywood ode to the Romantic American myth of the solitary white frontiersman who 'goes native' (virtually feral) in the nineteenth-century climes of the Rocky Mountains. Like Anderson, Pollack simultaneously valorises and deflates the myth of the wild as a place to 'find' oneself, although he does so much more

brutally: caught between town and country, Jeremiah is refused his pastoral middle ground and instead devolves into a brutal killer out of necessity.

Chapter 6

1. The press likes to emphasise Coppola's use of interjectory filler speech such as 'um', 'like' and 'whatever', perhaps to paint a portrait of her as cluelessly grasping and even inconsequential, although these placeholder words do lend a characteristic impressionism and ambiguity to her thoughts. One 2006 *Guardian* article characterises Coppola as a pampered and indolent adolescent not unlike Marie Antoinette: 'Sofia Coppola could easily be a character in one of her own films, a day-dreamy, slightly disconnected but immaculately stylish waif who seems all at sea in a world of extraordinary privilege. She is tiny and speaks quickly and quietly, her sentences sometimes petering out as if from the sheer effort of formulating them' (O'Hagan 2006). The writer goes on to describe Coppola as 'like a slightly out-to-lunch teenager' and 'sulkily beautiful' and describes her much less accomplished filmmaker brother Roman (who directed the second unit on *Marie Antoinette*) as the 'male heir apparent' of the Coppola clan (O'Hagan 2006). To my mind, such troublesome characterisations of Coppola go hand in hand with the often thinly veiled contempt for her work; they evoke negative connotations about feminine authority and female authorship in general.
2. There is no shortage of statistical and anecdotal evidence to support the conception of a so-called 'gender gap' in both Hollywood and European filmmaking. See Cwik 2016; Lang 2015; Siegel 2015.
3. Vivian R. Gruder examines whether the public attitude toward Marie Antoinette in the pre-Revolutionary era was actually as derisive as it is now portrayed, or if this idea is indicative of revisionist history. While various 'scandal' pamphlets on Louis XV and his mistresses, de Pompadour and du Barry, circulated widely during his reign (2002: 271–2), according to Gruder, 'The young king, and especially the young queen who had so visibly disliked du Barry, seemed initially to heighten the moral tone of the court' (2002: 273). However, she also concedes, 'fresh scurrilous gossip quickly circulated against the young royal couple, in particular against the queen' (2002: 273). Regardless of the severity or number of actual attacks against Marie Antoinette's character, she persists as a symbol of decadence and the subject of popular ridicule in the post-Revolutionary imagination.
4. Such statically composed long takes with slow zooms either in or out appear regularly in Coppola's films and usually represent a crucial moment of introspection or a psychological turning point on the protagonist's part, such as the silent, lengthy shot of Johnny Marco (Stephen Dorff) being fitted for a prosthetic mask in *Somewhere* (Focus Features, 2010).
5. It should be noted that the film's title explicitly relates to the sensationalist 1979 novel *Flowers in the Attic* by V. C. Andrews, a modern gothic tale involving incest and abuse. In Coppola's film teenage girls obsessed with the story, and its instance of attempted murder via rat poison, alter the phrase 'Kill the rats' into its mirror image, 'Lick the star'. The novel's subject matter aligns closely with the gothic fiction that

Coppola invokes in *The Virgin Suicides*, with its themes of sexual repression and familial oppression. It is also a very obvious example of the 'women's fiction' that Wordsworth and his contemporaries would likely deride as frivolous, superficial and dangerously feminine.

6. Coppola uses similar imagery in *The Virgin Suicides*, when Lux (also played by Dunst) reaches her hand outside an open car window in a fantasy sequence, enjoying the moving breeze. Lux is tellingly characterised by her therapist as being a 'dreamer' and 'completely out of touch with reality', criticisms that could certainly be applied to Marie Antoinette.

Conclusion

1. I define 'humanism' here in its most general terms, as a philosophy that 'gives special importance to human concerns, values, and dignity' (Law 2013: 264). I do not mean to relate it to any kind of 'atheistic world view' (2013: 263), and I especially do not mean to suggest that humanism in this context denotes rationalism or 'scientism', 'the view that every meaningful question can in principle be answered by application of the scientific method' (2013: 265). In fact, I hope I have shown that the humanism (with a 'small h') of these filmmakers lies in the veneration of the obverse.

FILMOGRAPHY

À bout de souffle. Dir. Jean-Luc Godard. Perf. Jean-Paul Belmondo, Jean Seberg. Les Films Impéria, 1960.

Adaptation. Dir. Spike Jonze. Perf. Nicolas Cage, Meryl Streep, Chris Cooper. Propaganda Films, 2002.

A.I. Artificial Intelligence. Dir. Steven Spielberg. Perf. Jude Law, Haley Joel Osment, Frances O'Connor. Warner Bros., DreamWorks SKG, Amblin Entertainment, Stanley Kubrick Productions, 2001.

Anderson, Wes. 'Director's Commentary'. *Fantastic Mr. Fox*. Blu-ray. The Criterion Collection, 2014.

Anderson, Wes. 'Director's Commentary'. *The Life Aquatic with Steve Zissou*. DVD. The Criterion Collection, 2005.

Anderson, Wes. 'Director's Commentary'. *The Royal Tenenbaums*. DVD. The Criterion Collection, 2002.

Anomalisa. Dir. Charlie Kaufman. Perf. David Thewlis, Jennifer Jason Leigh, Tom Noonan. Starburns Industries, 2015.

Baisers volés (Stolen Kisses). Dir. François Truffaut. Perf. Jean-Pierre Léaud, Delphine Seyrig. Les Films du Carrosse, Les Productions Artistes Associés, 1968.

BBC Newsnight. 'Newsnight: An exclusive BBC interview with Spike Jonze, director of *Her*'. 14 February 2014. <https://www.youtube.com/watch?v=3vAJGE97e4A> (last accessed 18 February 2019).

The Beguiled. Dir. Sofia Coppola. Perf. Nicole Kidman, Kirsten Dunst, Colin Farrell. American Zoetrope, 2017.

Being John Malkovich. Dir. Spike Jonze. Perf. John Cusack, Cameron Diaz, Catherine Keener. Propaganda Films, 1999.

The Bling Ring. Dir. Sofia Coppola. Perf. Emma Watson, Leslie Mann. American Zoetrope, 2013.

Blue Velvet. Dir. David Lynch. Perf. Kyle MacLachlan, Isabella Rossellini, Dennis Hopper. De Laurentiis Entertainment Group, 1986.
Bottle Rocket. Dir. Wes Anderson. Perf. Owen Wilson, Luke Wilson. Columbia Pictures, Gracie Films, 1996.
Carrie. Dir. Brian De Palma. Perf. Sissey Spacek, Piper Laurie. Red Bank Films, 1976.
Cléo de 5 à 7. Dir. Agnès Varda. Perf. Corinne Marchand. Ciné Tamaris, Rome Paris Films, 1962.
Confessions of a Dangerous Mind. Dir. George Clooney. Perf. Sam Rockwell, Drew Barrymore. Miramax, Mad Chance, 2002.
The Darjeeling Limited. Dir. Wes Anderson. Perf. Owen Wilson, Jason Schwartzman, Adrien Brody, Anjelica Huston. American Empirical, Fox Searchlight, 2007.
Eternal Sunshine of the Spotless Mind. Dir. Michel Gondry. Perf. Jim Carrey, Kate Winslet. Focus Features, Anonymous Content, This Is That, 2004.
Fantastic Mr. Fox. Dir. Wes Anderson. Perf. George Clooney, Meryl Streep, Michael Gambon, Bill Murray. Blu-ray. The Criterion Collection, 2014.
The Fighter. Dir. David O. Russell. Perf. Christian Bale, Mark Wahlberg, Amy Adams. The Weinstein Company, Closest to the Hole Productions, Mandeville Films, Relativity Media, 2010.
Frances Ha. Dir. Noah Baumbach. Perf. Greta Gerwig, Mickey Sumner. Pine District Pictures, Scott Rudin Productions, RT Features, 2012.
The Grand Budapest Hotel. Dir. Wes Anderson. Perf. Ralph Fiennes, F. Murray Abraham, Jeff Goldblum. Fox Searchlight, Indian Paintbrush, American Empirical, 2014.
Her. Dir. Spike Jonze. Perf. Joaquin Phoenix, Scarlett Johansson, Amy Adams. Annapurna Pictures, 2013.
Human Nature. Dir. Michel Gondry. Perf. Patricia Arquette, Tim Robbins, Rhys Ifans. Fine Line Pictures, StudioCanal, Good Machine, 2001.
I Heart Huckabees. Dir. David O. Russell. Perf. Dustin Hoffman, Lily Tomlin, Jason Schwartzman. Qwerty Films, Scott Rudin Productions, 2004.
'I'm Here'. Dir. Spike Jonze. D&E Entertainment, 2010. *Absolut*. <https://vimeo.com/103948718> (last accessed 30 November 2018).
'In and Around Schenectady, New York'. *Synecdoche, New York*. DVD. Sony Pictures Classics, 2009.
Isle of Dogs. Dir. Wes Anderson. Perf. Bryan Cranston, Koyu Rankin. American Empirical, Indian Paintbrush, 2018.
Jeremiah Johnson. Dir. Sydney Pollack. Perf. Robert Redford, Will Geer. Sanford Productions, Warner Bros., 1972.
Les deux Anglaises et le continent (Two English Girls). Dir. François Truffaut. Perf. Jean-Pierre Léaud, Kika Markham. Les Films du Carrosse, Cinétel, 1971.
'Lick the Star'. Dir. Sofia Coppola. Perf. Christina Turley, Audrey Kelly. Film Movement, 1998.
The Life Aquatic with Steve Zissou. Dir. Wes Anderson. Perf. Bill Murray, Owen Wilson, Anjelica Huston. American Empirical, Touchstone Pictures, 2004.
Lost in Translation. Dir. Sofia Coppola. Perf. Scarlett Johansson, Bill Murray. American Zoetrope, Focus Features, 2003.
The Magnificent Ambersons. Dir. Orson Welles. Perf. Joseph Cotten, Anne Baxter. Mercury Productions, 1942.

Marie Antoinette. Dir. Sofia Coppola. Perf. Kirsten Dunst, Jason Schwartzman, Steve Coogan. American Zoetrope, Columbia Pictures, 2006.

'The Midnight Coterie of Sinister Intruders'. *Saturday Night Live*. NBC. 26 October 2013.

Moonrise Kingdom. Dir. Wes Anderson. Perf. Edward Norton, Bruce Willis, Frances McDormand, Bill Murray. Indian Paintbrush, American Empirical, 2012.

The Royal Tenenbaums. Dir. Wes Anderson. Perf. Gene Hackman, Anjelica Huston, Luke Wilson, Gwyneth Paltrow. American Empirical, Touchstone Pictures, 2001.

Rushmore. Dir. Wes Anderson. Perf. Jason Schwartzman, Bill Murray. American Empirical, Touchstone Pictures, 1998.

The Science of Sleep. Dir. Michel Gondry. Perf. Gael García Bernal, Charlotte Gainsbourg. Gaumont, Partizan Films, Canal+, 2006.

Silver Linings Playbook. Perf. Jennifer Lawrence, Bradley Cooper, Robert De Niro. The Weinstein Company, 2012.

Somewhere. Dir. Sofia Coppola. Perf. Stephen Dorff, Elle Fanning. American Zoetrope, Focus Features, 2010.

Spanking the Monkey. Dir. David O. Russell. Perf. Jeremy Davies, Alberta Watson. Buckeye Films, Swelter Films, 1994.

The Squid and the Whale. Dir. Noah Baumbach. Perf. Jeff Daniels, Laura Linney, Jesse Eisenberg. American Empirical, Peter Newman Productions, 2005.

Synecdoche, New York. Dir. Charlie Kaufman. Perf. Philip Seymour Hoffman, Michelle Williams, Samantha Morton. Sidney Kimmel Entertainment, 2008.

Three Kings. Dir. David O. Russell. Perf. George Clooney, Mark Wahlberg, Spike Jonze. Warner Bros., Atlas Entertainment, 1999.

Tout va bien. Dir. Jean-Luc Godard. Perf. Jane Fonda, Yves Montand. Anouchka Films, Vieco Films, Empire Films, 1972.

The Virgin Suicides. Dir. Sofia Coppola. Perf. Kirsten Dunst, Kathleen Turner, James Woods. American Zoetrope, 1999.

'Wes Anderson Reteams with Favorite Objects for Grand Budapest Hotel'. 25 October 2013. *The Onion*. <https://entertainment.theonion.com/wes-anderson-reteams-with-favorite-objects-for-grand-bu-1819595515> (last accessed 30 November 2018).

Where the Wild Things Are. Dir. Spike Jonze. Perf. Max Records, James Gandolfini, Catherine Keener. Warner Bros., 2009.

BIBLIOGRAPHY

Aaron, Michele (2014), 'Cinema and Suicides: Necromanticism, Dead-already-ness, and the Logic of the Vanishing Point', *Cinema Journal*, Vol. 53, No. 2 (Winter), pp. 71–92.
Abel, Richard (1984), *French Cinema: The First Wave, 1915–1929*, Princeton: Princeton University Press.
Abrams, M. H. (1953), *The Mirror and the Lamp: Romantic Theory and the Critical Tradition*, Oxford: Oxford University Press.
Abrams, M. H. (1970), 'English Romanticism: The Spirit of the Age', in Harold Bloom (ed.), *Romanticism and Consciousness: Essays in Criticism*, New York: Norton, pp. 101–18.
Adamowicz, Elza (2001), 'Bodies Cut and Dissolved: Dada and Surrealist Film', in Alex Hughes and James S. Williams (eds), *Gender and French Cinema*, Oxford: Berg, pp. 19–34.
Aftab, Kaleem (2017), 'Sofia Coppola Has a Race Problem – and There's No Excuse for It', *The Telegraph*, 14 July, <https://www.telegraph.co.uk/films/2017/07/14/sofia-coppola-has-race-problem-no-excuse/> (last accessed 29 November 2018).
Allen, Richard (2007), *Hitchcock's Romantic Irony*, New York: Columbia University Press.
Alpert, Robert (2014/15), 'The Artificial Intelligence of *Her*', *Jump Cut*, No. 56 (Winter 2014/15), <https://www.ejumpcut.org/archive/jc56.2014-2015/alpertHer/index.html> (last accessed 15 November 2018).
Andrew, Dudley (2013), 'Every Teacher Needs a Truant: Bazin and *L'Enfant sauvage*', in Dudley Andrew and Anne Gillain (eds), *A Companion to François Truffaut*, Malden, MA: Wiley Blackwell.
Andrews, V. C. [1979] (2014), *Flowers in the Attic*, New York: Pocketbooks.

Astruc, Alexandre (1948), 'The Birth of the Avant-Garde: La Caméra-Stylo', *L'Écran française*, 30 March, <http://www.newwavefilm.com/about/camera-stylo-astruc.shtml> (last accessed 29 November 2018).

Backman Rogers, Anna (2012), 'The Historical Threshold: Crisis, Ritual and Liminality in Sofia Coppola's *Marie-Antoinette* (2006)', *RELIEF*, Vol. 6, No. 1, pp. 80–97.

Backman Rogers, Anna (2015), *American Independent Cinema: Rites of Passage and the Crisis Image*, Edinburgh: Edinburgh University Press.

Baggini, Julian and Gareth Southwell (2012), *Philosophy: Key Themes*, 2nd edn, London: Palgrave Macmillan.

Bainbridge, Simon (2008), 'Introduction', in Simon Bainbridge (ed.), *Romanticism: A Sourcebook*, London: Palgrave Macmillan, pp. 1–19.

Barth, John (1984), 'The Literature of Exhaustion', in *The Friday Book: Essays and Other Nonfiction*, London: Johns Hopkins University Press, pp. 64–76.

Bate, Walter Jackson (1970), 'The English Romantic Compromise', in Harold Bloom (ed.), *Romanticism and Consciousness: Essays in Criticism*, New York: Norton, pp. 149–69.

Bate, Walter Jackson (2012), *Negative Capability: On the Intuitive Approach in Keats*, New York: Contra Mundum Press.

Baudrillard, Jean (1983), *Simulations*, trans. Paul Foss, Paul Patton and Philip Beitchman, New York: Columbia University Press.

Baxendale, Sallie (2004), 'Memories Aren't Made of This: Amnesia at the Movies', *BMJ: British Medical Journal*, Vol. 329, No. 7480, pp. 1480–3.

Behler, Ernst (1988), 'The Theory of Irony in German Romanticism', in Frederick Garber (ed.), *Romantic Irony*, Budapest: Akadémiai Kiadó, pp. 43–81.

Bell, James (2014), 'Computer Love', *Sight and Sound*, Vol. 24, No. 1 (January), pp. 20–5.

Benjamin, Walter (1969), 'Paris: Capital of the Nineteenth Century', *Perspecta*, Vol. 12, pp. 163–72.

Benko, Stephen (1993), *The Virgin Goddess: Studies in the Pagan and Christian Roots of Mariology*, Leiden: E. J. Brill.

Benton, Richard P. (1966), 'Keats and Zen', *Philosophy East and West*, Vol. 15, No. 1/2, pp. 33–47.

Bertram, Christopher (2012), 'Jean Jacques Rousseau', in Edward N. Zalta (ed.), *The Stanford Encyclopedia of Philosophy*, Winter 2012 edn, <http://plato.stanford.edu/archives/win2012/entries/rousseau/> (last accessed 29 November 2018).

Biskind, Peter (1999), *Easy Riders, Raging Bulls*, New York: Touchstone.

Blake, William (2011), 'The Auguries of Innocence', in Morris Eaves, Robert Essick and Joseph Viscomi (eds), *The Pickering Manuscript: Electronic Edition*, Chapel Hill, NC: Carolina Digital Library and Archives, <https://www.poetryfoundation.org/poems-and-poets/poems/detail/43650#poem> (last accessed 29 November 2018).

Bloom, Harold (1970), 'The Internalization of the Quest Romance', in Harold Bloom (ed.), *Romanticism and Consciousness: Essays in Criticism*, New York: Norton, pp. 3–24.

Bone, J. Drummond (1999), 'A Sense of Endings: Some Romantic and Postmodern Comparisons', in Edward Larrissy (ed.), *Romanticism and Postmodernism*, Cambridge: Cambridge University Press, pp. 73–89.

Bordwell, David (1988), *Narration in the Fiction Film*, London: Routledge.
Bordwell, David (2007), 'Shot-consciousness', *Observations of Film Art*, 16 January, <http://www.davidbordwell.net/blog/2007/01/16/shot-consciousness/> (last accessed 29 November 2018).
Boreham, Judy and Duncan Heath (2005), *Introducing Romanticism*, Cambridge: Icon.
Borges, Jorges Luis [1962] (2000), *Labyrinths*, London: Penguin.
Botting, Fred (1999), 'Virtual Romanticism', in Edward Larrissy (ed.), *Romanticism and Postmodernism*, Cambridge: Cambridge University Press, pp. 98–112.
Bradshaw, Peter (2006), 'Marie Antoinette', *The Guardian*, 20 October, <https://www.theguardian.com/film/2006/oct/20/drama.romance> (last accessed 29 November 2018).
Bradshaw, Peter (2009), 'Fantastic Mr Fox', *The Guardian*, 22 October, <https://www.theguardian.com/film/2009/oct/22/fantastic-mr-fox-review> (last accessed 29 November 2018).
Branigan, Edward (1992), *Narrative Comprehension and Film*, London: Routledge.
Brevik-Zender, Heidi (2011), 'Let Them Wear Manolos: Fashion, Walter Benjamin, and Sofia Coppola's *Marie Antoinette*', *Camera Obscura*, 78, Vol. 26, No. 3, pp. 1–33.
Brooks, Xan (2007), '"One Does Feel Misunderstood"', *The Guardian*, 8 November, <http://www.theguardian.com/film/2007/nov/09/2> (last accessed 29 November 2018).
Buckland, Warren (2012), 'Wes Anderson: A "Smart" Director of the New Sincerity?', *New Review of Film and Television Studies*, Vol. 10, No. 1, pp. 1–5.
Burke, Edmund [1757] (1792), *A Philosophical Enquiry into the Origins of the Sublime and Beautiful*, Basil: J. J. Tourneisen.
Byron, Lord (1837), *Don Juan: In Sixteen Cantos, with Notes*, Halifax: Milner and Sowerby.
Byron, Lord (1974), *'Alas! The Love of Women!': Byron's Letters and Journals Vol. 3, 1813–1814*, ed. Leslie A. Marchand, London: John Murray.
Byron, Lord (2008), *Cain and other Shorter Works*, Cabin John, MD: Wildside Press.
Byron, Lord [1812–18] (2011), *Childe Harold's Pilgrimage*, CreateSpace Independent Publishing.
Byron, Lord [1816–17] (2014), *Manfred*, CreateSpace Independent Publishing.
Campbell, Colin (2005), *The Romantic Ethic and the Spirit of Modern Consumerism*, n.p.: Alcuin Academics.
Caughie, John (1981), 'Cahiers du cinema', in John Caughie (ed.), *Theories of Authorship*, London: Routledge, pp. 35–47.
Cavell, Stanley (1979), *The Claim of Reason*, Oxford: Clarendon Press.
Cavell, Stanley (2002), 'The Avoidance of Love', in *Must We Mean What We Say?*, 2nd edn, Cambridge: Cambridge University Press, pp. 267–353.
Chabon, Michael (2013), 'Wes Anderson's Worlds', in Matt Zoller Seitz (ed.), *The Wes Anderson Collection*, New York: Abrams, pp. 21–3.
Clayton, Alex (2016), 'V. F. Perkins: Aesthetic Suspense', in Murray Pomerance and R. Barton Palmer (eds), *Thinking in the Dark: Cinema, Theory, Practice*, London: Rutgers University Press, pp. 208–16.

Coleridge, Samuel Taylor [1817] (1980), *Biographia Literaria*, London: Everyman's Library.
Coleridge, Samuel Taylor [1908] (2009), *Rime of the Ancient Mariner and Select Poems*, ed. Frederick Sykes, Auckland: The Floating Press.
Collin, Robbie (2014), 'Wes Anderson Interview', *The Telegraph*, 19 February.
Collins, Jim (1993), 'Genericity in the Nineties: Eclectic Irony and the New Sincerity', in Jim Collins, Hilary Radner and Ava Preacher Collins (eds), *Film Theory Goes to the Movies*, London: Routledge, pp. 242–64.
Coppola, Sofia (2006), *Marie Antoinette*, New York: Rizzoli.
Cox, Gordon (2007), 'Hollywood Diversity and Inclusion See Little Rise in 10 Years (Study)', *Variety*, 31 July, <https://variety.com/2017/film/news/hollywood-diversity-little-rise-study-1202510809/> (last accessed 28 November 2018).
Creed, Barbara (1993), *The Monstrous-Feminine: Film, Feminism, Psychoanalysis*, London: Routledge.
Crouch, Christopher (2015), 'Architecture, Design, and Modern Living', in Peter Brooker, Andrzej Gąsiorek, Deborah Longworth and Andrew Thacker (eds), *The Oxford Handbook of Modernisms*, Oxford: Oxford University Press, pp. 618–34.
Cunningham, David (2005), 'The Futures of Surrealism: Hegelianism, Romanticism, and the Avant-Garde', *SubStance*, Vol. 34, No. 2, Issue 107, pp. 47–65.
Cwik, Greg (2016), 'Female Filmmakers Have It Just as Rough in Europe as They Do in Hollywood', *Vulture*, 1 May, <http://www.vulture.com/2016/05/female-directors-have-it-just-as-rough-in-europe.html> (last accessed 29 November 2018).
Dahl, Roald [1970] (2016), *Fantastic Mr Fox*, London: Puffin.
Dargis, Manohla (2013), 'Disembodied, But, Oh, What a Voice', *The New York Times*, 17 December, <http://www.nytimes.com/2013/12/18/movies/her-directed-by-spike-jonze.html> (last accessed 29 November 2018).
Davers, Rebecca (2011), '"I know how to do the play now": A Part of Willy Loman in *Synecdoche, New York*', *The Arthur Miller Journal*, Vol. 6, No. 2 (Fall), pp. 25–45.
DeLillo, Don (1986), *White Noise*, New York: Penguin Books.
Deming, Richard (2011), 'Living a Part: *Synecdoche, New York*, Metaphor and the Problem of Skepticism', in David LaRocca (ed.), *The Philosophy of Charlie Kaufman*, Lexington: University Press of Kentucky, pp. 193–207.
Docherty, Thomas (1993), 'Introduction', in Thomas Docherty (ed.), *Postmodernism: A Reader*, New York: Columbia University Press, pp. 1–32.
Dorey, Tom (2012), 'Fantastic Mr Filmmaker: Paratexts and the Positioning of Wes Anderson as Roald Dahl's Cinematic Heir', *New Review of Film and Television Studies*, Vol. 10, No. 1 (March), pp. 169–85.
Downing, Lisa (2009a), 'The Cinematic Ethics of Psychoanalysis: Futurity, Death Drive, Desire', in Lisa Downing and Libby Saxton (eds), *Film and Ethics: Foreclosed Encounters*, Abingdon: Taylor & Francis, pp. 134–46.
Downing, Lisa (2009b), 'Foucault in Focus: Ethics, Surveillance, Soma', in Lisa Downing and Libby Saxton (eds), *Film and Ethics: Foreclosed Encounters*, Abingdon: Taylor & Francis, pp. 121–32.

Downing, Lisa (2009c), 'What If We Are Post-ethical? Postmodernism's Ethics and Aesthetics', in Lisa Downing and Libby Saxton (eds), *Film and Ethics: Foreclosed Encounters*, Abingdon: Taylor & Francis, pp. 147–59.

Eisner, Lotte H. (1977), *The Haunted Screen: Expressionism in the German Cinema and the Influence of Max Reinhardt*, Berkeley: University of California Press.

Elam, Diane (1992), *Romancing the Postmodern*, London: Routledge.

Emerson, Ralph Waldo (1836), *Nature*, Boston: James Munroe.

Emerson, Ralph Waldo (1841), 'Circles', in *Essays: First Series*, Project Gutenberg, <http://www.gutenberg.org/files/2944/2944-h/2944-h.htm#link2H_4_0010> (last accessed 29 November 2018).

Esterhammer, Angela (2010), 'The Scandal of Sincerity: Wordsworth, Byron, Landon', in Tim Milnes and Kerry Sinanan (eds), *Romanticism, Sincerity and Authenticity*, London: Palgrave Macmillan, pp. 101–20.

Eugenides, Jeffrey [1993] (2002), *The Virgin Suicides*, 2nd edn, London: Bloomsbury.

Evans, Joel (2014), 'Figuring the Global: On Charlie Kaufman's *Synecdoche, New York*', *New Review of Film and Television Studies*, Vol. 12, No. 4, pp. 321–38.

Ezra, Elizabeth (2010), 'Cléo's Masks: Regimes of Objectification in the French New Wave', in *Noeuds de mémoire: Multidirectional Memory in Postwar French and Francophone Culture*, New Haven: Yale University Press, pp. 177–90.

Fender, Stephen (1997), 'Introduction', in *Walden*, Oxford: Oxford University Press, pp. ix–xliii.

Ferriss, Suzanne and Mallory Young (2010), '*Marie Antoinette*: Fashion, Third-Wave Feminism, and Chick Culture', *Film/Literature Quarterly*, Vol. 38, No. 2, pp. 98–116.

Festival de Cannes Daily (2014), 'Interview – Sofia Coppola', 24 May, <http://org-www.festival-cannes.com/en/theDailyArticle/61113.html> (last accessed 26 November 2018).

Fischer, Russ (2009), 'Wes Anderson Speaks About "Directing Via Email" Controversy on *Fantastic Mr Fox*', *Slash Film*, 14 October, <https://www.slashfilm.com/wes-anderson-speaks-about-directing-via-email-controversy-on-fantastic-mr-fox/> (last accessed 21 November 2018).

Fletcher, John (1999), 'The Sins of the Fathers: The Persistence of Gothic', in Edward Larrissy (ed.), *Romanticism and Postmodernism*, Cambridge: Cambridge University Press, pp. 113–40.

Flores, Pamela (2013), 'Fashion and Otherness: The Passionate Journey of Coppola's *Marie Antoinette* from a Semiotic Perspective', *Fashion Theory*, Vol. 17, No. 5, pp. 605–22.

Foucault, Michel (1998), *The Will to Knowledge: The History of Sexuality Volume I*, trans. Robert Hurley, London: Penguin.

Fraser, Antonia (2001), *Marie Antoinette: The Journey*, London: Weidenfeld & Nicolson.

Fraser, Antonia (2006), 'Sofia's Choice', *Vanity Fair*, 17 October, <http://www.vanityfair.com/news/2006/11/fraser200611> (last accessed 29 November 2018).

Fraser, Kennedy (2006), 'Kirsten Dunst: Teen Queen', *Vogue*, 1 September, <http://www.vogue.com/865326/kirsten-dunst-teen-queen/> (last accessed 29 November 2018).

Freeman, Barbara (1995), *The Feminine Sublime: Gender and Excess in Women's Fiction*, London: University of California Press.

French, Philip (2006), 'Marie Antoinette Review', *The Guardian*, 22 October, <http://www.theguardian.com/film/2006/oct/22/philipfrench> (last accessed 29 November 2018).

Freud, Sigmund [1919] (2003), *The Uncanny*, London: Penguin.

Frye, Northrup (1970), 'The Road of Excess', in Harold Bloom (ed.), *Romanticism and Consciousness: Essays in Criticism*, New York: Norton, pp. 120–32.

Fukuyama, Francis (1989), 'The End of History?', *The National Interest*, No. 16 (Summer), pp. 3–18.

Galperin, William H. (1993), *The Return of the Visible in British Romanticism*, Baltimore: Johns Hopkins University Press.

Galt, Rosalind (2009), 'Pretty: Film Theory, Aesthetics, and the History of the Troublesome Image', *Camera Obscura*, 71, Vol. 24, No. 2, pp. 1–41.

Galt, Rosalind (2011), *Pretty: Film and the Decorative Image*, New York: Columbia University Press.

George, Albert Joseph (1955), *The Development of French Romanticism: The Impact of the Industrial Revolution on Literature*, Syracuse: Syracuse University Press.

Gevinson, Tavi (2013), 'Girls with Power and Mystique: An Interview with Sofia Coppola', *Rookie*, 17 June, <http://www.rookiemag.com/2013/06/sofia-coppola-interview/> (last accessed 29 November 2018).

Gibson Lockhart, John ('Z') (1818), 'Cockney School of Poetry. IV', *Blackwood's Edinburgh Magazine*, Vol. III (April–August), pp. 519–24.

Gigante, Denise (2002), 'The Monster in the Rainbow: Keats and the Science of Life', *PMLA*, Vol. 117, No. 3 (May), pp. 433–48.

Gigante, Denise (2010), 'Foreword', in Thomas H. Schmid and Michelle Faubert (eds), *Romanticism and Pleasure*, New York: Palgrave Macmillan, pp. ix–xv.

Goethe, Johann Wolfgang von [1774] (1989), *The Sorrows of Young Werther*, ed. and trans. Michael Hulse, London: Penguin.

Goethe, Johann Wolfgang von [1808–31] (1999), *Faust*, trans. John R. Williams, Ware: Wordsworth Editions.

Gooch, Joshua (2007), 'Making a Go of It: Paternity and Prohibition in the Films of Wes Anderson', *Cinema Journal*, Vol. 47, No. 1 (Fall), pp. 26–48.

Goodman, Russell (2011), *American Philosophy and the Romantic Tradition*, Cambridge: Cambridge University Press.

Goodman, Russell (2015), 'Transcendentalism', in Edward N. Zalta (ed.), *The Stanford Encyclopedia of Philosophy*, Fall 2015 edn, <http://plato.stanford.edu/archives/fall2015/entries/transcendentalism/> (last accessed 30 November 2018).

Gould, Stephen Jay (1996), *The Mismeasure of Man*, London: W.W. Norton.

Grayson, Susan (1986), 'Rousseau and the Text', in Lynne Layton and Barbara Ann Schapiro (eds), *Narcissism and the Text: Studies in Literature and the Psychologies of the Self*, New York: New York University Press, pp. 78–96.

Gruder, Vivian R. (2002), 'The Question of Marie-Antoinette: The Queen and Public Opinion Before the Revolution', *French History*, Vol. 16, No. 3, pp. 269–98.

Guillén, Michael (2008), '*Synecdoche, New York*: Interview with Charlie Kaufman', *The Evening Class*, 22 October, <https://theeveningclass.blogspot.com/2008/10/synecdoche-new-york-evening-class.html> (last accessed 26 November 2018).

Guyer, Paul and Rolf-Peter Horstmann (2015), 'Idealism', in Edward N. Zalta (ed.), *The Stanford Encyclopedia of Philosophy*, Fall 2015 edn, <http://plato.stanford.edu/archives/fall2015/entries/idealism/> (last accessed 25 November 2018).

Habermas, Jürgen (1992), 'Modernity – An Incomplete Project', in Patricia Waugh (ed.), *Postmodernism: A Reader*, London: Bloomsbury Academic, pp. 98–108.

Hamilton, Paul (1999), 'From Sublimity to Indeterminacy: New World Order or Aftermath of Romantic Ideology', in Edward Larrissy (ed.), *Romanticism and Postmodernism*, Cambridge: Cambridge University Press, pp. 13–28.

Hanisch, Carol (1970), 'The Personal Is Political', in *Notes from the Second Year: Women's Liberation*, <http://www.carolhanisch.org/CHwritings/PIP.html> (last accessed 30 November 2018).

Hartman, Geoffrey (1970), 'Romanticism and "Anti-Self-Consciousness"', in Harold Bloom (ed.), *Romanticism and Consciousness: Essays in Criticism*, New York: Norton, pp. 47–56.

Hartman, Geoffrey (2002), *Scars of the Spirit: The Struggle Against Inauthenticity*, New York: Palgrave Macmillan.

Hegel, G. W. F. [1807] (1977), *The Phenomenology of Spirit*, trans. A. V. Miller, Oxford: Oxford University Press.

Henderson, Andrea K. (1996), *Romantic Identities: Varieties of Subjectivity, 1774–1830*, Cambridge: Cambridge University Press.

Hill, Derek (2008), *Charlie Kaufman and Hollywood's Merry Band of Pranksters, Fabulists, and Dreamers: An Excursion into the American New Wave*, Harpenden: Kamera Books.

Hill, Derek (2011), '"There's no more watching": Artifice and Meaning in *Synecdoche, New York* and *Adaptation*', in David LaRocca (ed.), *The Philosophy of Charlie Kaufman*, Lexington: University Press of Kentucky, pp. 208–23.

Hoby, Hermione (2009), 'The Ultimate Postmodern Novel Is a Film', *The Guardian*, 13 May, <https://www.theguardian.com/books/booksblog/2009/may/13/synechdoche-postmodern-novel-film> (last accessed 25 November 2018).

Hohenadel, Kristin (2006), 'French Royalty as Seen by Hollywood Royalty', *The New York Times*, 10 September, <https://www.nytimes.com/2006/09/10/movies/moviesspecial/10hohe.html> (last accessed 30 November 2018).

Hoskin, Bree (2007), 'Playground Love: Landscape and Longing in Sofia Coppola's *The Virgin Suicides*', *Literature/Film Quarterly*, Vol. 35, No. 3, pp. 214–21.

Huddleston, Tom (n.d.), 'Interview: Charlie Kaufman', *Time Out London*, <http://www.timeout.com/london/film/interview-charlie-kaufman-1> (last accessed 25 November 2018).

Hunt, Leigh (1832), *The Poetical Works of Leigh Hunt*, London: Edward Moxon.

Ivanchikova, Alla (2016), 'Machinic Intimacies and Mechanical Brides: Collectivity Between Prosthesis and Surrogacy in Jonathan Mostow's *Surrogates* and Spike Jonze's *Her*', *Camera Obscura*, Vol. 31, No. 1 (91), pp. 65–91.

Jaeckle, Jeff (2013), 'The Shared Verbal Stylistics of Preston Sturges and Wes Anderson', *New Review of Film and Television Studies*, Vol. 11, No. 2, pp. 154–70.

Jameson, Fredric (1984), 'Postmodernism, or the Cultural Logic of Late Capitalism', *New Left Review*, Vol. 1, No. 146 (1 July), pp. 53–92.

Jameson, Fredric (1992), *Postmodernism: Or, the Cultural Logic of Late Capitalism*, London: Verso.

Jarvis, Robin (2004), *The Romantic Period: The Intellectual and Cultural Context of English Literature, 1789–1830*, Harlow: Pearson Longman.

Jollimore, Troy (2015), '"This endless space between the words": The Limits of Love in Spike Jonze's *Her*', *Midwest Studies in Philosophy*, Vol. 39, No. 1 (September), pp. 120–43.

Kafka, Franz [1925] (2015), *The Trial*, London: Penguin Modern Classics.

Kant, Immanuel [1790] (2007), *Critique of Judgement*, Oxford: Oxford University Press.

Kant, Immanuel (1764), *Observations on the Feeling of the Beautiful and Sublime*, Königsberg: Johann Jakob Kanter.

Keats, John (1970), *Letters of John Keats*, ed. Robert Gidding, Oxford: Oxford University Press.

Keats, John (1976), *Complete Poems*, 2nd edn, ed. John Barnard, New York: Penguin Books.

Kertzer, Adrienne (2010), 'Fidelity, Felicity, and Playing Around in Wes Anderson's *Fantastic Mr. Fox*', *Children's Literature Association Quarterly*, Vol. 36, No. 1, pp. 4–24.

King, Geoff (2014), *Indie 2.0 Change and Continuity in Contemporary American Indie Film*, London: I. B. Tauris.

Knight, C. Ryan (2014), '"Who's to say?": The Role of Pets in Wes Anderson's Films', in Peter C. Kunze (ed.), *The Films of Wes Anderson*, New York: Palgrave Macmillan, pp. 65–76.

Kolker, Robert Phillip (1988), *Cinema of Loneliness*, 2nd edn, New York: Oxford University Press.

Kredell, Brendan (2012), 'Wes Anderson and the City Spaces of Indie Cinema', *New Review of Film and Television Studies*, Vol. 10, No. 1, pp. 83–96.

Kunze, Peter C. (2014), 'From the Mixed-up Films of Mr. Wesley W. Anderson: Children's Literature as Intertexts', in Peter C. Kunze (ed.), *The Films of Wes Anderson*, New York: Palgrave Macmillan, pp. 91–108.

Laine, Tarja (2013), *Feeling Cinema*, London: Bloomsbury Academic.

Laine, Tarja (2015), *Bodies in Pain: Emotion and the Cinema of Darren Aronofsky*, Oxford: Berghahn.

Landon, Letitia (1829), 'History of the Lyre', in *The Venetian Bracelet, the Lost Pleiad, and A History of the Lyre and Other Poems*, London: Longman, Rees, Orme, Brown and Green.

Lang, Brent (2015), 'Women Comprise 7% of Directors on Top 250 Films', *Variety*, 20 October, <http://variety.com/2015/film/news/women-hollywood-inequality-directors-behind-the-camera-1201626691/> (last accessed 19 November 2018).

LaRocca, David (2011), 'Introduction', in David LaRocca (ed.), *The Philosophy of Charlie Kaufman*, Lexington: University Press of Kentucky, pp. 1–20.

Larrissy, Edward (1999), 'Introduction', in Edward Larrissy (ed.), *Romanticism and Postmodernism*, Cambridge: Cambridge University Press, pp. 1–12.

Lauzen, Martha (2016), 'Still Too Few Women Behind the Scenes in Hollywood', *Women's Media Center*, 28 January, <http://www.womensmediacenter.com/feature/entry/

still-too-few-women-behind-the-scenes-in-hollywood> (last accessed 30 November 2018).
Law, Stephen (2013), 'Humanism', in Stephen Bullivant and Michael Ruse (eds), *The Oxford Handbook of Atheism*, Oxford: Oxford University Press, pp. 263–77.
Lefort, Claude (1986), *The Political Forms of Modern Society*, ed. John B. Thompson, Cambridge: Polity Press.
Lippit, Akira Mizuta (2000), *Electric Animal*, London: University of Minnesota Press.
Locke, John (1689), *Second Treatise on Government*, Public domain e-book, <http://www.earlymoderntexts.com/assets/pdfs/locke1689a.pdf> (last accessed 30 November 2018).
Lokke, Kari (2008), 'The Figure of the Hermit in Charlotte Smith's "Beachy Head"', *The Wordsworth Circle*, Vol. 39, No. 1–2 (1 January), pp. 38–43.
Lüthy, Michael (2002), 'The Consumer Article in the Art World: On the Para-economy of American Pop Art', in Max Hollein and Christoph Grunenberg (eds), *Shopping: A Century of Art and Consumer Culture*, Exhibition catalogue, Ostfildern-Ruit: Hatje Cantz, pp. 148–53, <http://www.michaelluethy.de/konsumgut-englisch.pdf> (last accessed 22 November 2018).
Lyotard, Jean-François (1992), 'Answering the Question: What Is Postmodernism?', in Patricia Waugh (ed.), *Postmodernism: A Reader*, London: Bloomsbury Academic, pp. 38–46.
Lyotard, Jean-François (1993a), 'Notes of the Meaning of "Post-"', in Thomas Docherty (ed.), *Postmodernism: A Reader*, New York: Columbia University Press, pp. 47–50.
Lyotard, Jean-François (1993b), 'The Sublime and the Avant-Garde', in Thomas Docherty (ed.), *Postmodernism: A Reader*, New York: Columbia University Press, pp. 244–56.
Lyotard, Jean-François (1997), *The Postmodern Condition: A Report on Knowledge*, trans. Geoff Bennington and Brian Massumi, Manchester: Manchester University Press.
MacDowell, James (2010), 'Notes on Quirky', *Movie: A Journal of Film Criticism*, No. 1 (August), pp. 1–16.
MacDowell, James (2014), 'The Andersonian, the Quirky, and "Innocence"', in Peter C. Kunze (ed.), *The Films of Wes Anderson: Critical Essays on an Indiewood Icon*, New York: Palgrave MacMillan, pp. 153–69.
MacDowell, James (2016), *Irony in Film*, London: Palgrave Macmillan.
McGann, Jerome J. (1983), *The Romantic Ideology: A Critical Investigation*, Chicago: University of Chicago Press.
McQuillan, Colin (2012), 'German Idealism', in James Fieser and Bradley Dowden (gen. eds), *Internet Encyclopedia of Philosophy*, <http://www.iep.utm.edu/germidea/> (last accessed 25 November 2018).
McSweeney's (2009), *Heads On and We Shoot: The Making of Where the Wild Things Are* ed. Michelle Quint, San Francisco: McSweeney's Publishing.
Maier, Charles S. (2010), '"Malaise": The Crisis of Capitalism in the 1970s', in Niall Ferguson, Charles S. Maier, Erez Manela and Daniel J. Sargent (eds), *The Shock of the Global: The 1970s in Perspective*, Cambridge, MA: Harvard University Press, pp. 25–48.

Manninen, Tuomas William and Bertha Alvarez Manninen (2016), 'David's Need for Mutual Recognition: A Social Personhood Defense of Steven Spielberg's *A.I. Artificial Intelligence*', *Film Philosophy*, Vol. 20, No. 2–3, pp. 339–56.

Margulies, Alfred (2016), 'Avatars of Desire and the Question of Presence: Virtual and Transitional Spaces Meet Their Liminal Edge – From *Pygmalion* to Spike Jonze's *Her*, and Beyond', *International Journal of Psychoanalysis*, Vol. 97 (30 May), pp. 1697–708.

Martin-Jones, David (2006), *Deleuze, Cinema and National Identity*, Edinburgh: Edinburgh University Press.

Marx, Leo (1964), *The Machine in the Garden*, New York: Oxford University Press.

May, Patrick (2014), 'Apple's Siri Goes to the Movies to Check *Her* Out', *San Jose Mercury News*, 9 January, <http://www.mercurynews.com/2014/01/09/apples-siri-goes-to-the-movies-to-check-her-out/> (last accessed 30 November 2018).

Mayshark, Jesse Fox (2009), *Post-pop Cinema: The Search for Meaning in New American Film*, Westport, CT: Praeger.

Mellor, Anne K. (1980), *English Romantic Irony*, London: Harvard University Press.

Mellor, Anne K. (1988), 'Introduction', in Anne K. Mellor (ed.), *Romanticism and Feminism*, Hoboken: John Wiley & Sons, pp. 3–9.

Mellor, Anne K. (1993), *Romanticism and Gender*, New York: Routledge.

Melville, Herman [1851] (1920), *Moby-Dick or The Whale*, London: Humphrey Milford.

Metz, Christian (1974), *Film Language*, New York: Oxford University Press.

Metz, Christian (1985), 'Aural Objects', in Elizabeth Weis and John Belton (eds), *Film Sound: Theory and Practice*, New York: Columbia University Press, pp. 154–61.

Milam, Jennifer (2011), 'Imagining Marie Antoinette: Cultural Memory, Coolness and the Deconstruction of History in Cinema', *French History and Civilization. Papers from the George Rudé Seminar*, Vol. 4, pp. 45–53.

Millan-Zaibert, Elizabeth (2004), 'What Is Early German Romanticism?', in Manfred Frank (ed.), *The Philosophical Foundations of Early German Romanticism*, Albany: State University of New York Press, pp. 1–21.

Milnes, Tim and Kerry Sinanan (2010), 'Introduction', in Tim Milnes and Kerry Sinanan (eds), *Romanticism, Sincerity and Authenticity*, London: Palgrave Macmillan, pp. 1–30.

Mitchell, W. J. T. (1986), *Picture Theory: Essays on Verbal and Visual Representation*, London: University of Chicago Press.

Mitra, Sayantanava and Seshadri Sekhar Chatterjee (2015), '"I do not exist" – Cotard Syndrome in Insular Cortex Atrophy', *Biological Psychiatry*, Vol. 77, No. 11 (1 June), p. 53.

Moats, David (2009), 'Charlie Kaufman's *Synecdoche, New York* Reviewed', *The Quietus*, 20 May, <http://thequietus.com/articles/01687-charlie-kaufman-s-synecdoche-new-york> (last accessed 30 November 2018).

Mohr, Hans-Ulrich (1996), 'The Picturesque: A Key Concept of the Eighteenth Century', in Frederick Burwick and Jürgen Klein (eds), *The Romantic Imagination: Literature and Art in England and Germany*, Amsterdam: Rodopi, pp. 245–68.

Monden, Masafumi (2013), 'Contemplating in a Dream-like Room: *The Virgin Suicides* and the Aesthetic Imagination of Girlhood', *Film, Fashion & Consumption*, Vol. 2, No. 2, pp. 139–58.
Monk, Samuel H. (1970), 'The Sublime: Burke's Enquiry', in Harold Bloom (ed.), *Romanticism and Consciousness: Essays in Criticism*, New York: Norton, pp. 24–41.
Moriarty (2008), 'Moriarty Reviews *Synecdoche, New York* and Interviews the Great Charlie Kaufman', *Ain't It Cool News*, 28 October, <http://www.aintitcool.com/node/38895> (last accessed 25 November 2018).
Mulvey, Laura (1975), 'Visual Pleasure and Narrative Cinema', *Screen*, Vol. 16, No. 3, pp. 6–18.
Nagib, Lúcia (2013), 'Film as Literature or the Truffaldian Malaise (*L'Homme qui aimait les femmes*)', in Dudley Andrew and Anne Gillain (eds), *A Companion to François Truffaut*, Hoboken, NJ: Wiley-Blackwell, pp. 530–45.
Nemoianu, Virgil (1998), 'Robert Southey's *The Doctor*: The Conservatism of Voracious Reading', in Larry H. Peer (ed.), *Romanticism Across the Disciplines*, Lanham, MD: University Press of America, pp. 187–205.
Nerval, Gérard de (1997), *Aurélia and Other Writings*, trans. Geoffrey Wagner, Boston: Exact Change.
Novalis (1997), *Philosophical Writings*, ed. and trans. Margaret Mahony Stoljar, Albany: State University of New York Press.
O'Hagan, Sean (2006), 'Sofia Coppola', *The Observer*, 8 October, <https://www.theguardian.com/film/2006/oct/08/features.review1> (last accessed 30 November 2018).
O'Pray, Michael (2003), *Avant-Garde Film: Forms, Themes and Passions*, London: Wallflower.
Palmer, Allison Lee (2011), *Historical Dictionary of Neoclassical Art and Architecture*, Plymouth: Scarecrow Press.
Papamichael, Stella (2006), 'Marie Antoinette', *BBC*, 19 October, <http://www.bbc.co.uk/films/2006/10/10/marie_antoinette_2006_review.shtml> (last accessed 30 November 2018).
Patterson, John (2013), 'Spike Jonze on *Jackass*, Scarlett Johansson's Erotic Voice and Techno Love', *The Guardian*, 28 November, <https://www.theguardian.com/film/2013/nov/28/spike-jonze-her-interview-scarlett-johansson-joaquin-phoenix-jackass> (last accessed 30 November 2018).
Pattison, George (2013), *Kierkegaard and the Quest for Unambiguous Life: Between Romanticism and Modernism: Selected Essays*, Oxford: Oxford University Press.
Pavel, Thomas G. (1986), *Fictional Worlds*, London: Harvard University Press.
Peer, Larry H. (2009), *Romanticism and the Object*, New York: Palgrave Macmillan.
Pelly, Rich (2014), 'Apple's Siri on *Her*: "Who is Whacking Phoenix?"', *The Guardian*, 12 February, <https://www.theguardian.com/film/2014/feb/12/apple-siri-her-spike-jones-joaquin-phoenix> (last accessed 30 November 2018).
Perkins, Claire (2012), *American Smart Cinema*, Edinburgh: Edinburgh University Press.
Perkins, V. F. (1996), 'Johnny Guitar', in Ian Cameron and Douglas Pye (eds), *The Movie Book of the Western*, London: Studio Vista, pp. 221–8.

Perloff, Marjorie (1999), 'Postmodernism/*Fin de Siècle*: Defining "Difference" in Late Twentieth-century Poetics', in Edward Larrissy (ed.), *Romanticism and Postmodernism*, Cambridge: Cambridge University Press, pp. 179–209.

Perry, Seamus (1997), 'Romanticism: The Brief History of a Concept', in Duncan Wu (ed.), *A Companion to Romanticism*, Oxford: Blackwell Publishers, pp. 3–11.

Pfau, Thomas (2005), *Romantic Moods: Paranoia, Trauma, and Melancholy*, Baltimore: Johns Hopkins University Press.

Plantinga, Carl (2009), *Moving Viewers: American Film and the Spectator's Experience*, Oakland: University of California Press.

Pottle, Frederick A. (1970), 'The Eye and the Object in the Poetry of Wordsworth', in Harold Bloom (ed.), *Romanticism and Consciousness: Essays in Criticism*, New York: Norton, pp. 273–87.

Price, Uvedale (1810), *Essays on the Picturesque, Vol. I*, London: J. Mawman.

Proust, Marcel [1922] (2005), *Swann's Way (In Search of Lost Time Vol. 1)*, trans. C. K. Scott Moncrieff, D. J. Enright and Terence Kilmartin, London: Random House.

Quinlivan, Davina (2017), 'A Dark and Shiny Place: The Disembodied Female Voice, Irigarayan Subjectivity and the "Political Erotics" of Hearing *Her* (Spike Jonze, 2013)', in Tom Whittaker and Sarah Wright (eds), *Locating the Voice in Film: Critical Approaches and Global Practices*, Oxford: Oxford University Press, pp. 295–310.

Raysor, Thomas M. and Samuel Taylor Coleridge (1925), 'Unpublished Fragments on Aesthetics', *Studies in Philology*, Vol. 22, pp. 529–37.

Renninger, Brice (2013), 'Spike Jonze, Why Are There No Brown People in Your Future Los Angeles?', *Indiewire*, 14 October, <http://www.indiewire.com/article/spike-jonze-why-are-there-no-brown-people-in-your-future-los-angeles> (last accessed 30 November 2018).

Respers France, Lisa (2018), 'Black Panther Proves that Diversity Sells. But Is Hollywood Buying It?', *CNN*, 27 February, <https://edition.cnn.com/2018/02/27/entertainment/hollywood-study-diversity/> (last accessed 28 November 2018).

Richardson, Alan (1988), 'Romanticism and the Colonization of the Feminine', in Anne K. Mellor (ed.), *Romanticism and Feminism*, Hoboken: John Wiley & Sons, pp. 13–25.

Richardson, Alan (2001), *British Romanticism and the Science of the Mind*, Cambridge: Cambridge University Press.

Rickey, Carrie (2013), 'Lost and Found', *DGA Quarterly*, Spring, <http://www.dga.org/Craft/DGAQ/All-Articles/1302-Spring-2013/Sofia-Coppola.aspx> (last accessed 30 November 2018).

Roberts, Andrew Michael (1999), 'Romantic Irony and the Postmodern Sublime', in Edward Larrissy (ed.), *Romanticism and Postmodernism*, Cambridge: Cambridge University Press, pp. 141–56.

Robinson, Jeffrey Cane (2006), *Unfettering Poetry: Fancy in British Romanticism*, New York: Palgrave Macmillan.

Rorty, Richard (2016), 'Getting Rid of the Appearance–Reality Distinction', *New Literary History*, Vol. 47, No. 1 (Winter), pp. 67–81.

Rose, Jacqueline (1984), *The Case of Peter Pan or the Impossibility of Children's Fiction*, London: Macmillan Press.

Roud, Richard (1977), 'The Left Bank Revisited', *Monthly Film Bulletin*, 46 (Summer), p. 143.

Rousseau, Jean-Jacques (1763), *Emile*, Public domain e-book, <http://www.gutenberg.org/ebooks/5427> (last accessed 4 March 2019).

Rousseau, Jean-Jacques [1762] (2007), *The Social Contract*, BN Publishing.

Rowland, Ann Wierda (2012), *Romanticism and Childhood*, Cambridge: Cambridge University Press.

Rushton, Richard (2014), 'Cavell and the Politics of Cinema: On *Marie Antoinette*', *Film-Philosophy*, Vol. 18, pp. 110–27.

Rybin, Steven (2014), 'The Jellyfish and the Moonlight: Imagining the Family in Wes Anderson's Films', in Peter C. Kunze (ed.), *The Films of Wes Anderson*, New York: Palgrave Macmillan, pp. 39–50.

Rzepka, Charles J. (1986), *The Self as Mind: Vision and Identity in Wordsworth, Coleridge and Keats*, London: Harvard University Press.

Sandhu, Suhkdev (2014), '*Fantastic Mr Fox* Review', *The Telegraph*, 31 December, <https://www.telegraph.co.uk/culture/film/filmreviews/6408554/Fantastic-Mr-Fox-review.html> (last accessed 21 November 2018).

Schapiro, Barbara A. (1983), *The Romantic Mother: Narcissistic Patterns in Romantic Poetry*, London: Johns Hopkins University Press.

Schlegel, Friedrich [1797–9] (1971), *Lucinde and the Fragments*, trans. Peter Firchow, London: Oxford University Press.

Sconce, Jeffrey (2002), 'Irony, Nihilism and the New American "Smart" Film', *Screen*, Vol. 43, No. 4 (Winter), pp. 349–69.

Scott, A. O. (2000), 'Evanescent Trees and Sisters in an Enchanted 1970's Suburb', *The New York Times*, 21 April, <http://www.nytimes.com/movie/review?res=9901EEDE1E31F932A15757C0A9669C8B63> (last accessed 30 November 2018).

Scott, A. O. (2001), 'Please to Not Feed or Annoy the Woebegone Prodigies', *The New York Times*, 14 December, <http://www.nytimes.com/2001/12/14/movies/film-review-please-do-not-feed-or-annoy-the-woebegone-prodigies.html> (last accessed 30 November 2018).

Scott, A. O. (2007), 'Movie Review: *The Darjeeling Limited*', *The New York Times*, 28 September, <https://www.nytimes.com/2007/09/28/movies/28darj.html?pagewanted=all&_r=0> (last accessed 30 November 2018).

Seitz, Matt Zoller (2009), 'The Substance of Style', *The Museum of the Moving Image Source*, 30 March, <http://www.movingimagesource.us/articles/the-substance-of-style-pt-1-20090330> (last accessed 30 November 2018).

Seitz, Matt Zoller (2013), *The Wes Anderson Collection*, New York: Abrams.

Shaw, Daniel (2011), 'Nietzschean Themes in the Films of Charlie Kaufman', in *The Philosophy of Charlie Kaufman*, Lexington: University Press of Kentucky, pp. 254–68.

Shaw, Philip (2005), *The Sublime*, London: Routledge.

Shelley, Percy Bysshe (1816), *Alastor; Or, The Spirit of Solitude: And Other Poems*, London: Baldwin, Craddock and Joy, <https://www.bl.uk/collection-items/alastor-by-p-b-shelley> (last accessed 14 January 2019).

Shelley, Percy Bysshe (1820), *Prometheus Unbound: A Lyrical Drama in Four Acts*, ed. Jack Lynch, Rutgers University, <andromeda.rutgers.edu/~jlynch/Texts/prometheus.html> (last accessed 30 November 2018).

Shelley, Percy Bysshe [1840] (1921), *A Defence of Poetry. The Four Ages of Poetry Etc.*, ed. H. F. B. Brett-Smith, Oxford: Basil Blackwell.

Siegel, Tatiana (2015), 'What Female Directors Are Telling the EEOC: "Very sad, disappointing, criminal details"', *Hollywood Reporter*, 11 November, <http://www.hollywoodreporter.com/news/what-female-directors-are-telling-839107> (last accessed 30 November 2018).

Silverman, Kaja (1988), *The Acoustic Mirror: The Female Voice in Psychoanalysis and the Cinema*, Indianapolis: Indiana University Press.

Singer, Irving (2009), *The Nature of Love 2*, Cambridge, MA: MIT Press.

Sinnerbrink, Robert (2012), '*Stimmung*: Exploring the Aesthetics of Mood', *Screen*, Vol. 53, No. 2 (Summer), pp. 148–63.

Smith, Charlotte (1807), *Beachy Head with other Poems*, London: J. Johnson.

Smith, David L. (2011), 'Synecdoche, in Part', in *The Philosophy of Charlie Kaufman*, Lexington: University Press of Kentucky, pp. 239–53.

Smith, David L. (2014), 'How to Be a Genuine Fake: *Her*, Alan Watts, and the Problem of the Self', *Journal of Religion and Film*, Vol. 18, No. 2 (October), pp. 1–37.

Smith, Ethan (n.d.), 'Spike Jonze Unmasked', *New York Magazine*, <http://nymag.com/nymetro/movies/features/1267/> (last accessed 24 November 2018).

Snell, Robert (2013), *Uncertainties, Mysteries, Doubts: Romanticism and the Analytic Attitude*, London: Routledge.

Sontag, Susan (1961), 'Notes on Camp', in *Against Interpretation and Other Essays*, London: Eyre & Spottiswoode, pp. 275–92.

Speight, Allen (2015), 'Friedrich Schlegel', in Edward N. Zalta (ed.), *The Stanford Encyclopedia of Philosophy*, Winter 2015 edn, <http://plato.stanford.edu/archives/win2015/entries/schlegel> (last accessed 25 November 2018).

Stam, Robert (1992), *Reflexivity in Film and Literature: From Don Quixote to Jean-Luc Godard*, New York: Columbia University Press.

Sternbergh, Adam (2015), 'In Conversation: Charlie Kaufman', *Vulture*, December, <http://www.vulture.com/2015/12/charlie-kaufman-anomaslisa-c-v-r.html> (last accessed 25 November 2018).

Swann, Karen (1991), 'Suffering and Sensation in The Ruined Cottage', *PMLA*, Vol. 106, No. 1 (January), pp. 83–95.

Thompson, Anne (2010), 'Exclusive Interview: With *Somewhere*, Sofia Coppola Grows Up', *Indiewire*, 14 September, <http://www.indiewire.com/2010/09/exclusive-interview-with-somewhere-sofia-coppola-grows-up-238428/> (last accessed 26 November 2018).

Thompson, Kristen (1977), 'The Concept of Cinematic Excess', *Cine-Tracts*, Vol. 1, No. 2 (Summer), pp. 54–63.

Thoreau, Henry David [1854] (1999), *Walden*, London: Oxford University Press.

Thorlby, Anthony (1988), 'Imagination and Irony in English Romantic Poetry', in Frederick Garber (ed.), *Romantic Irony*, Budapest: Akadémiai Kiadó, pp. 131–55.

Thorslev, Peter L. Jr. (1962), *The Byronic Hero: Types and Prototypes*, London: Oxford University Press.
Tobias, Scott (2000), 'Sofia Coppola: Virgin Territory', *AV Club*, 3 May, <http://www.avclub.com/article/sofia-coppola-13656> (last accessed 30 November 2018).
Tobias, Scott (2008), 'Interview: Charlie Kaufman', *AV Club*, 22 October, <http://www.avclub.com/article/charlie-kaufman-14322> (last accessed 25 November 2018).
Todorov, Tzvetan (1975), *The Fantastic: A Structural Approach to a Literary Genre*, Ithaca: Cornell University Press.
Trilling, Lionel (1965), 'The Fate of Pleasure', in *Beyond Culture: Essays on Literature and Learning*, London: Penguin, pp. 57–87.
Trilling, Lionel (1972), *Sincerity and Authenticity*, London: Oxford University Press.
Tzioumakis, Yannis (2006), *American Independent Cinema: An Introduction*, Edinburgh: Edinburgh University Press.
Vermeulen, Timotheus and Robin van den Akker (2010), 'Notes on Metamodernism', *Journal of Aesthetics & Culture*, Vol. 2, No. 1 (November), <https://www.tandfonline.com/doi/full/10.3402/jac.v2i0.5677> (last accessed 30 November 2018).
Vermeulen, Timotheus and Robin van den Akker (2017), 'Periodising the 2000s, or, the Emergence of Metamodernism', in Robin van den Akker, Alison Gibbons and Timotheus Vermeulen (eds), *Metamodernism: Historicity, Affect, and Depth After Postmodernism*, London: Rowman & Littlefield, pp. 1–20.
Vidler, Anthony (1992), *The Architectural Uncanny: Essays in the Modern Unhomely*, London: MIT Press.
Vincendeau, Ginette (2010), 'Introduction: In Focus: The French New Wave at Fifty', *Cinema Journal*, Vol. 49, No. 4 (Summer), pp. 135–8.
The Virgin Suicides Production Notes (n.d.), *Cinema Review*, <http://www.cinemareview.com/production.asp?prodid=959> (last accessed 30 November 2018).
Walton, Saige (2016), *Cinema's Baroque Flesh: Film, Phenomenology and the Art of Entanglement*, Amsterdam: Amsterdam University Press.
Ward, Geoff (1999), 'A Being All Alike? Teleotropic Syntax in Ashbery and Wordsworth', in Edward Larrissy (ed.), *Romanticism and Postmodernism*, Cambridge: Cambridge University Press, pp. 86–97.
Waugh, Patricia (1992), *Practicing Postmodernism, Reading Modernism*, London: Edward Arnold.
Webb, Samantha (2010), 'Exhausted Appetites, Vitiated Tastes: Romanticism, Mass Culture, and the Pleasures of Consumption', in Thomas H. Schmid and Michelle Faubert (eds), *Romanticism and Pleasure*, New York: Palgrave Macmillan, pp. 149–66.
Weber, Caroline (2007), *Queen of Fashion: What Marie Antoinette Wore to the Revolution*, London: Aurum Press.
Weiner, Joshua (2007), 'Unbearable Whiteness', *Slate*, 27 September, <http://www.slate.com/articles/arts/culturebox/2007/09/unbearable_whiteness.html> (last accessed 30 November 2018).
Weston, Peter (1988), '*Hyperion* and *The Fall of Hyperion*: Progress Through Suffering', in Linda Cookson and Bryan Loughrey (eds), *Critical Essays on Keats Poems and Letters*, London: Longman, pp. 101–11.
Wharton, Edith [1934] (1962), *A Backward Glance*, London: Constable.

Whitworth, Michael H. (2007), *Modernism*, Malden, MA: Blackwell Publishing.
Wiedmann, August K. (1979), *Romantic Roots in Modern Art: Romanticism and Expressionism: A Study in Comparative Aesthetics*, Old Woking: Gresham Books.
Winakur Tontplaphol, Betsy (2010), 'Pleasure in an Age of Talkers: Keats's Material Sublime', in Thomas H. Schmid and Michelle Faubert (eds), *Romanticism and Pleasure*, New York: Palgrave Macmillan, pp. 39–59.
Wolf, Mark J. P. (2012), *Building Imaginary Worlds*, London: Routledge.
Wollstonecraft Shelley, Mary [1818] (1980), *Frankenstein, or, The Modern Prometheus*, Oxford: Oxford University Press.
Wordsworth, William [1800] (1957), *Wordsworth's Preface to Lyrical Ballads*, ed. W. J. B. Owen, Copenhagen: Rosenkilde and Bagger.
Wordsworth, William (1979), *The Prelude: 1799, 1805, 1850*, ed. Jonathan Wordsworth, M. H. Abrams and Stephen Gill, London: W.W. Norton.
Wordsworth, William (1999), *The Complete Poetical Works*, London: Macmillan, 1888, *Bartleby.com*, <http://www.bartleby.com/145/ww287.html> (last accessed 30 November 2018).
Yeager, Patricia (1989), 'Towards a Female Sublime', in Linda Kauffman (ed.), *Gender and Theory*, Oxford: Basil Blackwell, pp. 191–209.
Zeitchik, Steven (2013), 'Five Days of "Her": Editing Samantha in (and out)', *Los Angeles Times*, 30 December, <http://articles.latimes.com/2013/dec/26/entertainment/la-et-mn-her-spike-jonze-cinematography-20131226> (last accessed 30 November 2018).
Žižek, Slavoj (1989), *The Sublime Object of Ideology*, London: Verso.

INDEX

Note: Page numbers in italics are illustrations and those followed by n are notes. Film titles are followed by the name of the director and the date.

À bout de souffle (Godard, 1960), 18
Aaron, Michele, 96
Abrams, M. H., 11, 32, 103–4, 142
Adaptation (Jonze, 2002), 101, 184n
Ader, Bas Jan, 15
aesthetics
    Anderson, 29–53
    eighteenth century, 30–3
    of pretty, 92–6
    suspense, 145, 149
A.I. Artificial Intelligence (Spielberg, 2001), 112, 115
Allen, Richard, 60
Alpert, Robert, 101
ambiguity, 54–78
American pastoralism, 121, 122, 127–33, *129*, 133, 135, 143
The American Supermarket, 131–2
Anderson, Eric, 139
Anderson, Wes, 29–53
    emotional reality, 175
    Fantastic Mr. Fox, 118, 121–43
    French New Wave, 18
    metamodernism, 15
    modernity, 177–9
    parodies of, 182n
    'quirky' cinema, 21–2
    and 'smart' cinema, 20
    sublime, 38

Andrews, V. C., *Flowers in the Attic*, 188–9n
anti-self-consciousness, 13
Astruc, Alexandre, 17
authenticity, 5, 10–13, 17–18, 21, 54–78

Backman Rogers, Anna, 85, 153, 167, 184n
'The Ballad of Davy Crockett', 134
Bate, Walter Jackson, 153, 165, 168
Baudrillard, Jean, 69
Baumbach, Noah, 182n
Bazin, André, 92
BBC, 112, 144, 187n
beauty, 29–53, 36, *109*
The Beguiled (Coppola, 2017), 96
Behler, Ernst, 14, 67
Being John Malkovich (Jonze, 1999), 101
Benjamin, Walter, 155–6
Bildungsroman, 149
Biological Psychiatry, 183n
Blackwood's Edinburgh Magazine, 161
Blake, William, 9, 107, 125
    'The Auguries of Innocence', 73
blankness, 20, 20–1, 86
The Bling Ring (Coppola, 2013), 96
Bloom, Harold, 4, 9–10, 124–5
Blue Velvet (Lynch, 1986), 90
Bone, J. Drummond, 175–6
Bordwell, David, 39, *59*

209

Borges, Jorge Luis, 60
  'Tlön, Uqbar, Orbis Tertius', 73–5
Botting, Fred, 2
Bottle Rocket (Anderson, 1996), 20, 33
Bowie, David, 44
Bradshaw, Peter, 135
Branigan, Edward, 68
bravery, 178–80
Brevik-Zender, Heidi, 152, 155–6
British Romanticism, 2–5
Brontë sisters, 83, 96
Buckland, Warren, 20
Burke, Edmund
  beauty, 35, 92, 98, 106, *109*
  obscurity, 34, 45
  A Philosophical Enquiry into the Origins of the Sublime and Beautiful, 30–1
  sublime, 10, 41, 82, 114, 179
  sublime and the beautiful, 30–2
  sublime form of language, 52
Byron, Lord
  Cain, 55, 70
  death, 70, 73
  Don Juan, 54, 59
  Manfred, 55, 73
  nihilism, 75
  revolution, 11
  Romantic irony, 56–9, 67
  Romantic pessimism, 55
  selfhood, 12

la caméra-stylo, 17
camp, 41, 48, 49–52
Campbell, Colin, 160–2
  The Romantic Ethic and the Spirit of Modern Consumerism, 158–9
Carlyle, Thomas, 103–4, 123–4
Carrie (De Palma, 1976), 91
Cavell, Stanley, 103, 104, 113, 117, 145
Chabon, Michael, 40, 52
chick flick, 144–5
childhood, 35–6, 49, 119–71
  and authenticity, 12
cinéma du papa, 18–19
cinema of gentrification, 18, 42
cinema of loneliness, 172–3
Clayton, Alex, 149
Cléo de 5 à 7 (Varda, 1962), 36
Coleridge, Samuel Taylor
  anti-sublime, 103–4
  Biographia Literaria, 83, 130
  'Dejection: An Ode', 104, 121
  film of familiarity, 107
  identity, 13
  imagination, 9
  'natural' genius, 130
  nature, 121
  radical fictionality, 177
  senses, 106
  sublime, 82–3, 114
Collins, Jim, 20
colours, 34, 44, 93, 185–6n
concrete idealism, 147
consumption, *152*, *155*, 158–60, 163–7
Coppola, Francis Ford, 19
Coppola, Sofia
  connections, 16–17
  egotistical sublime, 179
  emotional reality, 21, 175
  father, 19
  French New Wave, 18
  'girl clusters', 93
  gothic, 178
  Lost in Translation, 181n
  Marie Antoinette, 143, 144–71, *163*
  mise-en-scène, *94*
  'quirky' cinema, 21–2
  Romantic tradition, 177
  The Virgin Suicides, 81–99
Cornell, Joseph, 40–1
Creed, Barbara, 113
Cybulski, Mary, 184n

Dahl, Roald, 121–2, 132, 133, 136, 142, 143, 187n
Dargis, Manohla, 111
The Darjeeling Limited (Anderson, 2007), 40
Davers, Rebecca, 73
De Palma, Brian, 91
Death of a Salesman, 183n
DeLillo, Don, *White Noise*, 131
Deming, Richard, 62, 183n
desire, *155*, *163*
diagetic space, 38–41
dialogue, 49–52
Dick, Philip K., 64
Docherty, Thomas, 32–3
Dorey, Tom, 130
Downing, Lisa, 148
Dunst, Kirsten, 146

'edible books', 145
egotistical sublime, 81–99, 147, 179, 185n
Eisner, Lotte, 88
Emerson, Ralph Waldo
  'Circles' (essay), 8, 14, 172
  Nature, 81, 125
  pastoral ideal, 132
  revolution, 11
  self-reliance, 167
  subjective versimilitude, 73
  transcendental philosophy, 125–6
emotion, 79–118
  as a form of revolution, 178–80
Empire magazine, 144
endings, 172–80

Enlightenment, 8–9, 67, 100
escapism, 32
Esterhammer, Angela, 12
Eternal Sunshine of the Spotless Mind (Gondry, 2004), 74–5, 184n
Eugenides, Jeffrey, 81
Evans, Joel, 55, 69, 183n
Ezra, Elizabeth, 36–7

fancy, 144–71
fantastic, 63, 69–70
Fantastic Mr. Fox (Anderson, 2014), 18, 118, 121–43, *129*, *131*, *135*, 173, 175
feminine sublime, 79–118
feminine 'voice', 148
femininity, 35, *152*
Ferriss, Suzanne, 170
Fletcher, John, 45, 49
Flores, Pamela, 155–6, 160
Fluxus, 131
Foucault, Michel, 153, 157
Fraser, Antonia, *Marie Antoinette: The Journey*, 149–50, 158
Freeman, Barbara, 98–9
French New Wave *see* New Wave
Freud, Sigmund, 45, 169
Fukuyama, Francis, 175
Fülle, 57, 66

Galt, Rosalind, 82, 92–3, 95, 146, 148–9, 150, 167
German Jena Romantics, 5
Germany, 184n
Gigante, Denise, 163–4, 166–7
Gilman, Charlotte Perkins, 96
Godard, Jean-Luc, 18, 40, 131, 134
Goethe, Johann Wolfgang von, 67
Gondry, Michel, 182n
Goodman, Russell, 103, 104, 112
Gorin, Jean-Pierre, 131
gothic, 49–50, 83, 96–8
Gould, Stephen Jay, 187n
Gruder, Vivian R., 188n
The Guardian, 182n, 188n

Habermas, Jürgen, 180
Hartman, Geoffrey, 4, 9, 13
Hazlitt, William, 11
Hegel, Georg Wilhelm Friedrich, *The Phenomenology of Spirit*, 115
Hemans, Felicia, 83
Hemingway, Ernest, 182n
Henderson, Andrea K., 174
Her (Jonze, 2013), 100–19, *105*, *109*, *116*, 173, 175
Hero of Sensibility, 55, 67–8
Hill, Derek, 64, 174, 180
Hitchcock, Alfred, 60
Hoffmann, E. T. A., 60
Hoskins, Bree, 98

Hunt, Leigh, 11, 163
Hunter, John, 167
hysterical sublime, 41

idealism, 56–7
'I'm Here', 113–14
imaginary history, 119–71
imagination, 8–10, 133–6
Indiewood, 17
intersubjectivity, *90*, 100–19
Isle of Dogs (Anderson, 2018), 134
Ivanchikova, Alla, 101–2, 186n

Jameson, Fredric, 14, 16, 39, 41, 92, 96–7, 184n
Jeremiah Johnson (Pollack, 1972), 187–8n
Jonze, Spike
  connections, 16, 182n
  emotional reality, 175
  Her, 100–19, *109*
  metamodernism, 15
  New Hollywood, 19
  'quirky' cinema, 21–2
  and 'smart cinema', 20
  subjecthood, 177–8

Kafka, Franz, 60, 64
Kant, Immanuel
  beauty, 82, 92–3, 146, 148
  Critique of Judgement, 72
  mathematical sublime, 72, 114
  modernism, 95
  monstrosity, 166–7
  Observations on the Feeling of the Beautiful and Sublime, 82
  reason and imagination, 125
  Romantic irony, 56–9
  sensible intuition, 83, 88
  sublime, 10, 41
  transcendental philosophy, 103, 107
Kaufman, Charlie
  connections, 16, 182n
  emotional reality, 175
  New Hollywood, 18
  'quirky' cinema, 21–2
  Romantic tradition, 177
  Romanticism, 174
  'smart cinema', 20
  sublime, 179
  Synecdoche, New York, 53, 54–78
  theatricality, 178
Keats, John
  anti-self-consciousness, 13
  To Autumn, 169
  egotistical sublime, 185n
  Endymion, 168, 169
  'Fancy', 144
  fancy, 144–71
  Hyperion, 168

Keats, John (*cont.*)
  'To J. H. Reynolds, Esq.', 147
  Lamia, 153–4, 157, 163–7, 169, 170
  material sublime, 143
  nature, 124
  'Ode on Melancholy', 162
  pervasive eroticism, 147
Kent, William, 38–9
Kertzer, Adrienne, 122, 132, 133–4, 187n
kitsch, 41–2, 91, 179
Knight, C. Ryan, 140–1
Kolker, Robert Phillip, 17, 18, 172
Kracauer, Siegfried, 92–3
Kredell, Brendan, 18, 42
Kubrick, Stanley, 184n
Kunze, Peter, 137

LaBute, Neil, 20
Laine, Tarja, 88–90
Landon, Letitia, 'History of the Lyre', 12
Lefort, Claude, 161
Lichtenstein, Roy, 131
The Life Aquatic with Steve Zissou (Anderson, 2004), 29–30, 40–52, *40*, 44, 122, 179
Lippit, Akira, 141–2
Lockhart, John Gibson ('Z'), 161
Lolita, 184n
Lost in Translation (Coppola, 2003), 96, 146, 181n
Lovejoy, Arthur, 3, 4
Lynch, David, 64
Lyotard, Jean-François, 13, 14–15, 32, 45, 179

MacDowell, James, 15, 20–2, 40
  'Notes on Quirky', 22
madness, 67
The Magnificent Ambersons (Welles, 1942), 183n
Manninen, Bertha Alvarez, 112, 115
Manninen, Tuomas William, 112, 115
Mansion of Many Apartments, 158, 170
Margulies, Alfred, 103
Marie Antoinette (Coppola, 2006), 144–71, *151*, *152*, *155*, *163*
  death, 175
  domestic in public sphere, 96
  'quirky' cinema, 22
  Weltschmerz, 173
Martin-Jones, David, 56
Marx, Leo, 7, 124–6, 128, 132, 134, 135
material excess, 147–53
material sublime, 13, 143, 153–8, 164
mathematical sublime, 56, 71–6, 114
Mayshark, Jesse, 7, 20, 22
McGann, Jerome, 3, 12, 32
Mellor, Anne, 15, 57–8, 59, 67, 70, 83, 107, 115
Melville, Herman, 103
metamodernism, 13–16
Metamodernism: Historicity, Affect, and Depth After Postmodernism, 15

Milam, Jennifer, 146, 153
Millais, John Everett, *Ophelia*, 184n
Miller, Arthur, 183n
Milnes, Tim, 12, 13
mimetic realism, 64
mirrors, 54–78
mise en abyme, 71–6
mise-en-scène
  Anderson, 30, 32–4, 40, 49–52, 122, 178, 182n
  Coppola, 94
  Fantastic Mr. Fox, 136
  Her, 108–12
  picturesque, 177
  'quirky' cinema, 21
  The Royal Tenenbaums, 36, 37, 42, 48
modern utility, 163–7
modernism, 34, 181n
modernity, 161–3, 177
  crisis of, 56
Monden, Masafumi, 184n
monstrosity, 164, 166–7, 169–70
monstrous-feminine, 113
mood, 86–92
Moonrise Kingdom (Anderson, 2012), 18, 182n
Morton, Samantha, 186n
Mulvey, Laura, 92

Narboni, Jean, 92
natural supernaturalism, 103–4, 123–4
nature, 43–5, 121–43, 123–7, 140–3
Nerval, Gérard de, 60, 68, 70
  Aurélia, 68, 70
New Hollywood, 16–22, 172–3
new sincerity, 19, 20
New Wave, 16–22, 36, 39, 134
New World, 125–6, 133, 138
New York City, 29, 42
New York Times, 146, 182n, 184n
Newsnight programme, 187n
Newton, Isaac, 166
Nietzsche, Friedrich, 76
noble savage, 36, 135
nostalgia, 16, 22, 32, 42, 48, 49
Nouvelle Vague, 18
Novalis, 3, 88
now time, 155–6

The Onion, 182n
Owens, Bill, *Suburbia*, 91

painful picturesque, 29–53
pastiche, 41–2
Pavel, Thomas, 60–1
Perkins, Claire, 19–20
Perkins, V. F., 145, 149
Perry, Seamus, 3, 32
Pfau, Thomas, 12, 88, 91

pleasurable excess, 144–71
Poe, Edgar Allan, 67
Pollack, Sydney, 187–8n
postmodernism, 13–15
postnostalgia, 92
post-pop, 19, 22
'post-youth' culture, 19
pretty, 81–99, 148–9
Price, Uvedale, *Essays on the Picturesque*, 31
primitivism, 36, 124, *135*
proto-sublime, 49

Quinlivan, Davina, 109
'quirky' cinema, 19, 20–2

Radcliffe, Ann, 83
realism, 59–64
reflexivity, 13
revolution, 19–20, 119–71
Richardson, Alan, 84
Robinson, Jeffrey Cane, 147–8, 150, 171
Romantic
    clarity and confusion, 27–79
    definition, 2–8
    filmmaking as quest, 1–26
Romantic child, 123, 136–40
Romantic depth model, 167–70
Romantic idealism, 180
Romantic Ideology, 15
Romantic imagination, 102–6
Romantic irony, 13–16, 54–78, 174
Romantic reality, 174–6
Romanticism, 2–8
    identity, 10–13
Rose, Jacqueline, 133
Rousseau, Jean-Jacques, 12, 136, 137
    Emile, 123
Rowland, Ann, 123, 138–9, 140–1
The Royal Tenenbaums (Anderson, 2001)
    aesthetics, 29–30
    beauty, 36, 52
    British Invasion, 134
    camera movement, 39
    camp, 49
    death, 175
    dreams, 174
    language, 51–2
    nature, 122
    painful picturesque, 33–8, 37
    pastiche, 41–2
    'smart cinema', 20
    sublime, *38*
    taxonomy of people, 48, 182n
Rubsamen, Glen, 15
Rushmore (Anderson, 1998), 20, 33, 133–4
Rushton, Richard, 145, 161, 167, 168
Ruskin, John, *The Stones of Venice*, 49
Russell, David O., 182n

Rybin, Steven, 139
Rzepka, Charles, 10, 11

Saturday Night Live, 182n
savage man, 137
Schapiro, Barbara, 168–9
Schenectady, 183n
    'In and Around Schenectady, New York', 63–4
Schlegel, Friedrich
    amor fati, 76
    fragment, 73
    Fülle, 57, 66
    Lucinde, 58
    Lyceum (Critical) Fragments, 58
    Romantic irony, 14, 22, 55, 56–9, 67
    Socratic irony, 61
    transcendental critical idealism, 68
Sconce, Jeffrey, 6, 19, 19–20, 86
Scott, A. O., 185n
Seitz, Matt Zoller, 46
Selbstbeschränkung, 59
self-consciousness, 176–8
self-identity, 6–7, 145–6
self-reflexivity, 43
self-reliance, 167
sentimental sublime, 29–53
Shakespeare, William, 13, 130
Shaw, David, 75–6
Shaw, Philip, 4
Shelley, Mary, 83
Shelley, Percy Bysshe
    Alastor; Or, The Spirit of Solitude, 4
    imagination, 8–9
    Mont Blanc, 124
    nature, 124
    Prometheus Unbound, 107
    revolution, 11
    savage, 123, 135
    sublime, 107
shock effect, 32, 45
Silverman, Kaja, 106
Sinanan, Kerry, 12, 13
Sinnerbrink, Robert, 87, 90
Sirk, Douglas, 95
Slate, 182n
'smart cinema', 6, 19, 20–1
Smith, Charlotte, 84
    'Beachy Head', 83
Smith, David L., 62, 66, 76, 115, 185n
Snell, Robert, 181n
Socratic irony, 61
Solondz, Todd, 20
Sontag, Susan, 41, 50
sound, 108–12
soundtrack, 133–4
'Space Oddity', 44
'speciality' cinema, 18
Spielberg, Steven, 112

Stam, Robert, 71
Stimmung, 88–9
Stolen Kisses (Truffaut, 1968), 134
sublime, 30–3, 84–6, 100–19, 178–9
sublime feeling, 114
sublime obscurity, 106–8
sublime point-of-view shot, *38*
Sunday Times Magazine, 182–3n
surrealism, 64
Swann, Karen, 145
Synecdoche, New York (Kaufman, 2008), 53, 54–78, *62*, *71*, *74*, 173, 175
  'In and Around Schenectady, New York', 63–4
syuzhet, 59–60

Tarantino, Quentin, 20
theatricality, 39–40, *44*, 157
Thoreau, Henry David, 11, 121, 125–8, 132–3, 135–6
  Walden, 11, 121, 128–9, 135, 140, 143
Thorslev, Peter, 67–8, 173
Three Kings (Russell, 1999), 182n
Todorov, Tzvetan, 45, 56, 63–4, 66–7, 69–70
Tout va bien (Godard, 1972), 131
transcendence, 178–9
transcendental critical idealism, 68
trauma, 88, 91
Trilling, Lionel, 148, 169, 170
Truffaut, François, 18, 19, 134
Two English Girls (Truffaut, 1969), 134
Tzioumakis, Yannis, 18

ugliness, 148–9

van den Akker, Robin, 13–14, 15, 16, 175
Varda, Agnès, 36
Vermeulen, Timotheus, 13–14, 15, 16, 175
Vidler, Anthony, 97
The Virgin Suicides (Coppola, 1999), 81–99
  beauty, 166
  death, 175
  emotional reality, 87
  femininity, *94*, 146, 153
  Flowers in the Attic, 188–9n
  humanism, 173
  intersubjectivity, 90
  material sublime, 171, 179
  out of place, 168
  'quirky' cinema, 21–2

Walden see Thoreau, Henry David
Walpole, Horace, 49, 50
Walton, Saige, 146, 157
Wandering Jew, 73
Ward, Geoff, 51
Warhol, Andy, 131
Watts, Alan, 185n
Watts, Robert, 131
Waugh, Patricia, 177, 178, 179
Webb, Samantha, 145
Weber, Caroline, 156–7, 160
Wellek, René, 3
Welles, Orson, 39, 183n
Weltschmerz, 67–8, 70–1, 73, 173, 176
Whale, James, 164
Wharton, Edith, *The House of Mirth*, 98–9
Where the Wild Things Are (Jonze, 2009), 101, 185n
Williams, Linda, 92
Winakur Tontplaphol, Betsy, 154, 157, 164–5
Wordsworth, William
  anxiety of hope, 7
  authenticity, 11, 12
  childhood, 125
  'edible books', 145
  egotistical sublime, 147
  'An Evening Walk, Addressed to a Young Lady', 29
  film of familiarity, 107
  imagination, 9–10, 83
  intersubjectivity, 112–13
  Lyrical Ballads, 104
  nature, 123–4
  overbalance of pleasure, 34, 51
  picturesque, 33
  pleasure, 160
  Preface to *Lyrical Ballads*, 11, 33, 51
  The Prelude, 7, 51, 100, 104, 112–13
  radical situatedness, 177
  'The Ruined Cottage', 145
  senses, 106
  sublime, 104, 185n
  'Tintern Abbey', 106

Yeager, Patricia, 113–14, 116–17
Young, Mallory, 170

Žižek, Slavoj, 48
Zumbrunnen, Eric, 110

EU representative:
Easy Access System Europe
Mustamäe tee 50, 10621 Tallinn, Estonia
Gpsr.requests@easproject.com

www.ingramcontent.com/pod-product-compliance
Lightning Source LLC
Chambersburg PA
CBHW071841230426
43671CB00012B/2024